BEING JULIA

by the same author

Collaborative Approaches to Learning for Pupils with PDA
Strategies for Education Professionals
Ruth Fidler and Phil Christie
ISBN 978 1 78592 017 2
eISBN 978 1 78450 261 4

Can I Tell You about Pathological Demand Avoidance Syndrome?
A Guide for Friends, Family and Professionals
Ruth Fidler and Phil Christie
Illustrated by Jonathon Powell
ISBN 978 1 84905 513 0
eISBN 978 0 85700 929 6

Understanding Pathological Demand Avoidance Syndrome in Children
A Guide for Parents, Teachers and Other Professionals
Phil Christie, Margaret Duncan, Zara Healy and Ruth Fidler
ISBN 978 1 84905 074 6
eISBN 978 0 85700 253 2

Being Julia

A Personal Account of Living with
Pathological Demand Avoidance

Ruth Fidler and Julia Daunt

Foreword by Dr Judy Eaton

Jessica Kingsley Publishers
London and Philadelphia

First published in Great Britain in 2021 by Jessica Kingsley Publishers
An Hachette Company

1

Copyright © Ruth Fidler and Julia Daunt 2021
Foreword copyright © Dr Judy Eaton 2021

PDA awareness card image reproduced with kind permission from the PDA Society.

Front cover image source: Lily Charnock.

Trigger Warning: *This book mentions underage sex, prostitution and self-harm.*

A CIP catalogue record for this title is available from the
British Library and the Library of Congress

ISBN 978 1 84905 681 6
eISBN 978 1 78450 188 4

Printed and bound in Great Britain by TJ Books Limited

Jessica Kingsley Publishers' policy is to use papers that are natural,
renewable and recyclable products and made from wood grown in
sustainable forests. The logging and manufacturing processes are expected
to conform to the environmental regulations of the country of origin.

Jessica Kingsley Publishers
Carmelite House
50 Victoria Embankment
London EC4Y oDZ

www.jkp.com

Contents

Foreword

I am a clinical psychologist and have been working in the area of autism for the last twenty years. Over this time I have developed a professional and personal interest in PDA, or Pathological Demand Avoidance. I first came across Ruth when I was asked to join the PDA Development group several years ago and was instantly impressed by her passion for supporting individuals and their families. I then met Julia and her partner Paul at various conferences across the country and ultimately got to know her well when she asked me to support her at a speaking engagement when Paul was not available. I am so glad that they have written this book. Although when you hear Julia speak she comes across as eloquent and knowledgeable, I know first-hand the struggles she has experienced and the personal cost to her of such high levels of anxiety. At one conference when I was wearing a Smart watch, we compared our heart rates. Although she looked outwardly calm and was chatting with other speakers and delegates, her heart rate was through the roof.

It is important to emphasise at this point that I am aware of the huge barriers to telling her story that Julia faced as a result of her high levels of anxiety and demand avoidance. She can seem to those who do not know her well as though she is managing better than she is. However, this can be so misleading. For Julia, as it would have been the case for many individuals with this profile, the key to the success of this project was finding Ruth with whom she could work collaboratively and as an equal partner.

This book has really been written from the heart. Julia has been incredibly open and brave in talking about the difficulties she has experienced. Paul too, has been honest and frank about his own challenges. Their love and commitment to each other shines through. Ruth has used her patience and knowledge of the PDA profile to support and encourage Julia through this.

The resulting book is a warm, insightful and, at times, humorous window on the world of an adult with PDA. It also captures and acknowledges the challenges faced by parents of children with this profile, but at the same time, provides hope for the future.

It will provide an excellent resource for anyone wishing to gain knowledge about this perplexing, and sometimes controversial, area. Both parents and professionals will be able to use this book to learn but also to ensure that appropriate support is provided for other individuals with this profile in the future.

Above all though, read this book because it is funny, sad at times and so heart-warming – not least because it actually got written at all! Well done to Julia and Ruth on this project and a big thank you too to Paul, for helping Julia to become the person she is today.

Dr Judy Eaton, consultant clinical psychologist in independent practice and research associate at Kings College London

Acknowledgements

From Julia:

Thanks to Mum – without you I wouldn't be where I am today. Not only literally because you brought me into the world but crucially because you never gave up on me, even though there must have been times when that was really tough. I don't like to admit that you're right, but I do know that you've taught me loads and always supported me. As I've got older and we've got closer I come to appreciate you more and more.

Thanks of course to Paul – for helping me produce this book over all the years it has taken. Thanks for proofreading, encouraging and loving me through everything. I love you.

Thanks to Ruth – for agreeing to help me tell my story and for making sure we finished it! I've learned a lot from you and really appreciate how you understood me and persevered with supporting me through the whole process.

Thanks to Ginny and Liz – you were some of the special professionals who took the time to get to know me and gave me some of my happiest childhood memories.

From Ruth:

Thanks to Julia – for sharing your story in all its multicoloured glory with me. It has been a privilege to continue to get to know you and Paul better and to have worked together on a book that I know will make a huge difference to so many people we will never have the pleasure of meeting.

Thanks to Lily – for your beautiful cover illustration and for working with us so patiently and creatively. We are so delighted with your artwork.

Thanks to my family and friends – to my Paul for your love and encouragement, to Martha and Suzanne for your insightful comments and for taking the time to read the draft, and to all my cherished family and dear friends for your ongoing support.

Introduction

Everyone has a story to tell, but not everyone's gets heard. I was offered the chance to tell mine back in 2016; in true Julia style, I spent the following three years producing precious little, then wrote the rest in the last six months! All things come to those who wait...if you can wait long enough.

I do not for a minute view myself as speaking for everyone with Pathological Demand Avoidance (PDA), although there may be many overlapping experiences and emotions that a lot of us have in common. But I do have something to say, and I am pleased to have a place to say it. I'm writing this at the age of 37. A lot has happened in those years and there's hopefully much more to come! All of our lives have many eras and multiple layers. Whether you are a person with PDA yourself or someone who lives with or supports others, I hope that my story will help you to reflect on the ebb and flow of life with PDA and the impact it might be having on individuals. If you really want to understand someone you know as a person, then I hope my story will inspire you to make the time to help *them* tell you *their* stories.

A few years ago Ruth and I decided to work together on this book. Initially I had lots of freedom and control: I planned to write when I was able, and Ruth would help to edit and extend what I had written. The problem with this strategy was that it came with responsibility, that is, the task of actually getting something written. Needless to say, it wasn't very successful!

I did have various periods of writing that resulted in getting some words onto paper, but not in a sufficiently consistent or structured way to turn into a publishable manuscript. They were put to one side and were followed by long periods without any writing. Previous drafts have still been useful, though, and snippets from them have been included in this book.

How have I managed to write this time around?

I'm not really sure. Maybe it has been fuelled by feeling that I had made a commitment and I stubbornly didn't want to dodge it any longer? People told me that they wanted to hear my story, and because I am capable of telling it, I felt that I should do so to try to help others and to try to make a difference. Maybe it was helped by having told other people that I am doing it, so I wanted to show them I actually could?

To be honest, it's probably been helped most by having someone to write with, someone who can keep up the momentum and who can take care of committing words to a page in an organised way.

Maybe it all just came together at a good time for me.

The successful formula Ruth and I came up with is that we agreed a structure of various chapter headings. We tried to cover the central issues related to the impact of PDA on my life and to include answers to questions I often get asked. Then, Ruth and I had lots of very long phone calls during which I could just talk freely about a topic at a time. I don't mind phone calls. In fact, I actually enjoy them. We had many hours of calls to get this book written, over many months. Ruth wrote our conversations into draft chapters that we then edited together. That way there was no demand on me to create the written content, to choose the right words to express an idea, to type, to get spelling or punctuation correct, to organise the chapters or to complete the tasks, but I still had a lot of influence over the content and we could decide changes together. It's much easier to add to or amend what someone else has written than to start with a blank screen. When I think about it, that must be the same for so many pupils with PDA being given a blank sheet of paper and being asked to write essays in school classrooms, let alone sit exams. It certainly was for me, and would still be now!

There is a range of terminology in current use to describe people with PDA. Some prefer 'identity-first' language such as PDA individual or PDA-er; others prefer 'person-first' language such as 'person with PDA'. Professionals often tend towards the second of these. Personally I like to be referred to as an adult with PDA. I also like the term 'PDA-er' as it's relaxed and rolls off the tongue nicely. PDA is certainly an integral part of what makes me who I am but it doesn't define me any more than other key aspects do such as that I am a white, British, heterosexual woman. In recognition that there are various different and often strong views on the subject, both forms of language are used in this book.

Included in this book are extracts from reports and documents spanning my life. When we started writing together, I gave Ruth an enormous box of files and papers dating back to my pre-school reports and she has worked her way through each one so we could find the most relevant and accurate examples to map my story.

About half way through writing the manuscript, Ruth asked me how I was coping, and I told her,

> Well, I am struggling if I'm honest. Not struggling in a bad or negative way, but still struggling. On the other hand, I am enjoying the struggle too, because although it's a demand, and that's hard, at the same time I still want to do it. I want to conquer it.

And I have conquered it! Working on this book has been a liberating and cathartic experience, even if quite depressing at times. It's allowed me the freedom to explore my childhood in greater depth than I have previously done before, which I think has done me the world of good. I don't regret anything from my past as such, as all those experiences, good and bad, have helped shape me into the adult I am now. The only 'regret' I have, for want of a better word, is the impact that my experiences had on those around me at the time. I'm proud of my achievements, which, let's face it, are more than most thought I'd ever achieve. My life now has a nice rhythm to it and it's one that I can manage and enjoy. I'm also proud of my relationship with Paul. It really is one of my greatest successes. He is my rock, and I love him with all my heart.

My story isn't about the things I've done or the places I've been. What I want to share is my journey – making sense of who I am and how I've learned more about myself. It would be impossible to say where my character, my personal history or my intelligence ended and my PDA started, because every aspect of me is part of 'being Julia'. Welcome to my world.

Chapter 1

What Is PDA?

Some of you may already have a good understanding of PDA. For others, this may be the first book you are reading about it, so it's important for those who want it to include a section offering a brief overview.

'Pathological Demand Avoidance' was a term first used by Professor Elizabeth Newson in the 1980s when she was working at the Child Development Research Unit at the University of Nottingham. She began to see a number of children who had been described as having 'atypical autism'. They were reminiscent of other autistic children but at the same time, also different from them. Then she realised that this group of children were similar to each other. They shared what she described as 'an obsessional avoidance of the ordinary demands of everyday life' – they used social strategies to evade, distract or avoid expectations, and were highly anxious.

It's crucial to note that although the avoidance can be 'strategic', it doesn't happen by choice; it's driven by anxiety and can be as distressing to the individual with PDA as it can be to others around them. It is a fundamental characteristic of the profile, hence Elizabeth Newson describing it as 'pathological', which refers to something that occurs outside the range of ordinary and is intrinsic to the condition.

The first peer-reviewed paper on PDA was published in 2003 (Newson *et al.* 2003) proposing PDA within the pervasive developmental disorders, which, in practice, is what we now look on as the autism spectrum. Her work on PDA, and subsequent work by a range of researchers and practitioners, has generated considerable interest and debate. Descriptions of the PDA profile have particularly resonated with practitioners and families who 'recognise' the person they know when they read them. While this book is not the place to write about diagnostic formulations and the debates surrounding the PDA profile, there is a wealth of further information and links to research and publications at the PDA Society website.[1] The discussion continues, and research over the last few years is helping to clarify understanding.

There is a growing push across the UK for better understanding of autism and for supporting the needs of autistic individuals and their families. In 2017, the All Party Parliamentary Group on Autism in the UK recognised that for some children on the autism spectrum, 'their educational experience becomes a pathway for failure' (APPGA 2017, p.31). The report went on to recommend that autism understanding should be 'embedded in the education system' and that there should be a specialist curriculum for those who need one. In 2018 the UK Government Autism Strategy announced the prioritisation of four key areas, one of which was 'improving understanding of autism and all its profiles including recently identified forms such as Pathological Demand Avoidance (PDA)' (Department of Health and Social Care 2018). It has been really encouraging to see awareness grow, although there's still more work to be done.

In this book I'm writing my story about my own experience; however, Ruth and I do have a position regarding PDA. We share the viewpoint that PDA is best understood as part of the autism spectrum.

---

1   www.pdasociety.org.uk

PDA describes a particular profile of autism that is characterised by high anxiety and by differences in social understanding, which lead to demand avoidance. What is more, autism is a dimensional condition, and each individual will have their own presentation of their features. For some, their profile will include overlapping features of other conditions along with personal circumstances and previous history. Needless to say, we are all individuals and none of us fits neatly into a set of tick boxes, but having a diagnostic conceptualisation can be invaluable in helping to understand individuals and to support them to understand themselves.

According to the *Diagnostic and Statistical Manual of Mental Disorders*, 5th Edition (DSM-5; APA 2013), autism is characterised by problems with communication and social interaction as well as the presence, since early childhood, of repetitive behaviour and limited interests that have a pervasive effect on everyday life.

Autistic people also often experience sensory differences in respect of sight, taste, smell, touch and hearing as well as in vestibular, proprioceptive and interoceptive processing (see Chapter 6 for more details on different sensory experiences). These factors contribute to the basis of a PDA profile as part of the autism spectrum, alongside other particular features that are characteristics of PDA, which include:

- **Resisting and avoiding the ordinary demands of life:** The key here is that the avoidance relates to ordinary, everyday demands. People with PDA may resist not only the things that lots of people don't want to do, like doing the housework or tidying toys away, but even things that they know how to do, things they might usually enjoy doing, things that are mundane, things that might have even been their own choice or suggestion, and things that are 'perceived' demands, that is, demands they anticipate or interpret as expectations even if they have not yet actually been asked to do anything. It can feel like being on a hair trigger, and the trigger is fired in response to demands. The response feels like a type of fear, even if the person understands there is nothing fearful about the task in itself. After all, some of the tasks might be life's everyday basics, like eating, sleeping, speaking, using the toilet or washing.

- **Resisting and avoiding in a socially strategic way:** There may be times when a straightforward 'no' is the automatic PDA-er response. Often social strategies are incorporated such as distracting the person making a request, renegotiating a previously agreed 'deal', offering excuses or reasons why they can't comply, some of which might be more credible than others, taking on a different persona or pretend character who is unable to comply or who is busy doing something else instead, or creating a dramatic diversion by doing or saying something shocking.

- **Appearing sociable, but having difficulty with social interaction and social identity:** People with PDA are often socially motivated and may have a certain level of skill in managing social interactions, with some awareness of other people's feelings and preferences. Their seeming social awareness can lead to some individuals being misunderstood or misdiagnosed because they don't come across as being similar to those with other autism profiles.

  However, there are usually significant gaps in social understanding and empathy as well as in how they understand themselves, their own emotions, the consequences of their behaviours or words and how they identify as a person. Sometimes, for example, children with PDA don't recognise the natural hierarchies that are usual in schools or in families in terms of the adults having more influence than the children. The same can be true of how adults with PDA might view some figures of authority. PDA-ers may challenge authority figures and have genuine difficulty in accepting responsibility for their own actions or accepting boundaries, even when they are in their best interests.

• **Experiencing mood swings and impulsivity:** Changes in mood can be extreme and sudden. Frequently they are in response to being highly anxious and/or to receiving a demand or expectation. Sometimes the mood swings can take others as well as the person themselves by surprise, which can be unsettling for everyone. Mood swings can be sudden spikes in agitation, but can also suddenly drop back to a calmer baseline, even following a meltdown, suggesting that they have got past the incident when others are still recovering. Responses to overload can be cumulative, that is, they might be expressions of lots of small but accumulated expectations and stressors that lead to a meltdown. They may be the straw that breaks the camel's back, so to speak. Having difficulty with understanding the social consequences of certain actions can make impulsivity especially challenging to relationships too.

• **Comfortable in role-play and pretend:** This is sometimes seen in how PDA-ers take on pretend roles or live their lives through a persona, a doll or a pet. They may be more comfortable in role-play than other autistic people, but their play can be quite controlling. For example, children with PDA might enjoy make-believe play but may restrict their playmates from making their own choices or going 'off script' in shared games.

• **Displaying obsessive behaviour:** This may present differently from other autism profiles. Fascinations may be more social in nature rather than about collecting a 'library of data'. Some people may say that the avoidance itself comes across as obsessive. Where there is raised anxiety that leads to controlling routines, there may be an obsessive feel to these too.

Implications of a PDA profile

Some people with PDA become very good at masking their difficulties, which means that they may come across quite differently in different settings. For example, some children might seem more compliant at school and then be more explosive at home, where the pressure to hold it all together is lifted. They may be described as 'masking', and this can lead to having their autism profile unrecognised. Masking behaviours are when a person may 'borrow' ordinary social behaviours that align with usual neurotypical ways of interacting. It can also be called 'social camouflaging'. There is increasing awareness that it is often seen in girls with autism as well as in children with a PDA profile. Masking is referred to in the recent book *Girls and Autism: Educational, Family and Personal Perspectives* (Carpenter, Happé and Egerton 2019, p.4):

> *Many autistic girls have a desire to fit in with their peers...many girls use protective and compensatory factors to give the appearance of social conformity and integration.*

Masking can lead to families running the risk of being disbelieved when they try to describe their child, or to their parenting ending up being blamed as the cause. Some people with PDA who mask may develop a compliant, socially successful persona who functions well, to a certain extent, for example, in the workplace or the classroom, but which is invariably exhausting and emotionally costly to the individual to maintain.

It is often the case that the more conventional strategies used to support autistic individuals, such as providing clear structures and schedules, are less likely to be helpful for PDA-ers. These tend to be less effective for people with PDA – although certain elements of structured approaches can be useful in managing anxiety as they can reduce uncertainty, they can be problematic for PDA-ers because they are too directive. Providing a set of structured tasks to be completed in a certain way by a particular time can feel overwhelmingly demanding. I definitely wouldn't be able to cope with it!

Whatever position people take on PDA, what is really important is that a way forward is found that supports individuals to thrive. Aspects of achieving this will include:

- Balancing time and energies spent on research and on debating the details of diagnostic frameworks with providing the services, approaches, training and time to help PDA-ers and their families.

- Remembering that the purpose of a diagnosis is in order to understand the individual so as to develop and refine the most effective strategies for them. This is what Elizabeth Newson refers to as viewing a diagnosis to help 'make sense' of the individual.

- Recognising there are some benefits in conventional autism strategies, but that they will undoubtedly need adapting and individualising for people with PDA.

- Personalising support strategies and learning opportunities with an emphasis on emotional wellbeing and preparation for adulthood.

- Using effective approaches that reduce anxiety; build trusted, genuine relationships; use indirect strategies; appeal to interests, strengths and personality; include a sense of humour; offer limited choices and flexibility; and promote emotional wellbeing. Approaches are most effective when they do all of the above in collaboration with everyone involved.

In previous publications (Christie *et al.* 2012, p.52; Fidler and Christie 2019, p.27), Ruth and her colleague Phil Christie describe effectively supporting children with PDA by imagining two dials.

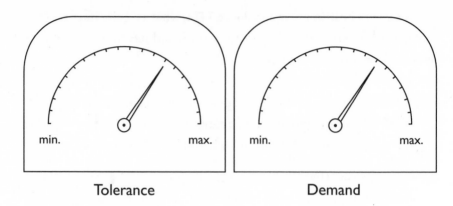

Tolerance   Demand

One of the dials measures the child's tolerance to demands at any given time; the other dial measures the amount of demand the adult is giving out. Both dials are sensitive to implied or anticipated demands as well as actual demands. The key to success lies in synchronising the dials so that there is harmony between the child's capacity or tolerance and the adult's level of expectation. Doing this skilfully requires tuning into the child's fluctuating moods and working flexibly around their anxiety and their social understanding. It does not mean simply going with the child's every whim without challenge, but it is about making careful, balanced decisions regarding how to navigate the process of synchronising the dials. The idea is that over time the child is supported to increase their capacity to tolerate uncertainty and expectations, and to manage their emotional wellbeing so they can be as well prepared as possible for adulthood. The goal is to encourage positive social relationships, to promote emotional wellbeing, maximise learning opportunities and help them contribute to their future as confident, valued adults.

Personally, what helps me is if you give me more time to process what you say to me; if you don't nag me; don't demand I do things your way but give me options; if you listen to what I say and how I feel, even if it's different from what you think; if you're willing to compromise. Don't rush me and don't treat me like a freak or like a baby. For me, it helps to have my PDA recognised. Not so that it is an 'excuse' for not stretching myself or for poor behaviour, but so that I can be understood. It's so that when I say, 'I just can't do that' I don't get the 'Oh come on, really?!' response, but that it prompts someone to ask me what they can do differently to help me.

That's why I wanted to write this book. So, enjoy!

Chapter 2

My Younger Years

It's hard to think what 'mini-me' was like because I don't have many clear memories until I was at school, but my mum and old reports have helped to fill in some of the gaps.

I was born in 1983, the youngest of three children. My half-brothers are 10 and 11 years older than me, and I was brought up by my mum and my stepdad. My parents separated when I was about 3 weeks old and I haven't had contact with my biological father since then. I have a couple of old photos of him holding me when I was tiny. My maternal grandmother also lived with us from when I was 6 until I was about 16. At the age of 9, we moved to Devon, where I remained until I was 34. Now I live in Nottinghamshire with Paul and our two cats, Louis and Ferdinand.

I have PDA, ADHD and psychosis: that is my personal profile, and it is by no means always the case that other PDA-ers will have co-existing conditions.

There are others in the wider family who may also have autism profiles or ADHD (attention deficit hyperactivity disorder), but they are not formally diagnosed. For instance, my mum looks back on her childhood and remembers being 'different' herself. She found it hard to learn in school, used to run away sometimes and would say she engaged in her own risky behaviours.

My mum had a straightforward pregnancy, apart from me being unusually active in the womb. I was described in the developmental history section of my diagnostic report as,

> *...a baby who did not sleep easily and screamed a good deal from her first night... At 3 months, Julia...still did not sleep well. She would scream for two hours at a time at night and was very difficult to comfort...she did not really play actively from 7–18 months; she would shuffle toys around but did not play with them as her brothers had...even in her first year her stepfather described her as already stubborn; her mother prefers the term 'actively passive' and feels this has always been part of Julia's make-up.*

At my initial assessment, Mum reported that by 18 months I demanded her attention, whatever she was doing, and couldn't wait for her to finish anything, yet at other times I showed no interest in her trying to engage with me. Right from an early age it was noticed by many people that I was 'different' from other children. I was very impulsive and in need of a lot of attention. I slept poorly and I was very aggressive. Even at pre-school age it was reported by teachers that I was very difficult to control and had a bad temper.

I do recall that I used to follow Mum around a lot, like her little shadow. As part of writing this book I asked Mum about some of the early differences she noticed. She said,

> *A comparison with your brothers isn't even relevant – there is nothing to compare! Your demands were out of this world, your non-compliance was extreme...*
>
> *Of course, in my ignorance I tried to treat you as I had your siblings.*

Nothing worked except my capitulation. Your brothers were justifiably outraged at the difference. As a parent I was very frustrated and concerned.

Reports give details of my unpredictable behaviour from a very early age:

At 2 years...she seemed very impulsive and difficult to control and at 2½ ran off from home without concern for the first time... Just before her 3rd birthday she ran away to Granny's house at midnight because she didn't want to go to bed... At 3 while on holiday in Malta she got up on her own at about 6am, crossed a busy road and was eventually found naked in the hotel dining room which was across the street, waiting for breakfast... The most noticeable thing was her complete lack of concern.

I went to a Montessori nursery from the age of 2½. My mum knew I was different, and while I hated structure, she also knew I needed to be challenged. I loved it at the Montessori nursery. We were able to pick and choose which lessons we went to and then, if we were bored, we were able to just get up in the middle of things and wander off to another room. This was perfect for me. No demands and only child-centred expectations. All in all, I seemed to manage pretty well while I was there. There was certainly no mention of the type of concerns about my development that my mum had noticed at home. One of my memories of this time is that I remember the big storm of 1987 when I was aged 4. This left an impression because I thought it was really exciting that we had to climb over a fallen tree to get to my nursery school, which was great fun, only to find that because the teachers couldn't get there, it was closed, so we had to go home again.

Reports when I left nursery a few weeks before my 5th birthday said that, 'Julia's communicative powers with both adults and other children are excellent and she possesses a full and wide vocabulary' (were the words 'powers' and 'full and wide vocabulary' some sort of code for other behaviours?). Anyway, they went on to add that I was, 'a polite and courteous little girl' who mixed well with the other children and liked to be helpful. A child who was 'lively, bright and inquisitive with a capacity to lead'. Apparently they also thought that my happy and cheerful presence was going to be missed by adults and children alike!

Meanwhile, at home, Mum said,

Most children, even babies, can be persuaded in some way. Not Julia, right from the start. It was her way or all hell broke loose... The ratio of adults to children at the Montessori nursery was 1:4 but Julia still managed to escape somehow. She once just left the building and went home.

At 3½ I tried to strangle a friend of the same age who had come over to play. My mum isn't sure whether it was a 'violent cuddle' that went too far, or whether there was real aggression in the incident. My little friend was certainly hurt and frightened, and needless to say, never came again. My mum was struck by how I didn't seem to understand what I had done or why people were upset with me about it. Apparently other children were often afraid of me as I was growing up.

Given the gap between the child described by my mum and the one described in the nursery report, it highlights how important it is that education placements try to understand the whole child. If a child with PDA is behaving very differently at home to how they respond at school, it's crucial that these differences are listened to. It can help professionals to interpret smaller events at school if they see the wider picture. This process of interpretation should bring the adults together to try to understand what is driving those differences and behaviours. It also matters that schools don't go so far in their attempts to encourage everyone that they are overly positive and optimistic to the point that the child they write about becomes unrecognisable to the family. Hearing that I was doing okay at school (even though it was short-lived) left my mum feeling rubbish about why she wasn't managing better at home. It fuelled her worries and self-doubt at a time when she needed to feel strong and supported.

Mum noticed that although I had developed language at the age that she would have expected and sometimes chatted incessantly as a child, my social use of language was not very fluent, and I wasn't quite 'in tune' with the person I was talking to. I wanted other people to be interested in what I wanted to show them, but she said it didn't feel reciprocal. Also, I wanted other people to show me affection and attention, but Mum said there was a feeling that even this lacked 'depth'.

What mattered to me most as a young child

As a young child I had a number of passions.

When I was really young, I had an old blanket that I used to call my 'tinkle'. It was shredded, chewed and frayed, but it was very precious to me. I used to use the frayed edges to tickle my nose until I sneezed, a sensation I used to love. (Nowadays I'm actually angered when I sneeze.) I also had dummies until I was 3 or 4. I don't remember the way these were phased out, but apparently my mum used to say we had lost one when we went out somewhere and we didn't get new ones. I was probably ready in my own way to give these up at that time, otherwise this could have been a bigger problem, but Mum may recall it differently.

I loved *Mary Poppins*. I used to watch it all the way through at least once a day, and I used to insist that Mum watched it with me. Mum remembers, 'Julia's main interests post toddler years were TV, playing schools – as long as she was the teacher – and watching *Mary Poppins* to the extent of being word perfect!'

I loved *Mary Poppins* so much because she looked like such a fun person to be looked after by, more fun than any of the adults I knew. They never took me for tea parties on the ceiling or to see dancing penguins! I desperately wanted her to be real and to come to our house. I thought that if I kept watching the film it would show how committed I was to her and how much I believed in her, and then she would be more likely to come. Plus, I loved to lose myself in the fantasy of her world, which, mixed with the familiarity of the script and the scenes that I adored, was really comforting. I don't know how *Mary Poppins* got phased out. I suppose something else slowly replaced it.

I loved Kylie Minogue when I was younger – specifically, her album 'Kylie' that was released in 1988. I used to listen to it over and over again on my little plastic cassette player. I also had a plastic speaker and microphone so I could join in when the mood took me. This music was on most of the time when *Mary Poppins* wasn't, so it must have been quite hard for the rest of the family, to say nothing of costing my poor Mum a fortune in batteries. When I hear 'I Should Be So Lucky' or 'Especially for You' it brings a smile, and I still know most of the words to all the songs on that album, even though I'm no longer a fan and haven't heard the songs in years; I only ever liked that particular album of hers. My next musical obsession was Take That followed by The Beatles and then Keith Urban, who I still worship! Keith is my longest lasting obsession and I recently got a tattoo of his logo and signature to prove it. If I get a new cat one day, I want to call him Keith. I was so upset when the Keith Urban concert I had tickets for was cancelled because of the Coronavirus pandemic, but hopefully it will be rescheduled.

I loved ALF (Alien Life Form), the cult American sitcom, and at age 3 was bought my own soft toy Alf and video by my brother. This is what started the whole Alf obsession. My original toy Alf is still with me to this day and is my most prized possession...way above any family silver! My family had an insurance broker come to the house once when I was about 9 or 10 to value some of my Nan's rings to see if they needed to be catalogued separately on the house insurance. I wanted to know whether Alf could have his own valuation as a specified asset and couldn't understand the difference between sentimental value and monetary value, no matter how many times it was explained to me. I was very pissed off by what I felt was the unfairness and obvious oversight of this. I remember very clearly how strongly I felt to this day.

Alf had to do school work. I made him exercise books and set him work that 'he' completed. He slept in my bed and then graduated to sleeping in his own cot in my room. There was a phase when he moved back to my bed, and now we only sleep separately because he's falling apart and he's very delicate. I bought him baby clothes from charity shops, and pushed him around town in a pram right into my teens, and a little way beyond, to be honest. I once gave him Holy Communion during an episode of *Songs of Praise* when I was about 7. On Saturday mornings I would wash his clothes and peg them out to dry. Sometimes he had adventures, like the time I made him a parachute and launched him out of the window. I became intrigued about whether he could fly, so also made him wings but, alas, he just landed in the bushes. When I spoke to him I wouldn't reply as Alf out loud, but I felt he did answer me. It certainly felt like we had two-way conversations.

My parents said that when I did something that I shouldn't have, I used to say 'Alf made me' or blame him and say 'Alf did it.'

I used to hope that Alf would help me at Christmas. I made lists of presents for each of us on the basis that if I put 50 per cent of the things I wanted on my list and 50 per cent of the other things I wanted on Alf's list, I could be well on my way to getting 100 per cent of my presents. Nice try, you might say, though not surprisingly, it didn't work. One year my Christmas list consisted of me simply handing over the whole Argos catalogue! Sometimes my Nan would buy Alf clothes when we saw an outfit in a charity shop, especially if I kicked up enough fuss about wanting it.

It's hard to determine to what degree I thought Alf was real, but I certainly treated him as though he was. When I went to my diagnostic assessment appointment with Elizabeth Newson herself, I immediately liked her when she talked directly to Alf as though he was a real person. When I was 12 my parents said that my interest in pretend, which started about age 2, still hadn't faded; indeed, that sometimes they felt like my whole life had been lived in pretence.

As a child, Alf did everything with me, even up to the start of my teenage years. I can remember when I was 13 wearing lipstick and smoking while holding Alf on my hip when we were out for the day! I remember that day out, but don't remember being remotely bothered by the strange looks others were reportedly giving me as a 'young adult' carrying a soft toy like a baby. I remember that people were looking at me, but I had no idea it was a negative stare or that they were questioning what they were seeing. It didn't register like that with me or bother me at all. It was noted that I also did this during a break in my diagnostic assessment at age 12½. I always take Alf away with me if we go somewhere overnight. This is partly about protecting him in case the house were to burn down while we are away, as well as because I need him near me to get to sleep.

There was a golden era when I had Kylie, dummies, tinkle and Alf to go to bed with simultaneously.

Alf, drawn when I was a child

At night I still need certain things to get me to sleep. I like Paul to tickle my feet – we call this having a 'wingle'. Even now I need a light on so there's enough light to be able to see all four corners of the room, and Alf needs to be close by.

I developed a real fear of the dark as a child. To be honest, this wasn't entirely my own quirkiness but came from my reaction to my brother letting me watch *Nightmare on Elm Street* (1 and 2, back to back) while he was babysitting me when I was only about 6. He got into big trouble for this. He had a bit of karma, though, because I got so scared I wet myself...and we were watching the films on his bed! After that I had recurring nightmares for years that Freddy (the evil character in the film) was chasing me down a dark lane and that I couldn't run. I was stuck to the spot. I would look back and see him coming just as he extended his bladed hand towards my back, then I would wake up. No surprise that I'm frightened of the dark to this day. On a positive note, though, I'm no longer scared of horror films and actually enjoy watching them, even *Nightmare on Elm Street*! In fact, it's one of my favourites...ironic or what?!

I slept in my own room until I was about 11, then in Mum's room until the age of about 14. This was at a time when my mental health plummeted and when my psychosis became very active. My mum and stepdad had separate rooms because he worked shifts and snored, so between about 11 and 14 years old I actually slept in my mum's bed until I moved to my own bed but in her bedroom. I used to wait up and go to bed when she did at about midnight, when we both used to fall asleep with the BBC World Service on the radio. I still find the 'Shipping Forecast' comforting. There's no way I would be able to stay up until midnight nowadays! Finally, at the age of 14, after my own bedroom had a big makeover – new paint, carpet, duvet set all yellow and blue themed, with stars and moons – I took the huge step of sleeping in my own room.

I had a PLAYMOBIL® doll's house that used to keep me occupied happily for hours. It was a wonderful Christmas present that my mum and brother stayed up until 3am one Christmas Eve constructing for me. Alf played with my doll's house with me, and we would be happy playing together for hours on end. I could spend whole days playing like this. He was a great playmate because I could control what he did or didn't do, what choices he made, when he got involved and when he sat quietly watching. It was a very pleasing and productive way to spend my time and it endured a long time. I would play happily like this until I was about 12 or 13.

I liked the LEGO® passed down to me from my brothers and used to enjoy building houses. In those days there weren't all the fancy LEGO® sets that are available now; we just had a box of LEGO® pieces, which suited me better because I didn't have to follow any instructions or be disappointed when my model didn't look like the one on the box.

As a child, I liked dolls and playing pretend babies. One doll I was particularly proud of could wet herself and be fed, after which she needed her nappy changing. I remember getting upset once when my brother had to poke a pipe cleaner down her throat to dislodge a bit of banana I had fed her instead of the special 'food' that she was meant to have, and the banana had begun to rot and smell.

Looking back, I think it must have been hard for my brothers to understand me and to accept that it seemed as though I was treated more leniently than them. Mum said to Ruth,

> Her brothers gradually became more resentful towards her. When we were all living without a diagnosis, from their point of view she got spoiled. Also, because of her ADHD she often didn't hear or retain whole sentences so used to get what people were saying completely wrong.

I became passionate about watching *EastEnders*, even though I was very young at the time. Some people may think that it wasn't the best TV show for a young child to be watching, but to be honest, I didn't understand much of the plots, although I didn't know that I didn't understand them at the time. However, it may not have helped in respect of teaching me some vocabulary such as 'rape', which I used despite not really understanding what it meant. I used to re-enact a lot of *EastEnders* scenes using my Barbie® dolls. I knew that there was a lot of shouting and people getting upset, but I only found out who had done what to who when I watched reruns recently. For example, I knew Michelle Fowler was a teenage mum but had no idea that Den Watts was the father of that child. What a shock that was! I'm no longer a fan of *EastEnders*, which I stopped watching regularly in the early 2000s, although I do enjoy the reruns of the early episodes.

My interest in soap operas led me to watch *Neighbours* when it first aired in the UK in the late 1980s. I fell in love with the characters, especially Scott and Charlene. I remember their wedding – it was great. This, in turn, led to my next obsession when Kylie (Charlene) released her album 'Kylie' in 1988. I was so invested in the characters of the show that I was bereft when Helen Daniels (one of the characters) died, and I actually felt like I was grieving. I remember saying that 'she was like a grandmother to me' and I cried for a couple of days. Having looked up how old I would have been, it's interesting to note that I would have been about 14 at the time. It's surprising that I truly didn't seem to understand that Helen Daniels wasn't real. I also cried when Take That broke up, but I don't think I was the only teenage girl doing so then!

I was very gullible as a child. To be honest I can still be really gullible nowadays. Maybe this is part of my PDA, maybe it reflects my way of thinking, maybe it's part of my personality, maybe it was part of being a much younger sibling to two older brothers? After I watched the film *Jaws* I got frightened about being attacked by a shark. I chose to watch *Jaws* myself aged about 8 – after the Freddy and *Nightmare on Elm Street* thing, I think Mum didn't see much point in trying to stop me watching horror films. The damage was already done! Well, given that I lived in England and didn't go on a lot of foreign holidays, I might have felt safe from shark attacks, except for the fact that one of my brothers told me that sharks can swim up through the plughole! For years I wasn't relaxed in the bath, and I definitely didn't want much bubble bath so I could keep my eye on the plughole at all times. I also got very concerned when one of my brothers told me that people only have so many sneezes in them and then they die, and he said that I had nearly used up all my sneezes so I was on borrowed time. I don't know if this was just a typical sibling tease or whether he was thoroughly fed up of my repeated sneezing so was trying to think of a way to make me stop.

I'm not scared of plugholes now, though I don't like the dark; I am frightened of vomiting, of spiders, and of germs.

Free time and holidays as a child were characterised by lots of time 'hanging out' outdoors, often with my friend and neighbour Daniella, known as 'Wella', who I have reconnected with recently via Facebook. We spent a lot of time on bikes and roller skates (sometimes both at the same time), and used to enjoy sneaking onto the grounds of the nearby school and making sandcastles in the long jump sandpit. The caretaker used to get cross with us and chase us off when he spotted us, but it didn't stop us coming back again! Locked gates were no obstacle to us.

Across the road from where we lived at the time was a sort of convent. Actually, it was a bungalow where missionaries who were associated with the Catholic secondary school lived (the school that was the home of the long jump sandpit). There were a lot of missionaries living there who had come from all over Europe, the USA and Canada. I liked to pop over to visit them, to hear them sing, and to listen to their stories of travel and their lives in other countries before they came to Reading. They were very kind and accommodating to me. They often gave me nice food and I enjoyed singing with them while someone played the guitar. Mum said,

> Julia would go to the convent opposite and tell them anything in order to get 'sanctuary' – the nuns were probably quite confused by her.

They led very simple lives and didn't even have a TV. Only the most senior Sister had a radio that she would listen to for a short, designated slot a day to hear the news so she could tell the others. I remember they used to sometimes borrow our lawnmower, and some of them, especially the German nuns, came over to our house to watch our TV when the Berlin Wall came down. I was 6½ and couldn't work out for the life of me why a wall being demolished in another country was worth anyone watching, least of all why they were laughing and crying about it.

We once went on holiday with the nuns to a priory they owned on the Isle of Wight. My brother's main piece of luggage was to take a TV and an aerial; I remember watching *Neighbours* on it. At the priory I enjoyed the storytelling about the nuns' lives in Europe and the guitar playing. I remember it felt like a very spooky place and it was hard to relax because there was a lot of bell ringing very early in the morning. Also, the pipes weren't lagged so they all made strange noises, day and night. Our Labrador, Benny, refused to go into the cellar of the house, which was very unlike him, because he followed Mum *everywhere*. It was a spooky but impressive place; I remember that it had about 15 bedrooms. The grounds were littered with old graves of nuns. One of the missionaries gave me a mug when we left that I had become attached to during our stay. I still have this mug, and even though it's cracked, it's in my china cabinet.

Primary school

I don't really remember starting school and my early memories of school days were fairly content and uneventful, so I guess that means I settled well, at least initially. I don't remember school being difficult until I was about 7, but looking back at how the school staff reported my first couple of years in school doesn't suggest they had an easy time of it.

At age 5, the class teacher fairly quickly said she could not cope with me, and this seemed to be because of my 'oppositional behaviour'. Then, having changed school at age 6 because of moving house, there were more problems with compliance and aggression coupled with my seductive behaviour towards a male teacher. Mum reflected,

With hindsight, 'ordinary' education was never a realistic option for Julia. Standard box ticking isn't feasible with children like her, but I hadn't the information I needed at this time. I was fighting though. DIAGNOSIS WAS NEEDED!

Throughout my primary school years I was often in trouble, with my mum being called into school on a fairly regular basis. I was suspended many times and my meltdowns at school were often extreme, violent and long-lasting. I was also very verbally reckless and was using swear words in their meaningful contexts from the age of 4 or 5. Other children often seemed to be frightened of me and I had few friends. The friendships I did have were short-lived and I was hardly ever invited to birthday parties or to another child's for tea. It seemed no one was safe from my meltdowns or extreme behaviours, although I did manage to keep the majority of them under control at school, letting them go when I got home. I was often accused of lying by both children and adults following an outburst, but actually I didn't usually have reliable memories about what had happened or understood what I was being accused of. I think the lines between my reality and fiction were frequently blurred. I lived in my own little world – I liked it there.

I began to behave in a sexually provocative way with male teachers even at primary school, and as I got older, one teacher said that they felt nervous of me. Mum said,

Her male class teacher was extremely worried, as was the male headmaster for his staff. Her teacher said, 'I can count on the fingers of one hand, children I have been unable to handle and I have 30 years of teaching but she is one of them.'

This was primary school! This was me being constantly contacted to come and take her home. This was me just being left with no support or guidance trying to control and help my daughter.

My brothers told me about sex when I was only 5 or 6. I began experimenting and had my first orgasm around age 8. They also taught me some colourful language that I began using in school around the same age. It didn't go down well, as you might imagine when I called my teacher a 'f****** c***'. He told me that little girls shouldn't use language like that when they didn't know what those words meant, at which point I proceeded to give him a definition of those words. He was dumbfounded, as you can imagine!

Mum first tried to get some advice about my development when I was about 7 because of my non-compliance and aggression at school and at home. Her biggest concern was my lack of awareness of consequences. In the absence of any diagnosis, the general conclusion people were working on was that it was as a result of her parenting. They recommended that I just needed firmer boundaries and more consequences!

Mum tried, but I hated things like star charts. I always have, and they have never worked. They only left me feeling pissed off. I think they are rubbish. They represent never-ending demands, back to back. They are also childish and patronising, which I felt even as a child. I certainly wasn't going to be placated by stupid stars on a silly chart!

I've never done very well with lists either, even ones I make myself. They feel too 'demandy'. When I was attending the Pupil Referral Unit (PRU), they had a good system that worked well for me. They gave me a weekly timetable and didn't care what order I did the work in, as long as I completed it. I would often lie and say I had done my history or maths when I hadn't. I don't remember being pulled up on it, but I don't know whether that means they truly didn't know or that they decided to let it go. They might have found another way of helping me complete it that didn't feel too direct, so it didn't register with me as a piece of work after all. There was a system whereby we had credits – the teachers awarded us credits per lesson and we awarded ourselves some too. It was out of 20 per lesson, so a maximum lesson score would have been 40/40. It was great because it meant that no matter how badly we had done, we still didn't score 0. It worked wonders for my self-confidence. Pupils could then use their credits to 'buy out' of an afternoon lesson. Buy-out activities were cashed in for things like playing pool, which I remember was worth 110 credits. It was possible to 'buy out' of all afternoon lessons if you saved up the credits, but I was too impatient to do that. Having control over some time out, though, was very beneficial.

In terms of extra-curricular activities, I tried Brownies, but after a week they asked Mum not to bring me back. I tried ballet at age 4 or 5, had a meltdown, swore at the teacher and again, Mum was asked not to bring me back. Then I tried trampolining for a short time, but gave that up when I was frustrated that I couldn't manage a somersault.

I did like swimming. I swam at my primary school, which had its own outdoor pool that I thought was cool. I went to the swimming pool in town, too. I went to an after-school art class with my friend Wella for a short while, which I enjoyed until we moved away and Wella went to secondary school. I liked this because it was only us and the teacher.

My last two primary school reports were surprisingly positive. In Year 5 my attendance was excellent, my academic potential was recognised and I was participating with learning opportunities. Having said that, the teacher's comments read,

> *Julia needs to maintain a more orderly management of impulses and energies.*

(Thanks, still working on that one!)

By the end of Year 6, my last in primary school, my attendance had dropped but wasn't dreadful, and I was continuing to achieve some learning and demonstrate further potential. There were, however, repeating themes about me only rarely completing pieces of work and being reluctant to write. The report summary said,

> *Julia has shown that she can be a very nice pleasant young lady when*

she tries to be. If she turned her attention to her work in school rather than chatting, she would probably do very well.

It seems that the lasting impression my teachers had, in the absence of an assessment, was of a personable child with potential, but one whose impulsiveness and behaviours made her her own worst enemy. It implied that if only she could get a grip on herself, she could do quite well! And that was the reputation I took with me to the busy world of secondary school.

Chapter 3

Growing Up

Looking back at my school teachers, I found them mostly disappointing, to say the least. They didn't 'get' me and didn't give me the impression they valued me much. To me, it felt that on the whole they were stuck up and rude. I was masking who I really was so I could fit in at school and played the 'class clown' to manipulate situations.

I remember being popular at school, but I'm not sure if that's really the case or just how I perceived it. I think it was more accurate to say I had what some teachers would call a 'reputation'! The other kids knew I was a bit of an oddball. I would do dares and I would do anything to be liked, including fighting others' bullies for them. My drive to fit in and be liked by everyone was strong, even from a young age. Mum said,

There was one person within education who did listen and do all he could. He was a special needs specialist. Teachers, in general, were actually scared of Julia; she could be very intimidating. I was told that three times and I think it's actually why she was removed from mainstream.

Once I had a Statement of Special Educational Needs (SEN), things began to change and attitudes towards me improved. Some children with special needs get issued with an Education, Health and Care Plan (EHCP). These were introduced in 2014 to replace Statements, which were current when I was a pupil. EHCPs are legally binding documents setting out a child's additional needs in the following areas: communication and interaction; cognition and learning; social, emotional and mental health; sensory and physical; health care and social care needs (DfE and DH 2014). They detail the agreed provision that the pupil has access to in order to meet their needs. This is linked to outcomes that are reviewed annually. Securing this kind of collaborative, individualised plan with the local authority can be a complex and lengthy process, but can open the way to a personalised plan, tailored to a child's particular profile.

I received my Statement at the age of 12. My mum wrote in the Statement assessment form,

> *I have been assured by a number of teachers that they would be able to handle Julia but the reverse has been the outcome. I'm not suggesting a lack of effort, more likely not anticipating she is so different. She certainly is; however, she has the same right as any other child to an education. She needs it even more and it is beyond my capabilities to educate her and keep her safe by myself.*

It was so important to have had a formal assessment and recognition of my needs so that my family and I could get some much-needed support.

My body started changing at quite an early age, and I had my first period around my 11th birthday. I knew what periods were, but my first one brought some brownish spotting rather than red blood, which alarmed me. Initially I thought what I saw in my pants was poo, and I couldn't work out how that could be happening in the wrong place until I wiped myself and understood. I was delighted to have started my periods and Mum was calm and clear and just told me what to do with the sanitary towels she provided. I was so pleased because it was a marker of being grown up, and I leapt on my bike and cycled straight over to my friend's house to tell her. But then the period pains started. I don't do well with pain, so the novelty wore off pretty quickly! My second period was heavier and more dramatic and I was freaked out by my first blood clot. I didn't understand how a piece of me could just fall out and that was okay. I was not happy about it, especially when I realised how often I would have to have periods over my lifetime.

As I entered adolescence my risky behaviours really took off. I was shoplifting and stealing, sometimes large sums of money. I tried to make sure no one found out about this so that I wouldn't be stopped from doing it again. I was smoking regularly and sometimes performed sexual acts with older boys for money. I was self-harming and threatening towards my family, verbally and physically. Mum remembers that once I ran off with £50 headed for Reading, a town about 160 miles away. I stayed in a Bed & Breakfast and was later picked up by the police in a telephone booth. I didn't understand how my reckless and threatening behaviour must have impacted on my mum.

I was also affected badly by PMT (pre-menstrual tension), and as my cycle seemed to synchronise with my mum's, this became problematic for us both. My behaviour became even more volatile when I was pre-menstrual. This letter was quite typical of a number of apologies I remember writing to Mum. I was probably about 13 or 14 at the time I wrote this one.

Dear Mummy,
I'm writing you this letter, cause I did not want to piss you off as you were in the middle of your "tellytime". I just wanted to say thanks for putting up with me & my "moods" and of crose my "P.M.T." I also wanted to say sorry for keeping you up when I have "P.M.T" (oh yer!) and for not going to science today. I think that I just got a bit to cross and I think you could say that I made a "Mountian out of a mole hill" yet again (It's me not A.D.H.D)! I will go back to science next week and Maths (oh god!) Any I had better stop this letter, cause you will kill me if I don't go to bed soon!

I love you lots & lots
& lots & lots & lots & lots & lots
× × × & lots & lots & lots & lots & lots
× × × × & lots & lots & lots & lots
× × × × × & lots & lots & lots & lots & lots
× × × × × × lots & lots lots & lots &
× × × × lots & lots & lots & lots & lots & lots
× × & lots & lots & lots & lots & lots
× × × × & lots & lots & lots & lots
× × × × × & lots & lots & lots & lots
× × × × × & lots & lots & lots & lots
× × × × × & lots & lots & lots & lots
× × × × × & lots & lots & lots & lots!
× × × × × × × × × × ×

Not long after I started my periods, I began to want a baby and talked about this, a lot. I didn't feel loved enough and I wanted a baby so I could have someone to love who would love me. I'm sure I was loved – even though my behaviour sometimes must have made me hard to like – but I seemed to have an insatiable need for hugs and cuddles, which were how I guess I got my sensory regulation and were the measure by which I determined how loved I was.

Understandably, talking about wanting a baby caused some concern to the adults around me, so I was put on the contraceptive pill. As far as I was aware at the time it was to help manage my PMT and period pain (which it did), but there was also a contraceptive rationale. Interestingly, taking the pill was very autism-friendly. It meant that my periods were not only better managed, but they were also now very predictable. I knew that when I had finished a packet of tablets, I would bleed for a number of days the following week. This really helped me cope with my periods, particularly when I was young as I didn't like the cramps and the bloating and my personal hygiene wasn't great in those days. I managed to take it routinely in the mornings along with my daily methylphenidate, prescribed for my ADHD.

After all that, as an adult, I actively do not want to have children, and this is not part of the plan in our relationship – I don't think I could deal with the physical sensations of being pregnant, least of all the process of giving birth, or the requirements of looking after a child every day.

Now I have a contraceptive implant, so I don't have periods at all and haven't had for at least 18 months. What bliss! I don't miss them; in fact, I wouldn't mind having an early menopause, which I hope might happen since I started menstruating early.

It was around the same time as starting my periods that I became aware of my psychosis, which has continued in various degrees since. It made for a tricky context in which to navigate my adolescence. To be honest, it's hard to say with any certainty whether this is when it started or whether this is when I recognised it for what it was. Maybe it did get worse as I got older and more pubescent. It's hard to say.

I remember talking to a psychiatrist who was encouraging me to reflect on my 'inner voice', intending me to connect with my conscience, presumably in an attempt to help me moderate my thinking and behaviour. I told her about my experience of the voices I heard, which, prior to this, I had assumed was normal for everyone. Once I realised it wasn't, I became very scared of my voice. We gave my voice a name,

'Jack', to try to make him less frightening. He was meant to be 'Little Jack Horner just sitting in the corner', but he did scare me. His voice is a voice from within, that is, I hear it like I would hear myself speaking. It's not like a whisper in my ear – he's as loud as you or I would be talking. His voice, when I hear it, is in the background, a throaty, guttural roar, like the vocalist in a heavy metal band. I can't tolerate listening to heavy metal music because it's too close to home. He tells me to harm myself and occasionally to do horrible things to other people. Mostly, he tells me to cut myself, to kill myself or to walk out in front of a bus. He also tells me I'm a horrible person, a waste of space and of oxygen, and he hopes I die soon. He's more like Monster Jack than a benign nursery rhyme character.

He is very repetitive, so it gets really annoying as well as anxiety-provoking. Almost like 'earworm', when you can't get the words of a song out of your head for a day. You can't reason with him; he just keeps saying the same things over and over. If I don't do what he says, I feel more physically unwell in terms of anxiety symptoms, such as feeling more nauseous, with an upset stomach, clammy skin, and racing heart. As an adult, I once had a nine-day psychotic episode during which he told me not to eat or drink anything. Fortunately I managed to sneak drinks past him, though only about 330ml (one can of Coca-Cola®) every two days. I didn't really eat for the duration. I knew I had to find the strength to drink something or else I would be so ill that I would have to go to the doctor, or worse still, the hospital.

I do have a conscience that I hear in more of a gentle tone in my own voice. That's the voice that may wonder whether I really should have that chocolate bar (the answer is always 'yes' by the way!). This is very, very different to Jack's voice. For a while Mum tried to identify the triggers for these psychotic episodes but couldn't really come up with a reliable answer. It does seem, though, that they usually accompany an event of heightened emotion, whether that is positive or negative. These experiences bring about bigger emotional responses that seem to make psychosis more likely.

Not surprisingly, it was then that I began self-harming.

Around this time, in an attempt to moderate my behaviour, there was a joint meeting where we all had to say what we wanted to change or improve. After the meeting I was sent a 'contract' by the social worker. I'm not sure exactly who was involved in writing this, but it was a spectacular failure. It was meant to be signed by myself, Mum and Nan, but none of us was prepared to sign it. It could not have been less PDA-friendly if it had been written as a spoof! It was simply a list of demands. And it directed me to control the very things that were part of my diagnostic profile! You can take a look and make your own decision. Not surprisingly, the paper is rather aged because I just screwed it up!

```
                        C O N T R A C T

                        JULIA DAUNT


    Participants :




    1.  JULIA WILL CONTROL HER TEMPER AND STOP HER TANTRUMS.  IF SHE FEELS
        STRESSED SHE CAN USE THE GARDEN SHED AS A BOLT HOLE FOR UP TO ONE AND
        A HALF HOURS.

    2.  JULIE WILL HELP AROUND THE HOUSE AND GENERALLY BE MORE HELPFUL AND
        COOPERATIVE.

    3.  JULIA WILL AVOID UNPLEASANTNESS.

    4.  NAN WILL "BE THERE" FOR JULIA.

    5.  MUM WILL BE MORE DEMONSTRATIVE WITH CUDDLES ETC. WHEN SHE IS ABLE TO
        LIKE JULIA MORE.

    6.  MUM WILL HELP JULIA IN ARRANGING HER "JOBS".

    7.  MUM WILL ARRANGE TRIPS TO BARNSTAPLE AS A FAMILY, WHEN JULIA'S
        BEHAVIOUR WARRANTS IT.

    8.  AFTER 4 WEEKS OF THIS CONTRACT REMAINING UNBROKEN, MUM WILL REWARD
        JULIA APPROPRIATELY.




    Signed ...................    ..................    ...................
           JULIA DAUNT
```

Then things really broke down at secondary school. I was permanently excluded after only one term. By this time, I was at breaking point, as was my family, and I hated my life. I felt isolated, angry, depressed and very confused. My relationship with my family was in tatters and I was taking part in some very risky activities, including providing sexual acts for money for blokes usually older than me. I was placed on the Child Protection Register and moving me to a residential school was even explored. At a Care Plan meeting when I was coming up to 12 years old, the summary of concerns about me included:

- My behaviour, mainly my impulsiveness and lack of concern or understanding of consequences.

- Protecting me and others in a manageable environment. Managing my explosiveness and my risk-taking behaviour.

- Maximising my learning potential.

- Maintaining positive relationships within the family, and, at the very least, causing no further damage to them.

- Ongoing assessment to try to understand what was driving my long-term difficulties.

We went to look round a residential school placement. It was for girls, many of whom had minor convictions and were mostly older than me. I thought they were really cool and exciting, and I loved the look of the place. The girls all had their own rooms with an en-suite bathroom; there was Sky TV, a relaxed teaching timetable, and they were allowed to smoke. There was a classroom and a minibus for going on day trips. Looking at it through the eyes of the adults, which I can see now, it was deemed to be an unsuitable peer group for me, so it didn't actually happen in the end.

Mum says she learned to manage me by giving herself and the PRU I started attending this piece of advice:

*As she got older I tried everything I could think of to correct her: brib-
ery, punishments, taking things away, but she didn't seem to experience
guilt or to understand consequences... In the end the best advice I could
give was to chuck away the 'good parenting rulebook' and find a way to
bend and twist everyday expectations.*

As I grew up and Mum understood more about which strategies
helped, she didn't ask me to do much. She let me take an autonomous
approach, which worked. Before my diagnosis we would argue and fight
all the time. Little requests used to result in me being in meltdown a
number of times a week, sometimes every day.

After my PDA diagnosis I started horse riding, which I loved. Mum
started a line dancing class with me when I was about 13, which soon
became an obsession, and I was often doing at least 15 hours a week.
This lasted about eight years and really helped.

Although I was getting up to all sorts out of school, my time in the
PRU was relatively uneventful. This was probably because I had my
dual diagnoses and was taking methylphenidate by then, plus, I was
spending time with adults who were using more effective and positive
strategies. By that time I had a lot of other professionals involved on a
regular basis: a consultant psychiatrist, outreach worker, health visitor,
social worker, school counsellor, PRU teaching staff, Child Protection
team and the police.

I was allocated an outreach worker called Ginny who was wonderful. She really 'got' me and seemed to like me for who I was. We
had lots of memorable times – making a doll's house, baking, crafting
and talking about my emotional regulation issues. Ginny helped me
see the funny side of things going wrong – for example, when we had
spent ages making a gingerbread house with icing that was too runny.
Fortunately, we managed to take a photo before it started to collapse,
but by the time I got it home from her house it looked more like the
leaning tower of Pisa. She helped me navigate my difficulties and mood

swings and she kept coming back for more! I am delighted to say that I am still in touch with her today.

These positive experiences help me to cope with new challenges, even today. I had my birthday in 2020 in Coronavirus lockdown, so had a very quiet celebration and decided to make myself a cake without any help from Paul (bad decision). I am usually a good baker, but whatever step I missed out in the recipe, I managed to make something rubbery and totally inedible. It tasted as bad as it looked. We binned it – it didn't seem fair to try to give it to the birds, given how dense it was! I just thought it was quite funny and even wrote something about it in my blog, so that goes to show I wasn't worried about other people knowing about it either.

I managed to get my Duke of Edinburgh Bronze award in my teens – no mean feat for me, walking seven miles across Exmoor and trying to light cigarettes in high winds. I got a First Aid qualification and Basic Food Hygiene, and we had sessions with a lady who came to teach us Life Skills. I learned how to write a cheque, wire a plug and change a fuse. I was also involved in planning, budgeting and preparing a three-course meal for the school inspectors. I remember that we made chocolate mashed potato cake. I was not prepared to try it, but they ate it politely and I didn't see anyone grimace!

I left school without any GCSE qualifications. I had tried to attend lessons for three subjects, which became two, then one, then none. By the end of the year I hadn't completed the required coursework. Anyway, we had to go to the main school to actually sit the exams, and I couldn't have done that.

I know that I have got a good brain and that I'm clever. In my mock GCSE exams I did really well. Goodness knows how but I got As in chemistry, biology and physics, a B in maths and an A in English. I was surprised I had done well in maths, but not about my results in the other subjects. Seems a bit strange that after those mock results I don't have any formal qualifications to my name, but I don't mind. I don't feel that having certificates defines me or truly reflects whether I am bright. I don't need them for the life I now lead.

I wasn't upset when it was time to leave school because I was desperate to become an adult. I wasn't worried about not seeing my friends because we had promised to stay in touch. That didn't happen in the end, with the exception of one boy who was the person I lost my virginity to aged 17. To be honest, there had been so many adults worrying about my sex life and vulnerability for years that I think I did pretty well to last that long!

After school, I did a taster course in Hair and Beauty, but didn't like it. Then I was enrolled on an 18-month Childcare NVQ. I stuck with the foundation part of the course for quite a few months, but had to drop out of the formal course because I hadn't completed enough written work. I was starting to go off young children around that time anyway, but I enjoyed some of the lessons and the work experience, so I was allowed to continue with those until the end of the course.

That was the last formal education I received. After leaving the course I was just at home with Mum and glad to see the back of school. I then fell into a void, and didn't do much to speak of. Then, at 17, I met a bloke who I went out with for three years. During our relationship we moved out into our own place, but that didn't go very well and we racked up a big credit card debt, mostly buying rubbish that I was convinced I urgently needed at the time. Mum offered to build an annexe onto her house and asked if we wanted to move in there, which sounded a lovely idea, so we did. We moved there in January, but by the October my boyfriend had left, and I was drifting. Fortunately I met Paul in 2004, shortly after my 21st birthday, and I can honestly say that he saved me. He gives me the strength to do what I do, and he's the reason I keep going.

Chapter 4

Making Sense of My PDA

I didn't think about what PDA meant to me when I was younger because I was simply me. I was just busy being myself, and I didn't know what it was like to be anyone else. I still don't. It's only since my early to mid-20s that I've really thought about it. Of course, none of us really knows what it's like to be another person, so I am both the best and the worst person to ask 'what's it like being you?' But I *can* talk about how I think and the things I do, and it's then up to you to decide whether that's similar to others or not.

I did have a sense of being rather unique at an early age, but I couldn't have articulated what that meant. It's still hard to describe it. I remember by about the age of 10 being aware that I was 'different' and most probably would have thought of myself as 'a bit weird'. One holiday to Euro Disney seemed to make it especially clear to me.

We had a catalogue at home from which we ordered clothes. I was delighted to choose a new summer outfit for our holiday, and I fell in love with a very bright blue and yellow shorts and t-shirt set covered with pictures of fish. I thought I looked incredible, so I was really surprised at Euro Disney to get some disdainful looks from strangers as well as from my own family when they saw me wearing it. Granted, looking back at photos it was a bit overpowering, and I was probably a bit too old for it. Plus, at age 10 I was already wearing a bra and was physically mature, so it was probably too snug in all the wrong places. Strangers might have been looking at the fact that I was carrying Alf too. I was not going to leave Alf behind, and I thought I looked the bee's knees, so I wore it with pride! I'm still proud now that I had the confidence to wear something that worked for me, despite what anyone else thought, but it was an occasion that was memorable because of being aware that people were looking at me and realising they were perhaps thinking something negative about me.

For me, developing self-awareness has been a slow and ongoing process. I was described in a report,

> Julia's image of herself as a 'child' has always been ambiguous. Her mother feels that she has never seen herself as a child; she has always been in some different role, as a mother, teacher or minder, or of equal status with adults. At the same time some of her play, notably with Alf, has remained childish and she doesn't seem to have any notion that this might be odd.

I went for my PDA assessment with Elizabeth Newson at the centre now named after her when I was 12. Strangely, Ruth worked at the school linked to the diagnostic centre at the time, although we didn't meet. Wouldn't it have been a nice story if I could say we'd come across each other back then? I knew I was going to be assessed, but wasn't really sure what that amounted to. I remember that Mum tried to explain it but I didn't understand, and I didn't try very hard to understand it. I must have been content enough to go through with it though. Mum wanted help to understand me. She said that she could tell someone else facts about me and even predict what I might have done in certain situations, but she couldn't 'explain me' or understand how I really felt.

By the age of 12, she was worried that I was becoming an increasing risk to myself and to others.

Looking back, I was already being seen about my ADHD, so maybe I thought the Elizabeth Newson assessment was related to that. I didn't understand that there was a difference between my ADHD and PDA diagnosis, and since I was having treatment and regular check-ups in relation to the ADHD, maybe I just thought this appointment was all part of the same thing. Back before taking methylphenidate, ADHD was undoubtedly my biggest problem. Without medication, this book could easily have been about ADHD instead of PDA! I suppose that reflects the complicated nature of overlapping and interlocking conditions.

In addition, there was my psychosis, which developed at puberty and ran alongside everything else that I was experiencing, although I can't really remember a time without it. For me, psychosis has consistently taken the form of a voice I call 'Jack'. I wrote when I was 12 that he's '...like a monster that pops out from somewhere to eat up the good bit in me then go.'

During one psychotic episode when I was about 13, I remember being alone in my room late at night, struggling to deal with hearing Jack tell me to kill myself. I somehow found the strength of mind to get past his voice and I wrote a poem. I called it 'If'.

If

If the trees grow where there is no rain,
If birds fly where there is no sky,
If fish swim where there is no sea,
If children play where there is no park,
If the sun moves where there is no land,
Then the world turns without any hope.

What I meant by it was that if these things are true, then there is no hope. Because these things are impossible, then there must always be hope. I was writing about remembering that even in bleak moments of despair, there is still hope. Difficult feelings will also end. Only later did Mum tell me someone called Rudyard Kipling had also written a poem called 'If', but I hadn't heard of it. I thought he was something to do with selling Kipling cakes, so I certainly didn't feel like I had copied him. I'm still proud of my poem. The only other one I remember writing was at school for Christmas, when I wrote from the perspective of the nativity donkey, being outraged that strangers kept coming to visit the stable all night and someone had put a baby in his food!

Nowadays I have become more used to my psychotic episodes (what a thing to have to say!) and I understand them better. When I am having one I am not delusional; I know that I'm having one. In fact, that is one of the things that makes them so alarming and unsettling, because I'm aware that I could be losing the plot. In some ways I think of them like a form of 'IBS (irritable bowel syndrome) of the mind' in that they are an unpredictable, disproportionate, heightened response. For me, they can be triggered by any extreme emotion, whether that's good or bad. They might be triggered by high anxiety, but they might also be set off by big positive emotions like attending a wedding, where I am so moved I am usually weeping the loudest! I know that Jack can't actually hurt me, but it's still terrifying when it happens because I'm always scared of what he might make me do. With each episode there's always a part of me that is worried that I might not come out the other side and I might stay like that forever. This terrifies me to the core. One step closer to madness, if you like! I've heard stories of people with psychosis who have, just one day, snapped and weren't able to recover and were stuck in that state permanently. I don't even know if those stories are true, but I hate even the thought of that more than anything.

At my assessment (age 12) I apparently described myself to the assistant psychologist as 'a problem child' who sometimes used 'bad behaviour'. At this time I was out of school and was being home tutored (at least, there were home tutors who were doing their best to try to teach me!). I guess I'd heard other people use those phrases about me.

My assessment report said, 'Julia has seldom attempted to evaluate herself, apparently lacking the concepts with which to do this i.e. conscience; however, a year ago (aged 11) she asked, 'Am I really bad?' as if confused, and it seemed that she felt herself out of control and unable to understand limits.'

Sometime later I was told that my PDA diagnosis was related to autism. I remember being told it was rare and more common in boys. Of course, we now know that this is not true. Interesting how things change as we learn more, and there's always more to learn. Anyway, back then I didn't think it was likely I would meet anyone like me, and it wasn't easy to find out more information about it, so I left it there. It was very early days for the internet, and I wasn't likely to seek out academic papers, which was mostly the information that seemed to be available. For me, life just carried on as it had prior to my diagnosis; I think being diagnosed was more significant for the adults around me who seemed to find it helpful in trying to understand me and give me the support I needed. My mum said,

> In the absence of a correct diagnosis the risk is that children get the wrong one rather than no diagnosis... The difference once two diagnoses had occurred was astronomical.

After being seen at the Elizabeth Newson Centre at age 12, I was seen again for a review just before my 15th birthday, having taken methylphenidate to manage my ADHD plus chlorpromazine as required for psychotic episodes. This time I didn't take Alf with me to the appointment – I had taken him to Nottingham but had left him in a drawer in our hotel while we were out. Some small progress! At that review appointment it was noted that,

> There is general agreement that methylphenidate has been successful for her; her mother describes the effect as 'brilliant', and indeed we immediately saw an enormous change in her, both in appearance and

manner. Julia is hardly recognisable...she has certainly lost weight, but more impressive is her general appearance and demeanour...much more able to hold her own socially...with little sense of the underlying instability and impulsivity that were noticeable at 12... However, despite the obvious improvements (Mrs Daunt says) the methylphenidate has 'not touched the PDA' except in indirect ways. Emergencies and crises can still easily arise.

Many years later, around the age of 25 or 26, I decided to Google PDA and I found the PDA contact group (which became the PDA Society in 2014). I made contact with some lovely people at the PDA Society, but I was very aware that they were parents and I really wanted to contact other individuals with PDA. So I set up a Facebook support group in April 2012, and I wrote this message,

I am a 27-year-old female who was diagnosed with ADHD and PDA when I was about 12 and I'm hoping to talk to anyone who can relate. I am sick and tired of (mostly professionals) not understanding PDA and if one more says that it doesn't exist I think I'll go mad...

...then I waited for someone to get in touch.

Slowly but surely people started to join. Eight years later, we now have a membership of around 2000 made up mostly of individuals who identify as having PDA. Some are diagnosed, others not, plus their parents and their partners. I'm very proud of this achievement. I tried an ADHD group previously, but I knew I didn't fit in there so well. In the PDA Facebook group I had finally found somewhere that felt right for me. I thrive on being part of a forum where I can be understood and can help others, but I still get frustrated when I hear about people who are cynical or even rejecting of the genuine profile of those of us with PDA.

In terms of the central features of my own PDA profile I totally identify with experiencing high anxiety (although when I was young I didn't know other people didn't all feel as anxious as me), avoidance, a need for control and mood swings. Other traits such as pretend play (Alf!) and being sociable, but nonetheless having difficulty navigating social relationships, also really ring true for me, as do other features of autism. Plus, I am affected by significant sensory differences. I have some rigid and repetitive patterns of thinking and behaving – for example, I need the lounge curtains shutting by the right-hand side one being pulled before the left, and I tend to flap my hands when I'm agitated. I prefer my Plan As to be available, though I try to have Plan Bs in place because my life is happier if I do that. However, I don't find it easy to generate a Plan B, and I would certainly struggle to make an alternative plan quickly, especially in the heat of the moment.

Apparently, I met most developmental milestones, such as walking, talking and toileting on time, but there were always some key differences in me. As a young child, if I played with toy cars I would prefer to spend my time spinning the wheels rather than 'brumming' them along a pretend road. When I did interact with other children, I played alongside rather than with them, and I was bossy and tried to control them rather than share games.

When I was younger, I tried to hide my diagnosis. Basically, it was because I was embarrassed. I didn't want to be judged. My own limited picture of autism at that time was of someone who was 'thick, unsociable and strange'. I wasn't any of those things and I didn't want to be viewed as if I were. I was also worried about showing any 'difference' that might have made me more vulnerable to being bullied. I knew a bit about bullying because unfortunately I used to bully some other children myself. Plus, I was interested in boys and I wanted to be seen as desirable. I thought that if they found out about my autism, I would be seen in a less positive light all round. It was another era in terms of general autism awareness in those days, and the whole difference rather than deficit model was not really being talked about back then.

I started to change my mind when I learned more about PDA and autism and also when I met other adults like me who were not 'thick, unsociable or strange'. I had found my tribe. I wanted to be understood in the context of my diagnosis but not defined by it. I regret not having had more opportunity to understand my diagnosis growing up, actually. I think it's really important to help children and young people know about themselves and what makes them unique. Self-awareness is a key aspect of emotional wellbeing, and makes such a difference to how we manage relationships and decision-making as we grow up.

When I did 'come out' and start to tell people about my diagnosis, there were a few people I had previously been friends with who distanced themselves from me and we lost touch. The same is sadly true for some members of my family too. However, there were others I grew closer to because of it. Understanding my diagnosis was not only a way of understanding myself as I was, but it made so much sense of everything that had gone before as I was growing up too.

I saw a saying on the internet:

Understanding your diagnosis later in life is like watching a TV show with a huge plot twist revealed at the end of the season, and then re-watching it with this new knowledge, picking up on all the foreshadowing and getting upset that you didn't see all of it before.

That's exactly how I felt!

The older I get, the more comfortable I am with the person I am, so I'm generally less stressed about being judged, though of course I don't like to be underestimated. If I needed to explain my diagnosis to someone now, I would say something like,

I have an autism spectrum condition (ASC) called PDA. It means I tend to avoid the everyday demands of life because they make me anxious.

Often, I tell people on a need-to-know basis, for instance if they are on a local committee with me. If I think that person might become a true friend, I will aim to tell them as soon as possible so there isn't a big moment of revelation later on.

When I first met Paul, I told him about my PDA, my ADHD and my psychosis because I wanted to be upfront from the start. When we started to see each other I also wanted to clear up other big topics like religion and pets. At that time I wasn't sure whether I wanted children, so I also asked him some questions about his family's genetic background, but we both decided against having children for other reasons anyway.

How do I view myself now? Well, I do think of myself as an adult but not an adult of a specific age or era of their life, even though I am 37 as I write this. I guess it's because I don't have the usual 'landmarks' that many people have as they get older. I don't have a paid job and never have had, so I haven't really had a 'career path', and we don't have children, which is usually another big life event. Therefore, although we do have our own home and a number of adult responsibilities and commitments, most of these are not age-related. I don't have any goals that are age-related like, 'I want to have done that by the time I'm X years old.' I feel that's been true of me forever, so I don't identify with a particular age. It takes me by surprise sometimes nowadays to meet teenagers who are old enough to be my own children, or when people younger than me get married, or when people who aren't that much older than me become grandparents!

Another thing that affects how I see myself is that I have looked old for my years from quite a young age. In fact, it was commented on in many reports, such as the one when I was nearly 13, describing me as someone who,

> ...is physically very mature and looks much older than her years...anyone who comes into contact with her has to constantly remind themselves of her age.

Understandably, the adults around me were worried about my vulnerability because I was frequently mistaken for being much older than I was, and I was making choices that I was not mature enough to deal with. At 11 I could buy alcohol, cigarettes, porn magazines and get into the cinema to see 18-rated films – all without being asked for ID. In fact, I've never been asked for ID in my life!

Elizabeth Newson recognised the pressure on my parents, who she described as, '...a major source of strength for Julia at great emotional cost to themselves.' I look back and realise I had no idea of the true impact I was having on them, only that they were hard to get along with and frequently blocked my plans or choices. It's only with the benefit of hindsight and maturity that I realise that my mum used to have lots of awful migraines when I was growing up, which were probably caused by exhaustion and stress. She is very artistic but didn't paint between me being born and me starting medication at about age 13. I thought that was just 'her normal'. It was only later when I found out that she had painted all her life (other than my childhood years) and that she stopped having regular migraines and restarted painting later on that I came to understand something of the effect of my younger years. I'm saddened at what I must have put my whole family through at times. Some days must have felt like a living hell. I wish I'd had a diagnosis and support sooner, and then perhaps things wouldn't have got as bad as they did. I still feel that there are massive issues and resentments remaining between myself and my brothers – I'm sorry about that.

The central concerns about me when I was growing up included: my violence, if thwarted; running away, if I was prevented doing something I wanted to do (Mum sometimes tried to stop me by holding onto Alf); cutting myself with razors; buying affection from boys; and generally causing damage to the house when I became distraught, sometimes to the point that the police were called out.

Coupling my risk-taking behaviour with my difficulties with social relationships, I can now see why the adults around me were worried, but interestingly I wasn't concerned myself at the time. Maybe that says a lot about where my understanding of social consequences was up to. Anyway, all to say that it meant that I didn't have the experience of 'entering adulthood' that most teenagers have because I kind of arrived there early, so I didn't have those key experiences of reaching 18 or 21.

Since I've been older than 30 I've become a bit more concerned about dying. I have a feeling I 'won't make old bones', as the saying goes. I've even made a will – with strict instructions about what I want, which must be followed. I don't know what I will do if they're not!

I recently applied for a voluntary role and I had to describe myself. I tried to let them know what I thought they needed to know. I just said that I had a wealth of lived experience of PDA, I had previous experience of being on a committee and I felt that I could make a worthwhile contribution.

If I reflect on the broader 'who is Julia?' question, I would say Julia is:

- A natural-born leader, some may say bossy.

- Warm, caring and loving to my nearest and dearest.

- Quite a 'black and white' thinker. I tend to love or hate most things I can think of, and there's very little in the middle.

- Weird, but in a good, quirky way.

- Very trusting when I get to know someone, sometimes overly so, and very loyal. But then, very unforgiving if I think that person has let me down.

- Strong-minded, fiery, sometimes short-fused, stubborn and can hold a grudge.

- Intelligent, but not particularly academic.

- Funny, quick to enjoy a laugh.

- Controlling, but I do try to take account of other people's feelings.

- Impulsive and disorganised (this is an attribute I wish I could improve; I'm always losing things because of my ADHD...and I blame Paul because of my PDA!).

- Practical and creative, good at crafts, setting up new devices and flat-pack assembly.

- Very emotional and prone to mood swings. It doesn't take much to create a real U-turn in my emotions.

- Pedantic, e.g. it really irritates me when people use the wrong grammar or spellings for things. On the other hand, my grammar and spelling are dreadful, so you could say I'm a hypocrite too!

- I like other people to follow rules, but I don't like to be bound by rules myself. I don't mind rules 'in the eye of the law', which I think everyone should follow; it's MY rules I like to have respected.

- Materialistic and poor sense of finances. This is why Paul takes care of our money because otherwise my impulsive materialism would mean I would be buying things we can't afford whenever I saw something I wanted!

It seems strange to me that there were so many years of not understanding my diagnosis, followed by more years of me rejecting it. That's so different from how I feel about it now. I spent a lot of my life wishing I was 'normal', whatever I thought that meant, just so that my pain and confusion would stop. I tried to fit in by attempting to copy more 'neurotypical' behaviour when I was younger. It's hard to know how successful I was. I longed to be accepted, but I was being fake, and it was utterly exhausting. It also left me feeling like I was a failure because I couldn't pull it off. Once I realised that I was not the same as everyone else but that being different didn't have to stop me being accepted or valued for who I am, the pain eased. I'm much happier now than I've been before since I've learned more about PDA. I haven't finished learning, though, not only about PDA, but also about myself. It's a life's work! However, I now feel more settled in myself. I realise it is okay to be me, that I do have a place and a purpose in this world, and that I can be loved. Paul has shown me that I am desirable and worthy of loving just the way I am. I couldn't view myself as me without my PDA. I am pleased to say that I actually like who I am now.

Chapter 5

My Avoidance

Anxiety-driven avoidance is probably the signature characteristic of PDA that stands out most. Our demand avoidance is affected by many different factors such as anxiety, mood, health, sleep, hormones, our relationship with the person asking, previous experiences, and personality, to name but a few! Overlapping with these are the issues that affect PDA-ers in terms of their autism profile, like their social and emotional understanding or sensory differences.

I've called this chapter 'My Avoidance' because I am writing about *my* experiences, my own experience of how demands feel to me and of how I respond to them. Some of this may ring bells with others reading this who have PDA or who are caring for someone with PDA, but I'm not making assumptions about how life is for others; I'm simply talking about what it's like for me.

I have tried to categorise a range of different demands here:

- **Direct demands:** These are the most obvious and are concrete demands such as, 'do this', 'put it there', 'pass me that', etc. I can take these from trusted people more than from strangers, but even so, there are some occasions when I am more sensitive than others. My more sensitive days usually correspond to days when I am more stressed or closer to overload, which may happen for a variety of reasons.

- **Social demands:** These are the unspoken demands of a social situation. They may differ depending on what social or cultural situation you are in. For me, these are the social 'norms' of living in the UK since 1983 (although some of these norms, like social distancing, are changing at the time of writing, in 2020, due to the Coronavirus pandemic). Social demands are the expectations that accompany all sorts of situations, and include special occasions as well as responses to social invitations.

- **Legal demands:** These are the laws of the land, things like respecting speed limits, not stealing, not murdering and not being fraudulent. I have no issues following these sorts of demands nowadays, even though I did used to find them hard when I was younger (I only had a problem with stealing, by the way, not murdering).

- **Implied and indirect demands:** These may be 'sneaky' demands, such as someone suggesting 'shall we try this another way?', which I can see right through, although I do appreciate why people may be trying to put a request to me carefully. Indirect demands may also be implied demands that come via praise – for example, if I have managed to complete a task or do a friend a favour and they praise me in a gushing way, I stop 'hearing' the gratitude and start hearing the expectation to do at least as well if not better next time. Also included in this category are choices and making decisions.

- **Self-imposed demands:** These are expectations I put on myself, such as getting on with making a card for a friend's birthday or feeling I should wash my hair today.

- **Inflexible demands, not open for negotiation:** These usually relate to systems in the wider world such as that a train is going to leave at that particular time, whether I am on it or not, or that the bins will only be collected on a Thursday, even if I prefer to put them out on a Monday. This is why I try to avoid public transport, as well as because of germs and having to deal with strangers, Anyway, Paul is kind enough to take responsibility for the bins because I don't want to put them out any day of the week, to be honest! If I can't avoid these inflexible situations, I can get very stressed by them.

- **Unexpected demands:** These are sudden changes or coping with sustained uncertainties. This group of demands reflects difficulties lots of autistic people experience. Like many of them I also struggle with flexible problem-solving, with predicting consequences, with impulsiveness, with anxiety-driven avoidance, with making choices and with processing time. These difficulties have been life-long for me, although there are certain periods of fluctuation in how they impact on me.

- **Other:** There always needs to be a category that scoops up any miscellaneous extras, even if I'm not sure what to include in it just now!

My responses to the different types of demands

I have an instinctive response to demands that I have only recently become aware of. If I am asked to do something that isn't immediately appealing, I tend to say 'no' straight away, even before I have had a chance to experience any anxiety. I wonder whether this is because subconsciously I know it could trigger a meltdown. Or it could be an ingrained habit. Or maybe it's because I want to give myself an opt-out or more time to decide about the request. I wonder if someone who was describing me as a child would have said that they knew this about me all those years ago, but I've only recently spotted it as a pattern.

For me, there are a number of reasons why I feel very strongly that it's right that the condition is called *Pathological* Demand Avoidance. Avoiding demands is not something I 'choose' to do; it is an integral part of who I am and how I process my world. That's why I'm comfortable with demand avoidance being called 'Pathological'. I think it's for a good reason. Most of the adults with PDA I am in contact with also feel the same. I would like those who want to have a debate about terminology to take account of all views, including those like mine.

The term 'pathological' was first used by Professor Elizabeth Newson when she wrote about PDA. I have a lot of respect for Elizabeth Newson and the work of her colleagues, who have dedicated their expertise and efforts to understanding PDA and getting it as recognised as it is today, but I worry that spending precious energies on how it should or shouldn't be classified takes time away from the important work of what can be done for families and individuals to support them to have calm, happy and fulfilled lives.

There are some individuals I know who have autism or who are 'Aspies' and who experience demand avoidance when they are particularly anxious, but their avoidance has a different quality to that of the people I know with PDA, myself included.

I feel that the degree of anxiety-driven avoidance in PDA is more significant than can be described as 'extreme'. Put simply, 'extreme' is at the far end of what you may expect of the majority of people, but it is still, just about, within that range of ordinary expectation. Pathological is outside that range.

If something is pathological, it means it is something that is happening to an out-of-the-ordinary extent, beyond the usual control or rational choice of the person affected. This doesn't mean to say that people with PDA can't or shouldn't be expected to increase their tolerance of demands, but it does mean that sensitivity to them is a core part of what makes us tick. Maybe it could be described like the startled reaction you have if someone suddenly claps their hands in front of your face. If it keeps happening, over time, you may manage not to flinch so much when they do this, but you may still not be able to stop yourself at least blinking when it happens.

My reaction to a demand depends on so many different factors, like my mood at the time, who is demanding something of me, why they are doing it and how often they've made demands of me before. They all play a role, and that role can fluctuate.

There are days when the demand on me is so great I quite literally can't get past it, and the avoidance takes over the whole day. I would never choose to spend a day like this, and it doesn't leave me feeling good about life when it happens. I wish the adults who support children with PDA would understand this point. Difficult days are not about deliberately making things difficult for other people; they reflect the person (or child) themselves having a tough time.

I like my 'badge' of PDA. It gives me a place to fit and a way of understanding myself.

Direct demands

If I am given direct demands, such as a 'do this now' type of demand, my usual reaction is to say or to think, 'No way, José!, p*** off'. Now that is not to say that I always act on this reaction, but I have to admit that internally, this is my first instinct. As I mature, though, I have got better at adapting my thinking so that I can appreciate another's point of view. I can see when something is the 'right thing' to do, even if I don't like it, and nowadays I understand more about what may happen if I either do or don't act on my first instinct.

Looking back, one of the things that has made a huge difference to me improving how I cope with the ordinary demands of everyday life was receiving medication for my ADHD. Once my ADHD became more manageable I had more processing time and I was less impulsive. It hasn't stopped me being sensitive to demands, but it certainly helps me to cope with them in a calmer and healthier way, causing less damage to myself and to those around me.

I realise some direct demands are necessary and in my best interests, such as hospital staff asking me to do something so they can examine me, or a doctor telling me how I need to take medication. In those cases I'm pretty good at following orders because I know it's for my own benefit and wellbeing in the long run, but I have to make a conscious effort to suppress my anxiety, and I'm not always successful. Also, the effort of doing so may mean that I am less able to concentrate on complicated information they are telling me, so I can miss some key points. That's why it can be really helpful to take someone with me to appointments to act not only as my support but also as my interpreter, and my memory!

Social demands

Social demands are ones I'm really motivated to manage because having good friends and positive relationships are important to me. If, for example, a friend asks me out for a meal, I know that will come with other expectations about how long I will be there, what I may need to talk about and for how long, how I will manage the environment of the restaurant, etc. So I try to achieve some balance of control by, for instance, deciding where we may sit. I prefer a table near a window or an air conditioning unit. It also helps if I order something that isn't on the menu. I avoid ordering a meal 'as is'. I always swap something for something else because menus always feel like a demand to me. I hate them! Well, I like reading them and seeing what's on offer, but I hate them when it comes to choosing. These are small adaptations, but they can make a big difference to me.

Legal demands

Legal demands are the easiest to deal with because these are enforceable rules, and I believe that it is wrong and immoral to break the law. There is no discussion to have because it's just the law of the land. Laws are there for a good reason to look after our community and not just to be annoying, even though sometimes they are both. To be honest, it annoys me to see other drivers blatantly ignoring the speed limit. And stealing is not okay – it doesn't matter how much you steal, it is still wrong. Now, I didn't always think like this, hence my earlier shoplifting era when I was younger, but I wouldn't dream of doing that now. Some people have moral debates such as, 'is it okay to steal to feed your baby?', and in that situation I think a judge should show some flexibility and humanity, but the crime has still been committed. In the right circumstances I can imagine stealing to feed my beloved cats, but I wouldn't steal to feed myself. Even if I did steal to feed my cats, it wouldn't be easy to live with my conscience, but I wouldn't really care about the consequences. I think we have a lot to answer for as a society if there are people who are driven to steal to feed themselves or their families. I do still like to bend rules if I can, although interestingly I get really cross if others try to do the same.

Implied and indirect demands

Implied and indirect demands are tricky to deal with because they are 'sneaky'. They can even creep up on me when I sometimes put them on myself! The world seems full of implied demands that are about the social environment we all inhabit. If you travel on a train, there is an implied expectation that you are going to sit on the chair in a carriage, not on the table or the floor. When I go out to a pub, there is an expectation that I will put my drink on the coaster left on the table and that I will be wearing ordinary day clothes, not pyjamas or beachwear.

Self-imposed demands

These are expectations such as if I think to myself, 'I want to make a card today'. What happens next is BAM! Now I can't do it because it's become a demand. Having said that, I do make cards for people I care about and I do bake for other people or give them presents, so I am able to get past the avoidance in the main, but it doesn't come easy. My point is that this process, which seems relatively effortless or even enjoyable for other people, is invariably complicated and stressful for me.

Writing this book is another self-imposed demand. No one has told me I have to do it. It is not a legal requirement that I write it. I have chosen to write it. It's pretty astounding to me that I have managed to complete it, not only because of the scale of the task, but also because of the extent of the demand. As I said earlier, I have only been able to do so by Ruth taking care of the workload and deadlines to minimise pressure on me. A good piece of PDA collaboration!

When I was younger I used to sabotage or cancel events that you would think I would be looking forward to. I still do. As a child, if an event was planned that I would usually enjoy but didn't feel I wanted to go to at the last minute, I was often still taken there. This is what lots of parents of young children would ordinarily do, especially if they're undiagnosed. I get that. But then, when I was at wherever the place was, I would misbehave so I was taken back home anyway. I don't remember it as misbehaving *in order* to be taken home. It was more because I was unable to stop myself being uncooperative or punching someone. I was extremely impulsive in those days and I couldn't predict the consequences of my actions. Sometimes I was then barred from going to certain places again. I was asked not to come back to Brownies or to my ballet lessons because I didn't do what I was asked. I used to overhear adults say things like, 'She's very strong-willed, isn't she?'

There are still times when I feel I can't do something at the last minute that has been planned. This includes things I had been looking forward to as well. Sometimes Paul and I have planned a nice day trip somewhere I wanted to visit, but I can't face it on the day. He is very understanding about late cancellations so I feel okay about that, but if I was meant to be seeing a friend, I wouldn't cancel unless I was genuinely ill, because I wouldn't want to let them down.

One of the things that helps me attend events like the Women's

Institute or Parish Council meetings is that I have a role or responsibility there. I don't want to be unreliable or to disappoint people, so as long as I can make other aspects of attending as easy as possible (such as getting a lift there, having someone else to take notes, doing very little else that day), then I can handle it.

I have mixed feelings about making myself go to events I struggle with. Also, about adults making children do the same. On the one hand, I can see that it helps us grow and mature to face challenges – as long as the challenges are manageable, even if they are tough. On the other hand, I understand that it doesn't always help to pile even more stress onto individuals who are already anxious on a daily basis. It's a very hard balance, and getting that right will be different for every individual. What is certainly easier now that I am an adult is two things: first, I have more control over lots of aspects of my day or my week so I can adapt other commitments to take account of a stressful event. Children are usually expected to come to school again tomorrow and the next day, whether today has been one of their best days or one of their worst, so they rely on adults to budget their capacities for them. Second, as an adult there are more socially acceptable ways to amend or postpone events than are available to children. There are also more acceptable ways to take even a short break, such as to leave a situation to have a cigarette or to take a call. Children can't just leave a house or a classroom whenever they feel the need (although maybe some of them do precisely that – I certainly did!).

Inflexible demands, not open for negotiation

The most frustrating type of demand that falls into this category is without doubt medical appointments, and mental health appointments in particular, which make me feel particularly agitated. Navigating systems that might block my access to a certain health professional or to getting a repeat prescription by being on the caseload of the right clinic within the right service causes me an incredible amount of stress and distress. Having had years of really difficult experiences I am delighted to say that I am now being seen by a thoroughly lovely and highly professional psychiatrist who is very good at listening and accommodating my needs.

Unexpected demands

Everyday life as both a child and as an adult seems to have a never-ending supply of unexpected events. Some are more significant than others, but hardly a day goes by without some degree of uncertainty. For people like me, this can create a constant backdrop of anxiety, which is why it may not take much to tip the scales some days. Sometimes an unexpected change triggers unmanageable levels of anxiety that might last for hours or even days. I like an element of routine with things, like what I eat or what I watch on TV. They need to be my own routines though, not ones imposed on me, and they need to be routines I can change whenever I want or need to. Strict routines actually make my skin crawl and my mind fuzzy.

Disregarding demands, boundaries and requirements

As a young child I didn't have a good grasp of right and wrong; I just knew what I wanted, for myself, here and now. Sometimes, even if I was caught red-handed doing something I shouldn't be doing, I would deny it. On some occasions it was as if I really couldn't remember or relate to having done that thing. Other times I was trying to charm my way out of it by using all sorts of denial, distraction and avoidance strategies. I liked to think that I had great charm, but looking back, I don't think I did. I wanted to be like Bart Simpson on TV, but I can't have been very good at charming my way out of trouble because I didn't get away with things like he did.

When I was about 7, I took the Barbie® doll I had taken a shine to from my friend's house. I don't remember the detail of how it was resolved, but I think I gave it back and said sorry, and then we all moved on. When I was 8 I stole the prized, unused, animal-shaped rubber collection from a girl in my class at school. She and I were arch-enemies, and I resented her for always trying to get me into trouble. Granted, 9 times out of 10 if there was trouble to be had I was involved, but every now and then I was innocent, yet she still tried to 'frame' me.

Mum says I used to insist that,

ALL mishaps were never as a result of you; they were always caused by other children.

I knew stealing would get me into trouble, but I didn't care because it was about revenge! In the end I did give her rubbers back to her, but only after I had used them all, which made them dirty and misshapen. She was very upset, but I just viewed it as karma.

When I was about 11, I started hanging out with a group of friends who were the best of friends because they accepted me for who I was, but at the same time they were the worst of friends because they encouraged me to do stuff that wasn't in my best interests. One of these things was shoplifting. I got a real buzz from shoplifting. At the time, I had not yet been given my ADHD diagnosis and it was another couple of years before I was to feel the benefits of taking methylphenidate.

I was often in trouble with the police for anti-social behaviour, for running away or for shoplifting (so looking back I can't have been that good at that either). However, I pride myself with the fact that although I was unofficially cautioned once, and despite being known to the local police by my first name, I was never arrested. One time, following a shoplifting incident aged about 11, my mum arranged for a policeman to come to the house to have 'a few strong words' with me. They sent their biggest, tallest policeman. He told me what I had done was illegal etc., and took away what I had stolen to be destroyed. Unfortunately, I told him to 'f*** off'. It really annoyed me that he came into my house telling me what to do and acting like he was better than me. I didn't have a well-developed conscience then, so I just felt like, who was this great big bloke coming to our house telling me what I should be doing? I genuinely didn't understand why I couldn't just have something I wanted, especially when it was only a small thing. My mum was very disappointed that 'PC Plod's' visit didn't have the desired effect, but back then I simply thought laws didn't apply to me. She wrote in her parental contribution to my SEN assessment around that time,

> *Julia imagines she doesn't need adult guidance or care. Actually the reverse is very much the truth. She is socially immature. Normal warnings and guidance don't apply to her. She exposes herself to extreme danger.*

I wasn't helped by my difficulties with impulse control and untreated ADHD. It took until I was about 14 for the criminal elements of my behaviour to reduce. My risk-taking anti-social behaviour calmed down about age 16 or 17.

What made me change? It's hard to say. Maybe a combination of natural maturation, plus the difference having a diagnosis made to the people supporting me, because they understood how to help me better. The effect of methylphenidate helped reduce my impulsiveness, and having my first serious partner also had a positive impact.

It's interesting to look back at the psychology report about me aged about 14, which said,

> *Julia and her mother are much calmer with each other, which is partly the result of her being easier to deal with on methylphenidate, and partly the result of Mrs Daunt's determined efforts not to be confrontational...she is back in full-time education (and) is showing more insight into herself...*

At first I had been very scared of taking methylphenidate, but I also knew that I needed it. I had been on amitriptyline for a while, and I was keen to come off this and swap it for methylphenidate because I didn't like how the amitriptyline made me feel, or the weight I had gained when I was on it. I wanted to do something else that would help. At that time, I didn't like being me and I was tired of how that felt. I wanted a positive life. I wanted quality relationships. I wanted to be 'good'. It was obvious to me I was doing something wrong because I was always in trouble, disappointing people or letting others down.

Mum reassured me that I was safe to take my first tablet. I decided to try one and see if I died! Not only did I not die, but I also felt better pretty much straight away. This was the real clincher because I could see immediately that methylphenidate was going to have a positive impact. All of a sudden my brain felt ordered, I was thinking in full sentences, not snatched phrases that jumped from one topic to the next. I could even see that I had brief pauses in thoughts so that I could process one before moving onto the next. Most exciting was that I could think about a thought. I mean, I could have an idea and stay with that train of thought for a while without something totally random popping into my mind on top of it that squashed and scrambled it. That was the start of me being able to achieve more learning because I could think about what I was learning; I understood more about empathy because I could consider how other people may feel; and I could make better decisions because I could weigh up whether doing that thing or not doing that thing really was a good idea.

Having a bit more thinking space helped me to curb my unhelpful impulses and to understand the impact of them on myself and on other people. I started to develop a moral code that really helped with my anti-social behaviour. Also, as I got to know myself better, I began to realise how much I needed to be adapted for me. I didn't know that much about the world, but I certainly knew enough to know that these accommodations weren't likely to be available in the criminal justice system, so it became really important to avoid going to prison! I still have some impulsive thoughts and ideas, but I'm better at thinking things through and checking them out with myself and with Paul. Then we can decide whether something is actually a good idea or not.

As an adult I find it hard not to disregard certain expectations or instructions, but they're only minor. If I see a sign that says 'Do not touch' or 'Keep off the grass', I usually need to touch it a little bit, which satisfies the urge!

Avoiding demands as a child

I asked Mum about what I did to avoid demands as a child. Her immediate reply was to say, 'What didn't you do would be a more relevant question! It wasn't possible to make you do what you didn't want to do, whether by discipline or bargaining.'

Mum also said, 'Never mind getting dressed, just getting you out of bed was a problem. Do you remember punching me in the mornings and me then having to wake you up from across the room so I wasn't within striking range?'

Teachers began commenting that they were 'struggling to cope with Julia because of her oppositional behaviour'.

I remember getting into trouble one time, at age 5, about colouring in a picture of 'Roger Redhat', a character out of our reading books. I was told to colour his hat in red, but for some reason I only wanted to colour it in blue. I remember a lot of shouting and stamping my feet. I was not going to give in so they called my mum who very sensibly asked whether I knew the difference between red and blue. The teacher said I did. So Mum said, *'Then why on earth does it matter what colour she uses on this worksheet?'* Apparently it was important for some school achievement records, so the teacher tried all sorts, even holding her hand over mine to get some red crayon on the paper, but I still wasn't having any of it. I don't know why this incident sticks in my mind because it must have been one of so many similar stories. I was a regular visitor outside the headteacher's office. There was always some green-faced child sitting there clutching a sick bowl...and me.

Sometimes I would fake injuries as a way of avoiding doing something. I often said I was in pain. This was hard for Mum, who reflected,

> *I could never be sure about your 'injuries' and yes, I did get it wrong on occasions. Sometimes you were hurt but had cried wolf so often, I didn't take any notice.*

Unfortunately, one of these occasions was when I said my wrist hurt, which was ignored, only to find out the following day that I had, in fact, fractured it.

I did sometimes say things like,

> *I can't do PE because my legs don't work.*

> *I couldn't do my homework because the clocks went back at the weekend.*

> *I can't water the plants because the sun's shining too brightly.*

I remember learning how to say 'the dog ate my homework' in Latin because I thought my teacher would be so impressed that he wouldn't insist on me doing the work. Unfortunately, my science teacher wasn't impressed at all. Maybe, with hindsight, I should have tried that one on a languages teacher instead?

There were times when I made up rather elaborate stories either to avoid or to distract, by getting sympathy. Talking to Mum recently she reminded me that,

> *...you didn't appear to care about adult scepticism or even remember (what stories you'd told) at times. Impossible to work out which. Remember the Christmas when you told the school you got no presents and were being starved?*

For the record, I did receive presents, and I wasn't being starved at home!

And at age 14, I was described by a developmental psychologist as having,

> *...an ability for social manipulation of others in pursuit of an obsession- al aim to avoid the ordinary demands made on children. She is a child without boundaries, with no sense of pride or responsibility...*

I would throw chairs at school and I punched anyone at any place at any time, regardless of whether they were a child or a teacher. And unfortunately I was even more violent at home.

I have included lots of the quotes from various reports and assessments here partly because I want to be honest and transparent, but also because I want to illustrate what had been happening, and how a range of people viewed it. It was, to go back to my point about the pathological part of PDA, way outside ordinary development, and often fuelled by genuine difficulties in social understanding as well as by anxiety.

Avoiding demands as an adult

The strategies I use now are not really so different to the ones I used (or tried to use, with mixed success) when I was younger. I had been under the impression that I had devised more strategies to avoid demands than I have to cope with them, but writing this chapter has helped me to see that this isn't actually the case, which is very encouraging!

Nonetheless, when I'm avoiding a demand, I may try to:

• Refuse the request or demand. This may include ignoring it is even there. It also applies to expectations I put on myself, such as making a cake that I have promised to bake for an occasion.

• Negotiate and renegotiate the terms and conditions. This applies to doing part of a task rather than all of it, to postponing a task, to getting an extension to a treat that was meant to be time-limited. Sometimes there is a bit of manipulation, such as telling Paul I will read his book on aircraft when he reads *Black Beauty* (one of my all-time favourites), which I know he will never do. I want to read his book because I know it's important to him, so therefore it's important to me, but I just can't. I know that the topic won't particularly interest me and I won't understand a lot of it. To put this into perspective – it takes me about a year to read a book I enjoy, so can you imagine how long it will take to me get through a book like Paul's!

- Be fun, flirty, funny. Another distraction or renegotiation tactic, I suppose.

- Change the subject. This works better with some people than others. People usually respond well if the subject is changed to something they like or something they are good at.

- Use compliments. Another distraction technique such as, 'I really like your nail varnish colour, where did you get it?'

- Say 'yes', but on my terms such as, 'Yes I can do that for you, but it won't be on Monday, it will be on Wednesday.'

- Delegate the task. This relies heavily on the wonderful kindness and cooperation of friends and especially of Paul. It means he has a number of jobs to do where there is a set date to work with, such as bin day.

Strategies that help me cope with demands

I continue to be sensitive to everyday demands, but it helps me if I can:

- **Negotiate:** This is a strategy I use to avoid demands, but it is also a strategy that helps me comply with demands. It's especially important to do this with kindness, to look after the friendships and relationships I want to maintain.

- **Split a task:** It helps if I can do part of a job and have some help with or postpone the rest. This stops one task being so overwhelming that it's too big to tackle. If the task needs completing as one, such as washing my hair in the shower, I may wash my body but Paul will help me to wash my hair.

- **Have projects:** It can help to have a number of projects on the go at a time, so that if I am able to get something done that day, I have a few things to choose from. I find it much easier to dip in and out of projects rather than feeling forced to do one all in one go. I often watch TV for a bit, reply to emails, carry out admin duties, do some crafting and then repeat. It helps keep the pressure off. Sometimes, though, with really important stuff, like replying to Ruth's emails, I feel I must do it straight away and I put everything else on hold. This is for two reasons: (1) if I put it off I will more than likely forget to do it at all and (2) if I postpone it, even for a bit, demand avoidance will kick in and I might not be able to do it at all.

- **Prioritise:** This may include an element of plain and simple refusal to do a task if it is not deemed a priority, but hopefully it eventually leads to some compromise. For example, we tend to do our grocery shopping on the internet. When it arrives, I am happy to put away fridge and freezer items, motivated by not wanting the food to spoil and to therefore have wasted money. However, I find it very hard to put away tins and boxes because that won't make a difference other than in terms of tidiness, so Paul does this part of the job. I'm happy to share this job, but if I'm honest, Paul tends to do it all most weeks.

- **Give myself extra time:** It helps me to have processing time and it can also help me to have additional time to finish a task, except that there are also occasions when having too much time means I just use that extra time to put it off for even longer, so I often feel that I am trying to catch up with myself.

- **Have a deadline:** Having a clear deadline can help to focus me on dealing with a task on some occasions. On others it adds to the stress, and then that doesn't help. Maybe a better way to describe it would be a 'guideline' rather than a deadline. This means that there is a degree of expectation, but with a hint of some flexibility.

- **Rely on myself:** As an adult I know there are some things that only I can do for myself and I understand that this is good for me. There are times when this is a pressure in itself, but it's one I want to work through – for instance, writing this book. Only I can provide the content, even if Ruth does the actual writing. So I need to commit to the telephone calls we have, otherwise it simply can't happen. This project is probably the biggest single task I have undertaken!

- **Have choices:** Having limited choices that are reasonably predictable can work well. Having too much choice or having to choose between too many variables that are unfamiliar becomes overwhelming, and then that isn't helpful at all. If I trust someone enough, I am comfortable with them making a choice on my behalf.

- **Make a task part of a 'most days' routine:** This sometimes works if I can set and change the routines any time I want. I generally aim to shower/brush my teeth/change my clothes a couple of times a week, always on a flexible basis, and I have Plan B options, such as if I couldn't manage a shower on a given day, I will at least use baby wipes or a wet flannel. I've realised I probably have more strict routines about what I can't do than what I can do!

- **Be asked politely:** Demands are on the whole easier for me to deal with now I'm an adult because adults have a lot more control in their everyday life than children. I still can't cope with being lectured at or having a long list of 'things I need to do' reeled off at me. If you do need to ask me to do something, one sure way to get a better response out of me is to at least be very polite about it. It sounds like a little adjustment, but starting a request with a 'Please do you think you could...' is much more likely to get the desired result. For me, being polite and asking rather than telling me to do something leaves the door open for negotiation and feels respectful.

- **Have caring and understanding support**: It is so important to have people in my life who accept me, who show me kindness and who I trust. This is important for everyone, of course, but specific to PDA, it is crucial to have people who can guide and support me to cope with everyday demands. Paul is obviously my 'rock' in this respect, as is my mum. I see now that Mum sacrificed her own happiness for me when I was growing up, certainly more so than would reasonably be expected of other parents. She took damage to her physical and mental health in trying to meet my needs and didn't get a break. Even the usual breaks that many parents have by arranging playdates invariably ended badly and weren't repeated. She's loved and supported me and never gave up on me. Thank you, Mum. When I was younger I was also lucky enough to have a couple of very special adults who understood me. One was my outreach worker and the other was my 1:1 at school. I'm pleased to say that I'm still in touch with them both. And finally, I got a lot of emotional support from the one and only Alf!

I want to include a note here to acknowledge the enormous difference it makes having Paul in my life. I appreciate him on a day-to-day basis, but this was particularly highlighted to me when I was ill at a time when he had to be away from home for a few days. I was in touch with Ruth at this time, and wrote emails to her saying,

It's Monday and Paul is currently away for a week. He's been away for three days now. There's some food in the house and I'm hungry but I

can't make dinner. This happens a lot when he's not here. I just can't. Lunch was basic – bacon, eggs, beans and instant mash. We had ready meals in for me, but I ate them all in two days! No chance of me leaving the house to buy something either. Two different friends have already come to my rescue – one with bird seed for the garden birds and one with cat food. We had plenty of cat food but they didn't like it so weren't eating it and were annoying me. I made my friends a cup of tea when they came but didn't feel I could make myself one. I haven't had a cup of tea for days and I really want one. Thankfully, another food shop is coming on Wednesday early morning so more ready meals at last! I hate this. I'm hungry.

...I have one of the worst abscesses I've ever had. I have a condition where they come up randomly on my body. I think I need a doctor but won't be able to go and see one...

...I had a rough night. Had a temperature with the abscess so called out of hours GP. They refused to do a home visit, so I had a rather uncomfortable night. I'm going to call my practice this morning and hope they'll be helpful...

I've been prescribed antibiotics over the phone so I'm pleased. Thankfully our pharmacy delivers if you're a patient unable to come in.

...They've delivered the antibiotics to me. I wasn't able to take the first dose on time but once I got started, I've been taking them regularly since. I'm hoping to do the washing up tomorrow before another friend comes over for a takeaway together because I wouldn't want her to see the house in a mess...

Just shows me what life would be like without Paul.

When you break down the different types of demands, it's easy to see that we are all surrounded by expectations every day. There are also demands that lurk within demands. For example, getting a child to put on their shoes, however gently you make that request, hides loads of other demands. First there is the question of which shoes, because they all feel different on your feet, and some may be more uncomfortable than others; then there is the sock issue, because socks may or may not feel right in the shoes; then there is the matter of getting the shoes on the right feet and fastening them; there may be more comments, questions or advice from a guiding adult at any time, and last but not least there is the biggest implied demand, which is the reason the shoes are necessary at all – because there is an expectation that we are going out somewhere (which comes with a load more lurking demands). All to say that for those of us who are highly sensitive to demands, our everyday lives are awash with them! The only positive aspect of this I can now say is that overcoming demands brings greater satisfaction and a greater sense of achievement than ever before.

Chapter 6

Sensory Differences

Sensory processing differences are a widely recognised aspect of ASC. As a child I wasn't particularly aware of having sensory differences, I guess because I was simply getting on with being Julia. I don't remember thinking that any meltdowns happened because of sensory overload, although of course, looking back now, I suspect that this will have been the case on some occasions. I'm not only affected by the problems caused by my sensory experiences, but my tendency to sensory overload also has a big impact on my general tolerance, anxiety and my ability to cope.

I sometimes wonder whether my sensory differences are getting even more pronounced as I get older, although it is possible I have just become more conscious of them now I know myself better and am able to articulate my thoughts. I will go through my senses one by one now, but it's important to remember that they don't function in isolation. What happens in one sensory mode can, in turn, affect what's going on in another, to say nothing of how they affect my mood!

Hearing

My hearing is very acute. I tend to hear everything at the same volume, which means that if an environment is too busy or full of too many people talking, I really struggle to pick out the sounds I need to be concentrating on, such as what the person standing in front of me is talking about. Background music also makes it difficult for me to hear because I am then hearing so many different noises. I find it very distracting and hard to pick out what to listen to.

Interestingly, on the other hand I don't like silence. When I'm at home I like to have music or the TV on.

I never liked balloons when I was younger (and I still don't) because I was always waiting for them to pop. Maybe this was in part not liking loud noises, but it was also about not liking things to be unpredictable or outside my control.

I feel like I am affected by delayed or disrupted processing across my sensory systems. In terms of my hearing, this has created one annoying little habit that frustrates Paul. If he makes any kind of vocalisation from across the room or in the next room, I ask, 'What did you say?' He usually didn't say anything – he may have coughed, burped or sighed. By the time I have processed what sort of vocalisation I have just heard, my irritating question has already popped out. Sorry Paul.

Talking of irritants, in spite of liking certain white noise, there is a long list of sounds I find somewhere between vaguely agitating and really hard to tolerate. This list includes:

• Clocks ticking.

• Washing machines on spin cycle (except for my Bosch machine which I chose for its low decibel specification).

• Vacuum cleaners (but not my Miele, which I also chose because of its quieter motor).

• Dogs barking.

- Bird song.

- The sound of crunching sand underfoot, although in contrast I love the sensation of walking barefoot in sand!

- The high-pitched squeals and laughter of children.

- Humming from street lights.

- Middle distance chatter, such as neighbours in their gardens.

- Traffic noise.

- Ferdinand's 'yodel' – Ferdie is one of my cats that makes a particular noise. It's not like a typical cat miaow, and he drives me mad with it, but it is part of his feline dementia so I try to be patient with him.

- People dragging their feet across the carpet when they walk (although, as Paul points out, I often do this myself, which, of course, I think is fine!).

- Mobile phones that make frequent bings and bleeps as notifications arrive.

Seeing

I don't like bright or fluorescent lights. Sometimes strong sunlight can be too much. Flashing lights can be annoying but also mesmerising, like Christmas fairy lights. Either way, they can dominate my attention.

At school fluorescent lights were distracting because I could see their flicker and hear their hum. During my teenage years Mum bought me a fibre optic light that we used when I had psychotic 'Monster Jack' attacks to help me relax. I remember going to a sensory room at a local special school once, which was awesome. I do remember coming out of it rather spaced out, however, like I was stoned but without the giggles or the munchies!

I like information presented visually – for instance, I like having pictures in a recipe book. I also love to watch video clips of things like cake decorating, paint pouring and waves breaking, etc.

Touching

I had a neurological examination carried out six years ago during which I was asked to identify whether my feet were being touched by a cotton pad or a needle. I had to name the touch as either sharp or soft. My responses weren't totally reliable, although sometimes they were accurate. The conclusion that was arrived at was that there was nothing fundamentally 'wrong' with my sense of touch, but that there was a delay in processing the neurological messages, which means that interpreting the sensation I've just felt can be disrupted.

At the age of 12, I had a psychology assessment which noted my,

> ...poor processing speed...Julia lost points in the Coding and Symbol Search subtests as a result of slow response speed as opposed to inaccuracy.

I have always liked being touched or stroked for reassurance. However, I don't like being touched when I'm having a meltdown because then I need space and to be left alone. At times like that, I hate to feel restricted or restrained by touch. During the assessment mentioned above, which my mum and half-brother both attended, my mum reported that:

> Julia herself has always come for comfort and responded to being cuddled...she has always been very demanding of affection and responds to approaches but there has been a feeling of a lack of depth in the contact.

I don't like being held too tightly and, because I don't like getting too hot, I don't like snuggling for long periods of time. Spooning in bed when I'm awake is fine but is simply not possible for me when I want to sleep.

I remember in my early teens wondering why other people didn't seem to have a problem with wearing shoes. I had a big problem wearing shoes and still prefer to be barefoot or in flip-flops. One of the drawbacks for me in moving further North in the country is that the weather is much colder, so the flip-flop season has become considerably shorter!

As a teenager I went through a phase of trying to wear high heels to look like some of the other girls, but I couldn't get my head around how anyone could tolerate wearing such uncomfortable shoes. Besides, I felt like they made me walk like a wonky elephant!

When I was a child, I was happiest barefoot, even when playing out in the street. There were a couple of years when, unless I was at school, I would have been either barefoot or wearing my roller skates. I would go a few houses away to play with friends wearing my roller skates, which I kept on, even inside their houses, including up and down their staircases. I did this in my own house, too. I mastered riding my bike wearing roller skates, which fitted neatly around the pedals (and had the advantage of giving me extra wheels to put on the floor if I needed them to tackle a bend). I once slept in a brand new pair of shoes. I loved them so much I couldn't bear to not be wearing them, so I slept in them for a few nights.

I have strong preferences about what clothes I wear now, but I don't remember any problems wearing school uniform when I was younger. The summer uniform was easiest, which was a traditional green-and-white-checked dress. Actually, this was very Julia-friendly for me because it was one cotton garment that was loose fitted, and after any annoying labels had been removed, it felt fine. Winter uniform was not bad, but I invariably added my own twist such as non-regulation socks, rolled-up sleeves, untucked shirt, and only rarely did I wear a coat.

I think Mum must have dressed me for school for many years, simply because I can't believe I would have been able to do it properly by myself, and since I don't remember being in trouble about it, it's most likely that someone must have helped me. I certainly do remember times when I got the planning and organising of getting dressed wrong. When I dressed myself I always seemed to look dishevelled, and sometimes even forgot the basics like putting on pants. After school swimming once I just put my school uniform back on top of my wet swimming costume, and after PE I would often arrive back at home missing some piece of clothing or wearing shoes but no socks in sight. Looking back now I really don't know if I was somehow avoiding the task or was not actually capable of organising myself for the task. This is where it's hard to separate the impact of my ADHD in terms of my ability to organise myself from my PDA.

At the age of 26 I had an adult assessment for ADHD, which confirmed the diagnosis that I had first received aged 12. As part of the developmental history, which my mum contributed to, the report said,

> As a child, Ms Daunt was very forgetful so she tended to forget what she needed for school, regular chores and what she had been asked to do; however, her mother was always unclear whether she was more forgetful or wilful. As an adult she continues to be forgetful with a tendency to have to go back for things which she has forgotten, she relies on other people to remember things and she tends to forget conversations she has had with people.

I still prefer loose clothing and natural fabrics. I don't know how I coped with wearing polyester when I was younger! I don't like tight underwear, so I have embraced 'big pants'. This makes up for having to deal with wearing a bra which has to fit how I am used to, and has to sit on my shoulders just right, or it's incredibly agitating and distracting. To be honest I am at my happiest in pyjamas and flip-flops, with my bra safely in a drawer.

When I get new clothes, it takes a couple of weeks to get them settled in and feeling right to wear. This usually involves giving them a number of washes and sometimes asking Paul, whose feet are a bit larger than mine, to wear a new pair of trainers for a few days to stretch them a bit wider for me. The only thing I like to use brand new is a soft fluffy towel; then I hate them when they get old and scratchy.

A few years ago, I was a bridesmaid for my brother. I wanted very much to make the day special for them and to do the right thing, so I wore a fitted burgundy satin dress, including control underwear, for the whole day. Fortunately, it was a long dress so I could put my slippers on after the first part of the celebration. I stayed dressed as a bridesmaid until midnight when I changed into my usual clothes and went back down to the party. Like some sort of a Cinderella story, except I was much happier dressed as me!

I don't like the feeling of being restricted physically, whether by another person or by tight clothes or underwear. I would actively try to avoid touching strangers and try to avoid touching people or things in the community that may carry germs, because I so hate getting a cold or a tummy bug. I've been like this for years. During the Coronavirus pandemic I wouldn't touch anything without gloves on, and I made Paul wear gloves and a mask when he went out.

I do like hugs, though, and am happy to hug someone if I know them well enough. Sometimes I find making good decisions about greeting people difficult. It's so hard to judge – is it a handshake? A hug? A hug and a hold? A hug and a kiss? All of the above?! At least at the time of writing this, in 2020, because of social distancing as a response to the Coronavirus pandemic, these expectations have all been suspended.

In some ways I have come to rely on Paul's gentle touch. I particularly like to be stroked in a certain way on my feet. The stroking needs to be quite slow and with a bit of scratching, such as with a longer fingernail. We call this having a 'wingle'. Most nights Paul gets me to sleep by stroking me in this way for up to an hour. An important part of the process is that he needs to give me a three-minute warning when the 'wingle' is coming to an end, followed by a final 30-second warning. At this stage I usually manage to negotiate a few extra minutes! I'm very grateful to him. It makes it hard for me to sleep if he has to work away because 'wingling' myself just isn't the same!

I think this stroking thing has been around for a long time. Mum remembers that I loved being stroked from being very young, and that the amount of stroking I craved, she felt, was 'excessive'.

Eating and taste

As a child I was pretty committed to eating typical kid-food and didn't want to try new tastes or unfamiliar-looking food. My menus of choice as a child featured Chicken Kiev, pizza, burgers, beans and chips with the odd rare appearance of vegetables! I've always had a big appetite and could easily eat a cooked school lunch and a proper dinner in the evening. Mum says, 'There were foods at school that you ate ravenously when other kids stuck to the dished-out amounts.'

As an adult, I'm not tempted by tapas restaurants with little tasting dishes; I would rather have a proper big meal that I don't need to share. Anyway, I hate food like olives and that sort of thing. I do enjoy eating out nowadays and even like Chinese; BBQ spare ribs, chips and spring rolls are my go-to choices, though I will sometimes eat other dishes. I like to go to a restaurant where I know the menu will include something I can be assured I will want to eat. Sometimes I find it extremely hard ordering off a menu and I invariably make substitutions, for example, I might order the vegetarian pizza but with bacon strips on top. I can't cope with eating fish or seafood, or even smelling it, for that matter, though I will eat tinned tuna occasionally.

I do not like toothpaste – I never have. I use a bicarbonate one now, but it's still too minty. All toothpaste feels like it's burning the inside of my mouth to some degree. I wouldn't want to try an unflavoured one because the mint is needed to deal with bad breath, so I have learned to put up with it.

I am aware that I have some other quirky little habits around eating. I'm sure lots of people do. Most other people probably keep quiet about theirs, but I'm happy to share mine here! If I eat something small, like peanuts, crisps or jelly beans, for instance, I need to eat them in amounts of either three, five, eight or ten. I only do it with quite small things, but if I'm having a sausage I would want to cut it into five pieces; I do this with bacon too. I also eat cereal bars or chocolate bars in five bites.

I know my three, five, eight, ten rule is ridiculous, but I just can't get away from how much it matters to me. If I have three of something and only a few minutes have passed, I can make that up to five by eating two more without feeling I've then had a set of two, which would be 'wrong'. If a longer period of time has passed I will need to go back to the start of the three, five, eight, ten rule. My systems, not surprisingly, are more rigid the more tense or anxious I am. If I'm having a really bad day, they can even affect Paul, who may be sitting there enjoying a handful of jelly beans when he gets asked how many he has just eaten. Paul always tells me the truthful answer, which is probably good for me to hear that he isn't sticking to my rules just because I am. However, on a bad day I will ask him to then adjust his number to 'correct' himself. I'm very lucky he is so kind and accommodating with me. It's important that I don't expect him to do this too often, and I try to remind myself that even though I may be in control of 'me', I can't and shouldn't try to be in control of him, or indeed any other person. I do find it hard to resist saying 'well done' to him if he eats the 'correct' number first time.

Mum remembers, 'when you were a child you would only eat from a certain bowl, cup and cutlery. If they were dirty and waiting to be washed you would have a big problem with that.'

I still have that bowl, plate and fork, which is an unusual one in having just three prongs. There's something uniquely pleasing about it, and I wouldn't want to get rid of it. I also have my old plastic orange set. I wouldn't want to use any of the sentimental crockery or cutlery and I would be very distressed if anyone else did so, but interestingly, I do keep the cutlery in the kitchen drawer, so it would be easy for a visitor to inadvertently make that mistake.

When I eat chips or French fries, I need to eat them in pairs that are evenly matched in length. Pasta needs to be loaded onto my fork three pieces at a time. When I get towards the end of a pasta dish, I need to amend the numbers of pieces I have left, maybe by counting a broken piece as one so that I am left with three for the final mouthful.

I have a specific system for eating toast, bread or sandwiches. I nibble the crusts off in a clockwise direction then fold the piece of toast (sandwiches are already effectively folded) and then eat the rest. I would still respect these rules if the bread was already cut into squares or triangles. When I was younger I used to eat puff pastry in single wafer-thin layers until there was only a thin covering left, say, over the contents of a Cornish pasty, then the middle could be eaten.

I like Mars® bars and I have a system for eating them too. I bite off all the chocolate around the edges and ends and then I eat the nougat, leaving just a long strip of chocolate and caramel, which I then eat in five bites, of course!

I realise that these comments are not so much about sensory sensitivities related to the texture or taste of the food. They're probably related to features of my autistic thinking, but there is certainly something that just doesn't 'feel' right to me about the notion of eating these things any other way.

Smelling

I have a sensitive sense of smell, which is sometimes a blessing and sometimes a curse. When I am enjoying a favourite smell it can be blissful, but when bombarded by an unpleasant smell it can be dreadful.

There are some smells that I have been able to get used to over time. For example, where we now live is a nice, quiet rural village, but it is near a pig farm. Most of the time this is fine, but there are days when we get a bit of a stench on the breeze. I have got used to this and it doesn't bother me now, although it did when we first moved here.

Bad smells can make me feel sick and dizzy. I feel that I can even taste very strong smells like heavy perfumes or some cleaning fluids. Having said that, my sense of smell keeps me oriented in my world.

One of the reasons I hate getting a cold is because then I lose my sense of smell, which is really disconcerting for me. I was quite upset when I had a cold over Christmas and I couldn't smell the mint-scented candle I was so glad to have received as a present. It was strange to be able to remember how it smelled when I saw it in a shop, to be able to see it was lit, but not to be able to smell it fragrancing the room.

Mum says she remembers that, 'Julia used to smell where people had been sitting. This behaviour went on for ages, unexplained and inexplicable.' And before you ask, I have no idea why I used to do it!

My ranking of smells looks like this:

Bad smells	Smells I don't like but have learned to tolerate	Good smells
• Plug-in room fragrances	• Pig farm next door	• My favourite scented candles
• Strong perfumes	• Cat food	• Sweet-smelling kitchen or bathroom cleaners (i.e. fruity, not pine)
• Spray deodorants	• Petrol and diesel	
• Some fabric softeners	• Aviation fuel and air shows	• Mint
• Green-coloured toilet cleaners	• A blown-out match	• Lavender
• Melted butter and popcorn	• Cigarette smoke	• Freshly cut grass
• Most public toilets	• Cat fur	• Natural woods, flowers
• Sewage farms	• Burned toast	• The smell of ironing – I don't do any ironing but I have a candle with this scent!
• Public transport		• Strong fruity shower gels
• London underground		• That crisp winter fresh air smell when people come in from outside
• Other people's body odour		• Freshly baked bread
• Fish and seafood		• Chocolate
		• Certain perfumes, like Chanel No 5 and my own perfume called 'Immense'

Proprioceptive and vestibular senses

These are the senses that deal with spatial awareness and balance. I've probably said enough already to have indicated that I have some difficulties with both of them. I'm quite clumsy and always have been. When I go through doorways I often bump into something. I find it really hard to tackle stairs if I can't see my feet, so if I am carrying something that stops me seeing my feet, I could easily trip. I feel lost and unsteady if I can't see my feet and I stumble frequently. I can even wobble if I'm standing still! My years line dancing helped with this, but I haven't danced for a while now.

I tend to overhug people, and as a kid would actually squeeze them until I hurt them.

When I tried to walk down stairs one foot per step, like most people do, I used to fall a lot. I even ended up in A&E a few times years ago when I was in a previous relationship because of having fallen down the stairs, and I attracted a bit of concern from the staff who were worried that I hadn't fallen on my own. Just to put the record straight – I had. Nowadays I climb downstairs sideways, especially carefully if I'm carrying something that makes it hard to see my feet.

I can even trip up over a slight bump in the carpet, or over those metal strips that separate different pieces of carpet between rooms. Lots of things seem to be able to set me off balance very easily. I also find it hard to judge joining an escalator as well as to balance when I'm on it. Getting off at the top is easier because it tends to tip or spill me off the other end.

Some things have just 'come to me' in a light bulb moment. For years I couldn't tie shoelaces despite lots of frustration trying to learn and no doubt lots of frustrated people trying to teach me. Then one day, about age 13, I could just 'see' how to do it and it hasn't been a problem since.

Interoception

Interoception is a less well-known sense, though people are starting to have a greater understanding of it. It refers to our internal senses, both conscious and subconscious. This means how we perceive and understand the internal condition of our bodies. It includes whether we are hungry or thirsty; whether we are in pain, and if so, how much and from which body area; whether we need the toilet, and if so, how urgently; our sense of the passing of time; and how we experience body regulation such as heart rate and body temperature.

Knowing how our bodies feel helps us to make sense of the emotions that we are experiencing because the two are linked. Having difficulty with interoception can affect all sorts of areas of learning, functioning and self-awareness.

Preferring natural fabrics is not only about my touch sensitivity, but it is also related to how I don't like getting overheated, which can happen very easily. When I get too hot I get fidgety and anxious and it makes me feel sick and dizzy. I need moving air on me all the time when I get like this. Last summer, during the UK heatwave, I had an electric fan trained on me all the time, and if I needed to leave the room for some reason, I had to swap to a mini hand-held fan until I was back in position in front of the large fan.

For me, feeling hot is probably associated with feeling anxious, so it's hard to feel hot and not to associate that with being anxious. I can get anxious even doing something I want to do, like going to choir, but I really need to take my trusty hand-held fan there too, to stop me feeling hot, sick and dizzy. For me, smoking is a handy regulating activity. It's been really helpful now that you can't smoke inside in the UK because it gives me a very socially acceptable way of stepping outside for a few moments. This means I can have a break from all sorts of anxiety-provoking situations. I can get some fresh air, no one feels obliged to follow me to 'see if I'm alright', plus I have the benefits of slow, deep breathing (unfortunately, along with nicotine and tar, but it soothes my anxiety all the same). I did try giving up smoking once, which only lasted for 22 hours. The additional agitation it brought on just didn't seem a price worth paying, for now. Even when I was just approaching my 15th birthday my mum told Elizabeth Newson at my review meeting that she no longer tried to stop me from smoking because she felt that 'it helps her get herself together and relax'.

I've always found sleep tricky and elusive. I take chlorpromazine every night to help with this, but I also have lots of other little habits and requirements to facilitate falling asleep, like the 'wingling'. I've tried all sorts of natural things like warm milk, no caffeine after 6pm, and lavender. I've even tried melatonin, but nothing really seems to help that much. Usually bedtime is between 9pm and 10pm; I might wake two or three times in the night, and I start my day between 5am and 6am.

Apparently I was not easy to settle to sleep, even as a baby, and never slept for long at a time. Mum must have been exhausted! I still have some trouble settling to sleep as well as staying asleep. If I get up in the night say to use the toilet, my body thinks it's morning and it's quite a lengthy process to persuade it to go back to sleep, even if it's 2am.

I am working on trying to sleep in a bed. It might come as a surprise to some of you reading this, but I haven't slept in a bed for about eight or nine years. I usually sleep on the sofa in the lounge, as does Paul, even though we have a perfectly good-sized bedroom with a luxury mattress and lovely bedding upstairs. I am not sure why it's so very difficult for me to sleep in a bed. I've been trying to get myself used to the idea by going to lie on the bed to watch something on my iPad or to have a drink. The last time I tried to actually sleep in it at night I had a panic attack. I really can't explain why that was the case. No one is making me sleep in a bed and I actually want to do it, but there's something about it I can't manage. I will keep trying, but for the moment I'm still on the sofa, with an old blanket and a mini Alf toy, whose left leg I hold in my right hand all night.

I don't find it hard to identify when I am in pain, although for me, there's no such thing as moderate pain. If I was asked to judge my pain on a scale of 1–10, I would either say it's level 1 (no pain) or 10 (extreme pain). What I do find really hard is to describe types of pain in words, for example it would be too difficult for me to say whether my pain is sharp, burning, aching, dragging or twisting. I would know if I had toothache, but if the dentist asked me where the pain was, I couldn't say left or right, upper or lower, front or back. We would have to go round my mouth, tooth by tooth, to identify which one was the culprit.

I can't easily identify even where I have an itch. I might ask Paul to scratch my back in a certain place but when he starts to do so I realise I was miles off. I begin a list of instructions, 'right a bit, no up, no down a bit, no left, actually the other left...ahhh the itch is running away!' In the end it's better if he just scratches my whole back to save time!

I struggled to learn to tell the time for years and then it just clicked, like tying shoelaces, also at about age 13. I don't think I have a very good body clock, and sensing the passage of time is not easy. I struggle to identify how long, for instance, five minutes is. If Paul says he will do something in five minutes, I'm asking him again after literally 30 seconds because I genuinely think more than five minutes has passed. One of the things that helped telling the time to make sense to me was the revelation that times can be more than one thing – for example, 20 to an hour can be the same as 40 minutes past the hour. Understanding this also fitted in with learning lots of social 'norms' about how people talk about time such as, it's fine to say it's 20 to 3, or it's 2.40 but not to say it's 40 past 2.

I have always found identifying the emotions I am experiencing tricky. If, for example, I start to feel a bit nauseous, I have to run through a list of questions: Am I hungry? Am I ill? Am I excited? Anxious? Usually, I begin to examine my emotions once I am feeling a physical indicator that something different is happening in my emotional landscape. The easiest emotions to identify are happy, sad and angry. It's much harder to determine variations or subcategories of these.

When I do get a strong emotion, especially irritation or anger, it seems to come over me very quickly. I don't feel the early warning signs, and even Paul sometimes finds it hard to spot a mood change coming. Also, when I'm angry it doesn't tend to be moderated by having empathy for the other person, it's just about how I am feeling in the moment. I have noticed that I can pick up emotions from other people, whether good or bad, so I try to avoid spending time with negative people because it rubs off on me too much.

Sensory regulation

I have learned a number of techniques to help keep my sensory system regulated. They are not always available, but these are the things that work for me:

- **'Wingles':** Paul is the expert here!

- **Fidgeting:** usually generally moving about or wobbling a leg. I also like fidget cubes.

- **Swaying:** used to be rocking, but is now more likely to be swaying from side to side when standing up.

- **Smells:** obviously needs to be the right kind of smells! Nice scented candles or wax melt blocks are good for this.

- **Fresh air:** this makes a huge difference. If I can't be near an open window, I like to have a fan close by, either a desk fan or mini hand-held fan.

- **Finger biting:** like nail biting, except it's the skin around my nails. If you're wondering how stressed I am, just take a look at my hands!

- **Baths:** I used to enjoy soaking in the bath that I could make lovely with the right smells. Now my hip has got more painful and the bathroom in our new house is a different layout I can't have a bath, though I'm pretty sure this would be nice if I was able to.

I've found it interesting to reflect on how many sensory sensitivities I have, when I lay them out here. I'm surely not unique in having certain preferences and intolerances, but I do wonder which are just 'Julia-quirks' and which are features of my autism profile. In some ways it might not matter, but I guess where it does start to matter is if someone's differences are having a significant impact on that person's functioning or quality of life, without being understood. For instance, one of the things I wish had been explained to me differently was the sensory challenge of having periods. I was told about the 'mechanics' of them, but what I found really hard were all the sensory experiences related to them. In the end, what's important is to know someone (me, in this case) as a whole person.

Chapter 7

Language and Communication

From being quite a little girl I remember having my own way of expressing myself. I liked to use vocabulary and phrases which I could make 'mine'. Many of these came from TV shows, films or the people around me. I would repeat or borrow and amend phrases I had heard simply for the enjoyment of the sound of them. To a lesser extent I still do that.

As a child I watched a lot of *EastEnders* and *Only Fools and Horses*. It was only when watching these many years later that I noticed, 'Oh look, Del Boy does that thing I do!' that I realised that I had lifted a phrase or mannerism from the show. I used to say 'Shut up you tart!' or call people a 'plonker', which Del Boy used to say to his brother Rodney. My Barbie® dolls used to say this a lot to my Ken™ doll! I also used to say 'Happy Christmas Ange,' which are the final words from an iconic *EastEnders* scene that I didn't understand at the time but I knew it was a phrase that had a big impact.

I also used to watch ALF (hence the origin of my beloved soft toy Alf). ALF was a character that was an Alien Life Form and his heart was in his ear. When he made a promise and was asked to cross his heart, he drew a cross with his hand on his ear. I did the same for a long time. I still sometimes like to do this, but try not to do so in public.

For a while now I have enjoyed the word 'tassel' and try to include it into sentences (no easy task!) so that I can have chance to say it. I like the word 'feral'. I use it to describe things like naughty cats, the car when it breaks down, or a malfunctioning machine, amongst other annoyances! I would also call it 'feral' to eat sweets straight from the treat jar.

Sometimes I repeat words or phrases that can start off giving me pleasure but then get stuck like an 'earworm' loop, by which time I want it to stop. When I was at school the same thing used to happen with spellings too – especially when I would write words ending in -er; it used to make me want to add another -er, and another. So 'weather' would become 'weather-er-er-er'. It was hard to feel that I'd added quite enough extra -er's.

I have a favourite scene in *Madagascar 3* where Marty, the zebra, puts on an afro wig and starts a very short circus dance sequence. I love this scene and, particularly when I'm stressed, I have this going round and round my head. The only thing that seems to get rid of it is to watch it on repeat for enough times until it sort of burns itself out. Actually, although I like the scene, I hate the song, but once it comes to mind it's in my head on an unwanted loop – like now, because I've just thought about it! Help!

I also find myself picking up accents from other people, and having recently moved up to North Notts from Devon I often mix and match how I speak. I'm trying to resist changing my own accent but I suppose it may happen to a degree over time. To be honest, I find broad Northern accents difficult to understand; the further North I go the harder I find it to attune to what people are saying. There are occasions when it's a bit awkward because there are only so many times you can say pardon before it starts to look rude.

Within the context of my relationship with Paul we have developed quite an extensive vocabulary that is our own. Some of this originates in me having trouble spelling words for shopping lists. Here are some of the words we use on an everyday basis:

Wingle	Tickle
Legg	Egg (hen's egg to eat)
Chewy	Tobacco
Cereal and cake	Cat food (as well as human food) (the cat even responds to the word 'cake' now)
Steek	Meat stick cat treat
Juice	Any drink I have, except tea (even though I never drink juice)
Woostle	Double-sided sticky tape backing paper (used for my crafting projects)
Foostle	Electric carpet sweeper (used to clear up from crafting, i.e. when we 'foostle the woostles')
Vak-oumme	Vacuum cleaner (name derived from an advert about cats)
Mouk	Milk
Mooperchin	Also milk
Liption	Prescription
Legs	Trousers (PJs or jeans)
Nest/nesting	Bed/going to bed
Nesty	Tired
Re-nest	Go back to sleep
De-nest	Get out of bed
Mushroom	Cat bed

Harr	Hair
He	His or him (e.g. look at he, I like he harr)
Hune	Bird's beak or other animal faces, e.g. cute puppy
Ticken	Chicken
Tycho surkey	Spoonerism for 'psycho turkey' which describes the clucking sound I make when I'm excited about something
Harm	Ham
Larmm	Lamb
Nilla	Vanilla
Pinch	Pink
Spoony	Cuddly, especially for cuddling the cats
Lint	Empty packets, wrappers or a small piece of rubbish
Tipacho	Tissue
Starbee	Strawberry
Skinny	Paul's nickname (I often have to remind myself not to call him this in public)
Baby Small	Ferdie the cat's nickname
Baby Tall	Louis the cat's nickname
Poo	My nickname, short for Julia-Poolia
Chippy	Guinea pig-type squeak (we sometimes communicate with these noises alongside mimed actions and pointing to request something of each other, e.g. something passing over)
Larry's	Paracetamol

Of the two of us, I create most of our personal language, though Paul does contribute too. To us, it just feels like 'our normal' and sometimes it's easy to forget that we are using it. There are times when using conventional vocabulary can become a pressure and I have to remind myself what the real word for something is, almost as though it's a second language. Having our own way of communicating feels very natural to us. It's one of the things that bonds us and it helps us to tune into one another.

I've never had personal experience of selective mutism, although I know this affects some PDA-ers, but there have been occasions when I have been so anxious or cross that I've been unable to talk for a while. As an adult this has happened mostly in stressful medical appointments. It is made worse when I feel that someone is misinterpreting me or trying to get me to say things that fit with their picture of me, but isn't what I'm trying to express. It brings on a mixture of anxiety, frustration and even anger. Combined, these three emotions leave me unable to speak. Hopefully, I can just about manage to let the person in question know what I think (and often what I think of them!) before I fall silent.

My understanding of language in a social context

I'm aware that although I think I am generally a very good verbal communicator, there are times when I misunderstand what someone says or vice versa, especially when it comes to reading between the lines. There are lots of expressions that I find confusing and irritating because there are too many potential interpretations instead of just one answer.

One example is when someone tells me they are going to be here in a couple of minutes or a few minutes. To me, 'a couple' means two because there are two people in a couple. 'A few' also means two because it rhymes with two. If they then arrive 15–20 minutes afterwards, I think they are late and rude, and I will have become anxious about whether they are actually coming at all. I would prefer it if they had said they would be there 'in a bit' or 'soon', which would give them up to an hour to arrive in my head. Now I do realise that not everyone thinks the same as me, so I always try to be polite and mature. This means that in real time I will try not to show that I am stressed or frustrated with them, but deep down I will be, so I will have had to use up some of my capacity for social and emotional energy by the time they arrive. Managing the emotion of all of this and trying not to show it in my interactions can be exhausting and inevitably does have an impact on my mood and therefore on how I am with them.

I started swearing at a young age, at about 3 years old, I'm told, largely coached by my older brothers. I used swear words appropriately in terms of meaning and intent but obviously not appropriately in terms of how people expected a little girl to speak. By the time I was in school I was often being told off by teachers for having told them to 'f*** off'. I even called one teacher a 'c***', which understandably caused a stir! The teacher in question said that it wasn't nice for little girls to use words they didn't understand so he didn't really have a reply when I explained to him exactly what I meant by it. I knew most of the swear/slang words for different body parts when I was in infant school (again, courtesy of my older brothers), and saw no reason not to use these words.

I used to get a bit of a buzz from the reactions I got to swearing, although this wasn't my aim. To me it was quite entertaining and more proof that adults were bizarre in how they overreacted to just a word. I used to incorporate shocking topics in conversations that had the impact of dominating the discussion. My school report at the end of Year 4 (age 9) said,

> *Julia is reluctant to join in whole class discussions. She is more relaxed in small group situations, but unfortunately she persists in using macabre themes.*

People have different views about what is and isn't 'socially appropriate', and whether such a social construct should even exist. Now I'm older I understand that even though you technically have the freedom, within reason, to say what you want to people, doing so isn't without consequence. It also means that they have the freedom to react to what you're saying and how you are saying it, and that won't necessarily turn out well for anyone. Yourself included.

I still swear quite a lot, mostly at home and with other people I know well. I guess that's similar to how it is for many people. I do find it hard to tone down my swearing but I can do so depending on the company I'm in. I would try, for example, to use 'ordinary' swear words rather than to blaspheme when I'm talking to the vicar. I try to say 'Oh geez' rather than 'Oh Jesus' or to say 'Oh crap' instead of 'Oh Christ'. Fortunately, our vicar is quite open-minded and I've even heard her drop the odd swear word herself! On a day when I'm really frustrated it can be like the opening scene from *Four Weddings and a Funeral* when there is just a stream of swearing. I do understand that just because I personally am not upset by swear words, some other people might be, so I do think it's important not to go around hurting and offending people without good reason. There is a difference, though, between saying 'Oh f*** it!' if I stub my toe and saying 'Oh f*** off!' directly to a person who would have every right to react.

Some people I know would say that I am articulate, sociable, kind, interested in other people and fun to spend time with. I know that I am not without social skills and I do have friends. I enjoy time with certain people at certain times in certain amounts. However, there are times when I don't quite understand a social situation or I misjudge something. It might be because of difficulties with social understanding or with my literal processing of the words spoken. It's really hard to explain what happens when I find social situations difficult, because I only know how I am, not how it is for other people. How would I be able to express difficulties I have with something when I have difficulty knowing what I've got difficulty with? Paul has described it as,

The stress of social situations affects Julia's ability to communicate and direct questions are met with strong resistance...timing and social etiquette are also issues as is knowing when to speak in larger groups.

I do realise there are times when I need to look quite intently at someone's face when I'm saying something because I'm trying really hard to read their reaction. I can see from their response that there are occasions when I misjudge things, but I find it hard to avoid doing so until it's already happened.

I was quite a literal thinker when I was younger, so I was an easy target for people to tease. I am still rather gullible – for example, if someone called me to the window to say, 'Look at that bird, it's just laid a square egg!' I would believe them at first. When I was a child, I had one very stressful Christmas when my brother told me that Santa had fallen off our roof and died, so half the children in the world wouldn't get their presents that year. I was extremely upset. I don't know if he thought I was old enough not to have believed him and to have passed it off as him just messing around. I still struggle with sarcasm, especially if I don't know the person well. I realise I am a bit gullible when I see fake news online too. I don't like how it leaves me feeling because I don't like to feel that I'm being teased or made to look stupid. I hate my intelligence being insulted.

As I say, I do enjoy socialising but there are limits to my tolerance and my processing. For example, I know that I can follow a conversation more easily when I've had my methylphenidate. I can sense this is much harder when I haven't had it. At times, people will ask me something and I start answering, only to realise I have no idea what point I'm making, or I can't remember their question. I hate that because it leaves me feeling like a fool.

Following the flow of a conversation when the topic shifts is not easy. If I am the one who changes the topic, that's fine because I don't have to predict or judge it happening because I am the one making it happen. If the discussion moves on before I have had a chance to say everything I want to about a subject, especially if I have strong feelings about it, then that makes me very agitated. I find it hard to 'let go' of my unfinished comments, which means I can't concentrate on what is then being talked about. Also, I find it hard if there is more than one person in the conversation, particularly if there were more than three of us. I've noticed that when most people talk, they start to cut across each other and sometimes begin to take their turn to talk just before the other one has finished speaking. They're not being rude, just bubbly and enthusiastic. They seem to be able to keep up with this pace, but I don't find it easy. It's hard to separate who is saying what. If I'm asked after a conversation what we talked about, I may, in these circumstances, have difficulty telling you who said what. There have even been times when I have talked to a person I know quite well but afterwards have described it as 'some woman who came to talk to me said...'

I'm aware I interrupt quite a lot too. Sometime this reflects me finding it hard to spot the 'gaps' in a conversation, but other times it's because if I've had an idea I need to say it quickly, otherwise it will have disappeared!

As a result of the Coronavirus pandemic, we have had to conduct more of our social interactions online. I have continued to have weekly phone calls and emails with Ruth, but otherwise lots of our social life has been via virtual online platforms. It's a real mixed bag! The advantages are that I don't have to go out to attend a meeting or see a group of people, plus there are fewer social niceties, so the whole process is usually quicker (as long as the technology works). The disadvantages are that the interaction is much harder to read. I can't tell who I'm meant to be looking at; I talk to people's pictures and not the device camera, so people think I'm not looking at them; I don't know when to take my turn to speak; the slight delay means I don't always know if someone if joking or not; and often no one speaks or everyone speaks at the same time: it's communication chaos!

I watch dramas on TV and have been interested in them since my childhood days of watching *Neighbours* and *EastEnders*. Nowadays I particularly like Linda La Plante crime dramas, the *Murdoch Mysteries* and *The Walking Dead*. When I'm watching this sort of show I often need to pause the TV. Sometimes I just need to swear at the telly. Other times I can't believe or make sense of what I've just watched so I need to talk to Paul about it and maybe need to re-watch that scene. I want to understand, why did that character just do or say that? What do they think is going to happen next? Sometimes I get the feeling that I am blurring what's real and what's pretend. For example, when I talk about what a character has done, I need to remind myself they are not a real person. It throws me when I might see a picture of an actor out of costume because I think their character is what they should really look like. I often muddle up actors who to me are similar, like Barbara Streisand with Bette Midler, or Morgan Freeman with Samuel Jackson, or Robert de Niro with Al Pacino, which can make joining in conversations about one of them very confusing!

On reflection, my autism shows itself quite clearly in how I communicate.

Generally, in the midst of a social situation, I think I manage pretty well, but this chapter sets out what's going on under the surface. That is, a degree of awkwardness managing the flow and turn-taking in a conversation, some risk of crossed wires regarding my literal thinking, plus a tendency towards social overload. I'm better in relaxed situations rather than formal ones, and I know I tend to dominate social interactions because that way I can reduce some of the unpredictability of the exchange; if I'm leading the conversation I don't have to work out how to follow it. I can get exhausted with trying to understand the gap between what people say and what they mean, and although I love spending time with my valued friends and loved ones, it's certainly true that my appetite for social occasions is quite low.

Chapter 8

Friendships and Relationships

Scattered throughout the book I've given lots of examples of my experiences of the relationships I've had, but in this chapter I will try to focus more closely on the nature of my relationships, what they mean to me and in particular, my relationship with my partner, Paul.

Childhood friendships

When I was growing up, although I wasn't really aware of how or why it was difficult, I knew I had more problems making friends than other children around me seemed to have. Fortunately, when I was a child, I was usually able to have at least one friend at any time, and I'm lucky enough to say that I have many now. Friendships have always mattered to me, even if sometimes they have been rather bumpy. I've always struggled to maintain friendships, although I don't seem to have as much difficulty in starting them. It feels easier in the early stages of a friendship, but when it carries on and you get to know someone better, you have to cope with the fact that sometimes you find them annoying, sometimes they let you down, sometimes they want a different pace of friendship than you do, and sometimes I may upset them or vice versa and then we have to find a way to repair what's happened. It's all very complicated!

I was a loud, active, bubbly child, so other children who didn't know me would often naturally gravitate towards me. I was fun, silly, daring and cheeky, and other children found that appealing. They didn't always cope well with getting into trouble, though, which often came with being my friend. They also tended not to respond well to some of my explosive ways of managing disagreements. Invariably they wanted to step away if I got annoyed with them and started beating them up, or if I was mean to them. Not a surprise, of course, but at the time I didn't see things that way.

Most of these friendships were inevitably short-lived. Sometimes I would physically lash out at another child even without an obvious reason for my behaviour. When I was about 5 I invited a friend over for dinner. For a reason I can't remember, if there even was one, I pushed her very roughly and abruptly off her chair and she hurt herself. I laughed because it looked funny. Another time I had had such a grip on her that I left fingermark bruises on her neck. Although I remember the events before and the incident itself vividly, I don't have any memory of why I did what I did. Not surprisingly, her mum didn't let her come over again. Maybe my 'friend' didn't want to come anyway. I remember being angry with her for taking it badly and being cross with her mum who I thought was being mean. Although this was the first 'attack' on another child that I can recall, it wasn't the first or last time I hurt another child. Mum wrote about me as a child,

> In comparison to her friends, Julia is unable to accept 'no' and has difficulty fitting in socially. She says outrageous things and does not understand the effect they have on other people.

I remember going to a friend's birthday party. She had been given a new doll as a present that I took a liking to and wanted to play with. She wasn't keen on sharing her new toy but I grabbed it from her and ripped its head off. Then, when I got into trouble, I sat in the garden refusing to join in and being rude. I was furious with her for not sharing and thought any fallout was her own fault for not letting me play with her doll. Needless to say, my mum was called, and that was another event that I was dragged away from, marched down the path with Mum grasping hold of my wrist. That sort of thing happened often. By about age 8, I wasn't often invited to parties and not many children came to mine. My mum resorted to 'enticing' other parents to bring their children to my parties by offering to pick their children up from school or some similar favour.

My assessment report at age 12 said,

> *Julia has never had any idea of how to negotiate with other children and still doesn't know how to make normal contact with them. She will select 'nice' children to become friends with and this works briefly because she can be entertaining, then she ruins the relationship by flaring up into sudden impulsive violence, which her parents describe as pressing her self-destruct button...other children have consistently been afraid of her.*

Having said that, during my childhood I did have a couple of long-standing friendships. One of those was with a girl called Wella who was a year older than me and lived down the road. We went to the same school. For some reason, known best only to her, she liked me and put up with all my antics and moods. We even had physical fights on rare occasions, but we always seemed to make up in the end. She stood her ground and I stood mine, but we stayed friends. Our friendship only ended when my family moved away from the area and I failed to keep in touch with her, although I'm delighted that we have made contact again recently through Facebook.

I remember getting along better with children who were a bit younger than me. I think it was because they didn't seem to mind being 'controlled' or 'influenced' by me as much as children my age or older. We used to play pretend schools a lot. I was the teacher and would set them lessons, etc. Maybe it worked well because our game had clear roles and one of us was in charge (that would be me, obviously!). It also meant that I could enjoy pretend games at an age when my peers might have finished being interested in playing like that.

At about the age of 7 I was caught in a bed with a boy of about 9. We were both naked. We had been touching each other. This left me feeling very confused, but I also enjoyed it. Not long after I had had this bedroom encounter, I reported to my mum that I had been raped by the boy. As you can imagine this caused mayhem. When my mum got to the bottom of what we had actually done, the panic was over. I think I'd picked up the term from *EastEnders*, but needless to say, I hadn't understood it beyond it being something to do with nakedness and beds. It says a lot about the dangers of interpreting a little bit of information with my limited understanding of complicated concepts, as well as the importance of adults asking the right questions.

Later, after I made another equally innocent but misleading statement, more action was taken to support me. All I really remember is being taken to visit a fancy playroom full of really cool toys, having the afternoons off school and getting to play with rag dolls that had 'hair and bits', which, of course, fascinated me! It meant that I could enact all of the things I was so interested in. Of course, I was unaware of just how serious this all was and even if I had been told, I doubt it would have registered. Most of the time, I didn't understand the implications of what I was doing or saying.

I would definitely say that one of the most precious relationships to me has been the one I have with Alf. I know this might sound a bit strange to some people, but he was the ideal friend for a child like me. He was loyal, always available when I wanted to spend time with him, he never judged me, would always stand by me, was never upset by anything I did or said and he loved me unconditionally. He still remains an important part of my life to this day and will always be so.

During the latter part of my childhood and into my teens my struggles with friendships continued and, in fact, got worse. After our house move, I really struggled to make new friends and to maintain the relationships that I did manage to make. When we moved I was just 10, so I only went to school for the final year of the primary phase, which, of course, didn't allow me much time to make long-lasting friendships before the big move to secondary school. By this age I think most children thought I was odd and a bit 'weird'. Most of them gave me a wide berth, and those who did like me were either the types of children it wasn't in my best interests to hang out with, or they had difficulties too, which made our friendships complicated. I longed to fit in, so I would be friends with anyone who offered, even if that meant that they ended up using me. This, of course, got much worse once I went to secondary school and I was no longer one of the oldest children.

Adolescent relationships

My primary school decided that in order to help me settle in at secondary school, and so that I wouldn't be a disruptive influence on my former classmates, it would be best if they placed me in a tutor group without any children from my previous class in primary school. This had a massively negative impact, and despite my mum telling the staff so, it happened nonetheless. From the moment I arrived at secondary school I was simply overwhelmed by everything. I was isolated. I couldn't make new friends, and those I had managed to make were then in separate groups and I hardly ever saw them, so we simply drifted apart. I started stealing money from home to buy cigarettes and occasionally alcohol so that I could impress the other children at school. Of course the kids who were impressed with this were much older than me and weren't my friends because they liked me – they were simply using 'the freak', which I, of course, didn't see at the time;

I just thought they liked me and thought I was cool. I might have had a niggle in the back of my mind, but if it was there, I ignored it. Any friend was better than no friend.

It was at this point that I first kissed a boy properly. He was 16 and I was 11. It was done as a dare in some bushes after school. How romantic! I don't think I even fancied him, but I was so desperate for any friendship that I would have done just about anything in order to get it. This dare opened up a whole new world to me: the world of boys and men, the buzz and excitement of kissing them, and the thrill of being valued and wanted.

At the age of 11 I looked considerably older than I was, and I was considerably less mature than most other 11-year-olds, which made me doubly vulnerable. To me, it was quite useful looking older than I was, because it removed some barriers to my behaviour that would otherwise have been there. At the age of 11 I was telling the adults around me that I wanted a baby. I was still playing with Alf as though he were a real baby. I had already started my periods and was putting myself in risky situations where an unplanned pregnancy could have been a real possibility. And I wondered why the adults around me were getting twitchy!?

I began kissing 15- and 16-year-old boys, and they were paying me to do it. I loved it! We aren't talking huge amounts of money but enough cash to buy a can of lager or a packet of cigarettes. It didn't go further than a kiss and a quick grope mostly, and I had to work hard to keep it secret so I could carry on 'earning'. I began drinking alcohol and playing truant. My behaviour was spiralling. My mum and my school couldn't cope. I thought I was coping, but looking back I wasn't.

One day I met this older bloke. He was 21 and I was 11, so I thought he was really cool and grown up. He must have known how old I was, more or less, because I was wearing my school uniform, but anyway, I spent the afternoon making out with him. Later, when his 17-year-old flatmate arrived home he said, 'Here, you try her'. And I swapped my attentions. It felt exciting to me and started to feel normal when this carried on for five months. The reason it stopped was because I was expelled from school so I wasn't around any more. I do wonder looking back whether getting expelled was in fact a lucky break and saved me from something much worse.

At about age 13, after something like 18 months out of school, I was reconnected to the outside world and sent to a local Pupil Referral Unit (PRU). My interest in sex and boys was still as strong as ever, and it was by accident one weekend that I discovered just what lengths I would go to to find the comfort, acceptance and love that I craved. I was out one afternoon in a small seaside town about 40 minutes from home. This wasn't unusual because it's where the PRU, and therefore my friends and social life, was. On this particular afternoon I was in a pub, drinking a shandy, and this man approached me and started talking to me. He was much older and extremely good-looking. I'm guessing mid-30s. I was 13, perhaps 14. Anyway, he asked me if I would like to earn some money and right away I knew exactly what he meant so I replied 'Yeah, sure'. He paid me £20 to perform a sexual act on him; I think you can fill in the blanks. I don't remember much about it. I had never done anything like it before. I didn't enjoy it, like I had when it was just kisses. This was something else. It felt wrong. It felt dirty. I felt used. I do remember thinking that I hoped he'd love me after, but it wasn't like it is in the films. Where was my happy ever after? Anyway, for reasons best known to myself, I met up with him again and I let him introduce me to a couple of his mates. Same thing with them. I won't say I enjoyed it, but I did learn to switch off and just get on with it. The money was good, and I did enjoy the attention from them. In a strange way I felt special. I felt loved during, but never after. I kept hoping that this would change and that one of them would fall madly in love with me, which obviously never happened.

I continued to meet these three men every few months until I was about 16. Just like selling kisses, no one knew what I was doing. I never told my mum. During the time I was also on the Child Protection Register because I was 'at risk from myself' – you can say that again!

Part of the buzz was that I had got away with it; that these adults who were looking out for my welfare had absolutely no idea about the magnitude of what I was doing. They knew I was high-risk and that I was overly sexualised, but never this. It's a secret I've kept hidden for too long. I do feel shame and guilt. I feel sad for my lost innocence, but I also feel that it's helped shape me into the adult that I am today.

Alongside my 'paid activities', I was also meeting boys of my own age in normal situations, like the local under-18s disco, and I think this helped me to hide my secret liaisons. The adults were more focused on this and not my secret. At 13 I met one boy who I fell madly in love with. I thought he was wonderful. We had a strange relationship. He was older than me and he had a car, which I initially thought was cool – except he couldn't have turned out to be more UnCool! He used to pick me up and we would go for a drive in the countryside together. I never told him in so many words about what I was doing for money, but he seemed to know. He used to make me feel so special and he always brought a smile to my face, so I was more than willing to perform sexual acts on him, for free. This didn't feel dirty or wrong. I loved him and I thought that he loved me too. When he was bored, he used to stop by my house, and we would go for a drive. Although it was all a bit bizarre, I enjoyed it.

Now I want to add a few important bits to this part of the story. This boy and I never kissed. Not once. Ironically, he refused to kiss me. And the sexual favours were never returned. Not once. Anyway, he kept asking me to sleep with him and I kept saying 'no'. Believe it or not, I felt like I wasn't ready. I was a virgin until I was almost 18. God knows how, but I was. Anyhow, one night, when he stopped by to pick me up, unannounced as usual, I had already decided that I would sleep with him – partly to make him happy, partly to see what all the fuss was about, and partly just to get it out of the way. So, we parked in some layby as we normally did, and I gave in. It was horrible. I lost my virginity in the front seat of a car. It was so mechanical. We still didn't kiss. I didn't even have time to take my seatbelt off. I just lay there and listened to the radio. I went into autopilot mode. My mind was blank. It was all over in minutes. He just reclined my seat, did his thing and then drove me to a line dance class where I was meeting my mum. Oh, and he bought me chips on the way home – how gallant!

Just before my 18th birthday I realised that men like him and all the others were toxic, but I knew he was a habit that was going to be hard to kick. I loved him, well I thought I did, and I couldn't think how to break away from him. Then one day I found the answer. I knew that if I were to meet someone else then I wouldn't be able to see him any more. Problem solved. I knew that I would never cheat on anyone, and I also knew that he wouldn't mess with someone else's girlfriend for fear of being beaten up. I went online and went looking for Mr Right-now rather than Mr Right, and that's when I met 'him'.

After Mr Right-now and I broke up three years later, Mr Cool Car returned. I was 20. Things were different now. I wasn't interested. I didn't love him any more and I wasn't going to be used. No man was ever going to hurt me again. So, when he made a move I told him 'no', and it was then that I saw a side to him that I had never seen before. He grabbed me and forced me to endure one last sexual act. I was so scared he was going to really hurt me, so I just complied. He held me with such force that he left finger-shaped bruises. I remember everything. Every detail. His hands smelt like petrol. I started crying and begged him to stop, but he just looked me in the eyes and smiled. I don't think I've ever been so scared in my life. I wanted to die.

After he was done, he made me make him a coffee and we sat and 'talked' for about an hour after. I was terrified. I just knew that I couldn't piss him off, so I played along. It was the longest hour of my life. After he was gone, I think I went into shock. Mum was holding a New Year's Eve party and I just went and pretended everything was fine. A few days later I had a text from Mr UnCool asking me how I was and that he'd see me soon. I panicked and I couldn't keep it in any longer so I rang Ginny, my former outreach worker, and told her what had happened. She advised me to call the police, so I did. I also told my mum. She said she would stay with me whilst the police were there, but I said I would be okay alone. I knew that certain topics would come up and I couldn't face going into all that in front of her.

I remember the moment they arrived at my house. There were two of them. A man and a woman. They interviewed me for about four hours, took photos of the bruises and took the clothes that I had been wearing as evidence. It was awful. Having to share every detail with them. I felt dirty all over again. I hated men. The police interviewed Mr UnCool and, of course, he denied it all, and because it was a matter of his word against mine, no charges were brought; however, it was logged on file so, should it happen to anyone else, God forbid, he'll be known to the police already. The assault really affected me. I was prescribed sleeping pills but I wouldn't take them in case he broke in during the night, and when I did sleep, I slept with a knife under my pillow. I resumed self-harming, a lot.

Interestingly, though, I did recover quickly. I don't know how or why. Perhaps all of my experiences before had in some way desensitised me, but less than six months later, I met Paul. When we met, I had a lot of issues around sex and men in general. He was very understanding and never once judged me. I felt loved and safe, finally.

A lesson learned: although these men took so much from me, they also gave me something – courage. I learned to fight. I learned to keep going. I learned I was better than how they treated me. I learned that it's not okay to be treated like that. No one has the right to make another person feel so rotten, ever. Yes, even to this day I have emotional scars that will never heal, but I'm okay. I'm loved, I'm safe and I won't let them win!

Relationships as an adult

When I fall out with friends as an adult there are usually two natural reactions: one is to think it's their fault for messing me about or not being more accommodating; the other is to go into a steep decline of self-doubt assuming it's all my fault and feeling horribly guilty. I would like to find a middle ground, but that seems rather elusive. It's easier to repair friendships if there's a basis of trust and care. In that context, it also helps me to moderate my reaction because there's more at stake that I might be risking if the relationship gets damaged.

Now, I try to surround myself socially with people who understand PDA. Of course, there are others I have to come across who don't, but they are less likely to be in my inner circle of contacts.

It appears that I misjudge boundaries, especially online. I do sometimes get blocked on social media, probably more often than most people. What irritates me is that people don't tell me when I'm overstepping the mark and explain why; they just react to it. I realise they are entitled to their own emotional reactions, but it's hard for me to read the situation and to modify what I'm doing if I only know where the edge is once I've tripped over it.

If I haven't heard from a friend for a while, I just assume everything's okay, otherwise they would have contacted me, so I need to remind myself that it's a kind and wise idea to check in with them every now and again. Doing so is certainly something I can do, but it doesn't come instinctively. I am better at apologising nowadays to mend a situation, although I have to confess there are times when I really have no idea what I'm apologising for; I just know it needs to happen to help the relationship.

I find it very confusing that there are so many different types of friendships. How on earth people know which ones fall into which categories is beyond me. I basically have two categories: people who are there for me in a crisis, and others. I aim to have one or two close friends I can rely on and then lots of others I can enjoy hanging out with. It's also confusing because sometimes people move category. I've made mistakes promoting people from the hanging out category to best friend category too quickly, only to be disappointed. Actually, there's a third category, which is acquaintances and people I try to respond positively towards, even if I don't know them well or don't immediately warm to them. This includes people I may meet in a queue at a shop or at an appointment.

When I'm in social situations I tend to mask. It's hard to tell how successful I am at it from the perspective of the person I'm with, but when I'm doing it, I'm certainly trying to behave in a sociably well-adjusted way, even if it's a bit off the mark by some people's standards. The reason I mask is so I can fit in and enjoy other people's company. Masking helps me to bring out my smoothest social skills. Without it I would be too nervous to socialise and I would worry about coming across negatively or too childishly. As long as I don't have to mask for too long or too often, it actually serves a useful purpose. To some extent we probably all mask, for example, when we behave differently with our boss than we do on a night out with friends. Masking is not all negative. It's about how often we do it, to what extent and how well we are in touch with our true selves the rest of the time.

I like online social media because it's social interaction that's more on my own terms and at my own pace. Plus, I can do it any time of day or night and from the comfort of my own sofa in my pyjamas. I do love meeting people but it does cause me varying degrees of anxiety, so I have to be careful about how much I do, how often and with whom. I don't really like to be alone and I find silence unbearable, it's just too loud for me. My favourite thing is being with Paul, whether that's at home or when we're out.

I try to pick friends more carefully now, but I'm still not very good at it. I think there's still a massive part of me that wants everyone to like me; this, of course, is unrealistic no matter who you are. A hangover from childhood, I guess. I've always rushed into friendships, but I'm now learning to distance myself until that person has proven to me that they have my back. Believe me, it saves a lot of heartache in the long run. I'm so trusting from the outset and I often don't think to question why. I just believe that this person likes me, for me, and for no other reason. This is, of course, a dangerous attitude to have. I'm also finding that because I'm so public with my PDA people who don't know me are often surprised at just how 'normal' I am. This confuses me. They treat me like PDA is the only thing about me and often talk down to me, like a child who needs them to tell me what to do. I'm now learning that these people, who don't take the time to get to know me, or who make sweeping judgements and treat me like I'm incapable of rational conversation, aren't worth my time, effort or friendship.

Fortunately, I get on well with most of my family. I think every family would say it has its own quirks and peculiarities – some more than others! I'm in regular contact with my mum. We have lots of text conversations and a video call every couple of weeks. Our relationship has had its ups and downs, as has every child with their parents, but we are in a good place now. I can't believe I'm saying this, but we have even reached that stage of life where we will talk about gardening and she's definitely my go-to person for plant identification! I value her honesty; she will tell me straight whether her view is something I want to hear or not. She's strong-minded (remind you of anyone?), but that has helped her be such a great mum to me. She fought my corner when I wasn't able to do so myself, and has never stopped believing in me. I'm not in touch with one of my brothers, which was initially upsetting, but I have accepted that now. I am in occasional contact with my other brother but he has lived abroad for a long time so we don't see each other. I'm in touch with some members of my extended family, including my stepdad, though not at all with my biological father.

I like to please the people I care about and it means a lot when they say thank you. I know I'm not an easy person to thank. One of my favourite thank you gestures is getting flowers. They are simple and lovely. Thank you cards are nice too. It's the face-to-face that I find uncomfortable. In fact, it makes my flesh crawl. If someone starts thanking me or praising me too much, I can feel a defensive wall going up, like it would in other people if that person was actually being nasty to you. For me, I have that reaction when they are trying to be nice to me. I also don't know what to say when someone thanks me and have been known to say thank you back when I'm the one who has done something for them! I also don't like the social attention of praise, which may be because I'm not very socially confident. Even now, I prefer to 'overhear' someone praise something I've done rather than say it directly to me. When a friend came to our house recently to collect a craft project I had worked on for her, Paul gave it to her in the kitchen while I stayed in the lounge, where I could hear her tell him how pleased she was with what I'd made. Having this bit of distance probably gives me some processing time too, which can help.

Paul

Paul and I have been together for 16 years now, since the spring of 2004. Our successful relationship is one of the biggest and most enjoyable achievements of my life. We don't agree about everything all the time, but we have worked out a good way of 'arguing constructively'. If we fall out it's usually because one of us is stressed about something outside our relationship, and we haven't talked about what's really bothering us. Paul and I often bounce off each other's moods. If one of us is anxious or agitated, the other one can be affected by that so we have to check in with how each other is feeling before we can tell what the shared dip in mood is all about. Generally we have a wonderful life together, and I'm delighted to be in a thriving relationship that works for us both.

I met Paul shortly after my 21st birthday and I can honestly say that he saved me. He gives me the strength to do what I do and he's the reason I keep going. It's funny how we met: I joined a dating site after the break-up of my previous relationship. I signed up for three months thinking that would be long enough to find someone, but I found Paul after only eight days! According to our matched data we weren't that compatible (56 per cent) but I ignored this and sent him a message anyway (PDA?). We sent messages backwards and forwards for about an hour, and then I asked him to call me. I needed to tell him about my 'issues'. I didn't want to waste his or my time getting to know each other if he wasn't going to be able to accept me, warts and all. So he rang me and I knew from the moment that I heard his voice that he was 'the one' and I've never doubted it once to this day. I asked him if anyone in his family suffered from a mental health problem or autism. He said 'no'. I asked because if the answer was 'yes', then it would have made the next bit easier! He listened while I explained PDA, ADHD and psychosis to him, then he went and researched on the internet for about an hour and called me back and said 'okay'. I had never experienced acceptance like it before with a man. It was as if he couldn't care less about it all, but in a good and positive way.

After a few weeks of talking on the phone, we decided that we should meet, so, on the 9th July 2004 we did just that. I remember it like it was yesterday. At the time he lived more than 200 miles away so he travelled down on the Friday after work. I remember waiting for him at the train station with a taxi driver who, when I told him why I was there, replied with 'I'll wait with you in case he's a weirdo'. That made me smile. He was really delayed because the train tracks had been damaged by heavy rain so he had to finish his journey by taxi. I don't think I've ever felt so nervous and excited all in one go. I knew that the moment he stepped out of the taxi would change my life forever. It was quite a first meeting. There was the overprotective taxi driver with Paul and me, who, both feeling extremely self-conscious, had removed our glasses, which then meant that neither one of us could spot the other in the crowd!

We went back to mine, had dinner, which neither of us could eat, and I spent the next two hours sitting with my back turned to him! I had warned him that when I'm nervous I can't bear to be looked at and that my idea of hell is to have someone look lovingly into my eyes. As you can imagine, it made conversation a little difficult, but he was so understanding and if it bothered him, he never let it show. I know it might seem like a crazy thing to do – have a complete stranger stay the weekend – but as far as I was concerned he wasn't a stranger, he was my soulmate. That weekend was the most amazing time. When I think about it I still get warm and fuzzy.

When his train pulled away on the Sunday I thought that I might die. I had never felt sadness like it in my life. We both cried. We then spent the next five months travelling up and down the country, spending the weekends together. I couldn't bear to be apart from him (and I still can't all these years later). With our bank accounts haemorrhaging money on train tickets and our phone bills rocketing, I knew we couldn't keep doing the long distance thing forever so I asked him to move in with me. It was a big step for him as he had never lived with anyone before, but eventually he said 'yes'.

We've had our ups and downs, like any other couple, and yes, we argue, but I wouldn't want a life without him. I can't imagine it. We've even been to Relate to learn how to argue productively! I think we work because we complement each other: the qualities he lacks I have, and vice versa. Now I'm the first to admit that I'm not the easiest of people to live with. I mean how can I be (!), but Paul knows that I try every day to keep my demands on him low. I really do try. I do worry sometimes that one day he'll have had enough and leave, but he tells me all the time that I'm wrong about this.

Paul works from home as a freelance aviation writer and photographer, which he has done for many years. This suits us both really well. He's here when I need him and he doesn't have any of the hassles of commuting or having to wear a tie! Seriously, it works for us. He has so many more freedoms than he would if he were chained to a desk somewhere – I mean, how many people get to say that they get to do their work in their dressing gown! I like having him at home. I guess it's another way of controlling our environment. He gets to work, earn money and do a job he loves and I get to choose what we have for lunch every day, what background noise we have, plus I'm not alone. Sometimes it's a bit of mess when the home-life and work-life lines get blurred, as tends to happen without the structure and routine of an office environment, but it's something we try to bear in mind.

Sometimes I forget that he needs to concentrate on his work, and he cannot help me at that precise moment, and sometimes he forgets that he can't sacrifice his work in order to please me. He once drew up a rota to try to help us organise our time better, but it wasn't terribly successful. There was never much chance of me being able to stick to a rota, but it wasn't flexible enough for either of us in the end. What we have found that works for us is to set aside certain blocks of time around his work commitments. We have what we call 'orange weeks', so-called because we first blocked them out in the diary with an orange highlighter. We recently started to use a pink pen in the diary, but we still called it orange week. During an orange week we don't organise anything non-essential that could be done at another time, so that Paul's availability for work is protected.

He works so hard and cares for me and then forgets about himself. Sometimes he has no alone or down time. I don't want him to burn himself out or end up resenting his job or worse, me. I am supportive of him, well, I always try, but sometimes my own stuff gets in the way. When he's working until midnight I'm up with him; when he has a super early start I get up with him and I try to arrange my day to fit around his. Every day I try to rein in my demands on him and I'm always apologising, but it's not easy. Sometimes I feel angry with myself that I feel like I have to apologise for just being me. It's hard to explain. PDA is my normal. I don't know any different. It would be like you feeling bad and apologising for being tall or having blonde hair. Crazy, but that's what it is like sometimes. Paul is very good, though; he just says it's okay and thanks me. I truly value and appreciate him.

I am totally committed to Paul. Despite my other variable relationships I have never cheated on him, physically or emotionally. It's my one perfect score in life! We celebrated our 16th anniversary in July 2020.

It's a happy coincidence that neither of us wants children. It's not only because it means there's no tension between us about it, but it also means that we can prioritise our own relationship, which is probably very good. I've never felt broody for children although I do sometimes feel that way about animals. For me, some of the reasons I don't want children include:

- It would be too much responsibility for me.

- It would be too much relentless hard work.

- I would worry too much.

- I would struggle to look after an ill child because of my fear of germs.

- My sensory system would get overloaded.

- I would resent or be unsettled by my life and my house having to change.

- I couldn't cope with all the different places I would have to be, e.g. school, playdates, parties, parents evening, doctor's appointments, out of school clubs, school assemblies...the list goes on and on.

- When I look at other parents, especially mothers, they seem to me to be like domestic machines and tireless servants to their offspring. I couldn't keep up the pace required, plus doing loads of thankless tasks doesn't appeal in the slightest!

It all boils down to me being too self-centred, too sensitive in my sensory needs and too variable in my PDA. I know that there are other PDA-ers out there who are parents and I have every reason to assume they are doing an excellent job. I'm just saying I don't think I'm cut out for it personally. I can hardly look after myself 24/7 least of all another dependent human being! Too much would then fall on Paul, and that wouldn't be fair.

Lastly, although I sometimes find relationships complicated and exhausting, they are also really important to me. I find my friendships easier to maintain than some of my family relationships. I strive to be there for my friends, although I'm probably best suited to providing practical help. If a friend needs help, I'm better at dropping off a casserole or walking their dog than spending many hours talking to them about a complex emotional event. But I'm lucky to say that I have lots of friends and family members who mean a lot to me and who I'm grateful to have in my life.

Chapter 9

Meltdowns

What is a meltdown?

First, I want to explain what I mean by 'meltdown'. It's a term that's being used more widely these days, and is sadly often over-used. A meltdown is so much more than the feeling many people would experience after a difficult day at work or when they are a bit emotional.

A meltdown is a significant reaction to overload. That overload might be caused by social, emotional or sensory factors, to name but a few. For me, hormones play a large part too. I don't have a very reliable monthly cycle so it's not easy to be specific about when my hormones affect my thinking or behaviour, but they definitely peak at certain times. Meltdowns happen when whatever is being asked of someone's energies or sensitivities outweighs their available capacity to cope with them. Meltdowns are not the same as tantrums or when someone occasionally overreacts. They are wholly overwhelming experiences. By the time my meltdown is happening, I have usually done everything I can to prevent it, but I can no longer contain it because it has all become too much.

In *Collaborative Approaches to Learning for Pupils with PDA* (Fidler and Christie 2019, p.64), meltdowns are described as,

> ...a response to being overwhelmed...meltdowns are not a deliberate action in order to make something happen or change. They are an emotional, anxiety-driven reaction to being overloaded. They are extremely distressing to the person experiencing them as well as to those witnessing and supporting them. Fear is the primary driver behind a meltdown which explains why they are linked to the flight, fight or freeze responses.

My meltdowns, like those of many other people with and without autism, are triggered by anxiety or overload, or both. I can only comment on my own experiences. I don't know what it feels like to be another PDA-er, or indeed someone who doesn't have PDA. To be honest, sometimes I find that a bit annoying because I am really curious to know how other people feel.

I like to use the metaphor of a stress or anxiety 'bucket' to describe ways of experiencing and managing stress and anxiety. The idea is that we all have our own bucket that fills up with the stresses of everyday life. For so-called 'well-adjusted people', their bucket has a formation of holes towards the bottom, like a colander, which allow a small amount of the 'stress water' to trickle out, leaving a manageable amount in the bucket at any given time. We learn to manage our buckets better over time as we mature. I think of my bucket (and probably the buckets of other PDA-ers) as much bigger than that of 'ordinary' people. This is because I have had to become accustomed to more anxiety-provoking experiences than most, so my capacity is larger, even though my ability to release the pressure is less. My bucket doesn't have holes in it. It relies on a few leaks, overspill and a bit of evaporation. These are not very efficient methods to deal with a constant flow of 'stress water', so when my bucket gets too full, it either leaks, slops or sometimes just tips right over. The key to managing the inflow is to reduce demands when needed. This allows time for the water level to drop.

I do notice that compared to many other people I know, I can be so highly sensitive to everyday stressors that they seem, to me, to be able to accommodate with relative ease. I can have meltdowns that are more extreme than most people seem to experience in response to similar triggers. As an adult, my meltdowns don't tend to come out of the blue, so I can usually spot what's led to them or when one is building. Sometimes a meltdown is not due to one single event, but is as a result of an accumulation of lots of other things. This was probably the same when I was a child. Nowadays, it's stopping a meltdown happening that's the tricky part, because once it's started it's there, and it won't be ignored!

Like everyone else, my threshold is impacted by other factors such as if I have slept well, if I am in pain, if I am unwell, if I am preparing for a challenging event, if I'm getting over an exhausting event, or if I have to cope with a change.

Childhood meltdowns

I think it's important to point out that many of the behaviours that I still experience today have been there right from the very beginning. For example, when Elizabeth Newson was taking my developmental history at my diagnostic assessment when I was 12 she reported that,

> Julia's parents had been questioning her development from babyhood; the salient problems were her screaming and tantruming for no apparent reason and...by age 5–6 they felt she was not only very difficult and out of control but also very 'different'...Julia has always had 'blinding' rages. She has rapid mood swings, changing from being happy to a total rage and back to being happy for no clear reason.

I remember having meltdowns from being a very young child, probably around age 3 or 4. My residing memory is of my wrist being held, as I used to be taken somewhere I clearly didn't want to go. Thinking of meltdowns that happened when I was, say, up to the age of 10, the words that spring to mind are 'rage' and 'injustice'. I used to be perfectly content, or extremely angry – nothing in the middle. I used to get overwhelmed by incredibly intense anger and I remember feeling that I was often blamed for things that I felt weren't my fault, or that I didn't even remember actually doing. Looking back now, I think I remembered things in my own way that often didn't match the recall of other people around me. Even if I was seemingly caught red-handed, I might still deny doing the thing. I also thought that lots of adults overreacted to what had happened. For example, shoving a pupil, breaking something or telling a teacher to 'f*** off' I regarded as minor but they seemed to view these things as major. As a pupil, I thought teachers in particular had it in for me and were trying to get me into trouble. It was too hard for me to understand the role I might have played in contributing to an incident, and I couldn't make sense of the bigger picture of what had happened or how others might interpret it. I believed my own version of events and didn't change my mind easily if those around me disagreed with me, even if they provided 'evidence'. Sometimes discussion after an incident would only lead to a renewed meltdown.

One Christmas holiday, when I was about 7 or 8, I wanted to have something to eat that I wasn't allowed. Looking back, I think it was probably that I wanted some Christmas sweet treat. Following an altercation about this I was sent to my bedroom, without said food item. I remember sitting in my room feeling cross and upset about it. When I went back to school I told my teachers that I had had no presents and no food over Christmas. My Christmas sob story! By this time my teachers were getting the measure of me, so they checked out my version of events before believing me. After all, I've never exactly looked like an undernourished child! I now think that what happened was that the image of sitting alone in my bedroom while everyone else was downstairs with presents and food became so inflated that this became what I held onto as my 'truth'. Still now, there are times when I struggle to remember what has caused a meltdown and what the details of a situation actually were. It's a bit like when you have had an argument with someone, and although you've moved on, to a certain degree you harbour a feeling of irritation with them, even after you have let the disagreement go.

As a child I also felt that I was 'framed' for things I didn't do by people who didn't understand me, who didn't like me, or more probably, who didn't interpret events like I did.

As a young child at primary school I had explosive meltdowns that often resulted in someone getting physically hurt. They usually went like this:

- Get cross about something.

- Get into a fight.

- Get into trouble or get blamed for something.

- Get removed from the situation.

- Sit outside the headteacher's office.

- Mum gets called in.

- Mum and I get told how unacceptable my behaviour is and that it must stop.

- Other child (and possibly their mum) is called in so that I can apologise to them.

- Get sent home for the rest of the day.

- Get in more trouble at home from Mum, e.g. get grounded.

- Go back to school the next day.

- Repeat.

Back then, meltdowns were an extreme 'red mist' of explosive hatred that would come over me. They were usually directed at the person telling me off or blaming me, but could also be directed at anyone who was in the wrong place at the wrong time. I didn't care what people thought of my behaviour. I didn't care about consequences; it's possible I wouldn't have been able to predict the consequences either. I wasn't bothered by who I vented at, whether that was another child, Mum, a police officer or the headteacher; I didn't discriminate. Nowadays I try to view my lack of discrimination positively, as a mark of how much I have always valued equality!

My behaviour must have been particularly hard for Mum to manage. I would regularly hit, punch, bite, kick and swear. For a long time, all of these were directed at Mum daily. I even remember trying to push her down the stairs once. At school, there was a lot of physical fighting as well as my intimidation of other children. I did it to reduce my anxiety over demands, which, in turn, would reduce the chance of a meltdown being triggered. I did it so I had control over myself, other people and my surroundings. I wasn't conscious of this then, so I couldn't explain it to myself or to another person. It's only many years later that I've come to understand it.

Teenage meltdowns

As a teenager, my mood regulation was on an absolute hair-trigger, much as it was in my younger years, but by now I was bigger and stronger. I could be triggered whenever I was asked to do something, or told what not to do. A lot of teenagers can be difficult, temperamental and confrontational, but this was to an extreme extent with me. Large-scale teenage meltdowns could easily happen more than a couple of times a day. These meltdowns included shouting, swearing, damaging property and often became physical. Although I can remember some of the meltdowns, it is really hard to remember what caused them. I presume they were triggered by being asked to do something I didn't think was reasonable or didn't want to do. It's interesting that although I can remember something of what happened during a meltdown, it's really hard to remember what caused them. It was almost like the word 'no' was toxic to me.

I don't know what had led to this, but around the age of 12 there was a three-day period when I went to live in the outside shed in protest about something or other. The shed was more of a playroom, not literally a garden shed, but it was still pretty basic as accommodation goes. I settled in there with my fold-out bed, kettle and a supply of instant soup. I have a memory of finding a sharp stone and scratching it all over the living room window panes whilst looking in directly at Mum, who was doing her best to ignore what I was doing. A lady from somewhere official came to talk to me to try to persuade me to move back into the house, but I told her to 'f*** off!' In the end I moved back into the house in my own time, when I felt calm enough to do so. Anyway, I had become cold and ready for a proper meal. My memory is that we all just moved on quietly from the whole incident.

Internal meltdowns and self-harm

At around the age of 12 or 13, I started having what I think of as internal meltdowns. These were happening as well as the explosive ones. I really didn't want to be different from other people, certainly not in such a way that meant my life was more difficult. I knew what the adults around me thought, which is that I would most likely end up in prison, and that didn't leave me feeling great about myself. What's more, I was worried they might be right. I wanted to be 'good'. I had always wanted that from an early age, but much more so as a teenager.

I knew what 'being good' looked like at school. It looked like sitting still on a chair, doing school work quietly and not getting into fights with other kids. It also meant achieving and making your parents proud. Not something that I could claim. I could see there were other children who could do this sort of 'good' and I knew that I wasn't like them.

From the age of 5 or 6 I was already confused and upset about being in trouble so much. The headteacher used to have an old margarine tub of 'reward rubbers' in the cupboard in her office. Some children seemed to get loads of them; I only ever got one. It seemed like an extra taunt to me that the headteacher kept the rubbers next to a set of papers that she filled in for sending home to report a behaviour incident. There was no shortage of her opening her cupboard to reach for these forms, but all I really wanted was a rubber!

I understood that being 'good' at home meant not causing upset or damage. I knew I wasn't doing well at that either, but I couldn't fix myself. It really hit me when my mum said to me at about 13, that although she loved me, she didn't like me at that time. I wanted to be liked. And loved. And respected. I wanted those things at home and at school.

Meanwhile, I thought I was invincible. I thought I was above the usual rules that applied to other people. And to be honest, I had begun to gather some evidence, which to my mind, seemed to back my theory up. It was around that time that Mum stopped trying to discipline me for the sort of stuff she had previously challenged. I was coming to realise that external services didn't seem to work very effectively, so I didn't feel accountable to them either. I wasn't scared of the police. I had learned that if I ran away, the police would bring me back home and tell me not to do it again, but they didn't arrest me, because, of course, running away isn't illegal. I thought that as long as I didn't commit an actual crime, there would be nothing the police could really do other than tell me off, which I didn't care about. I had been told at some point that it was against the law not to go to school, but then when I wasn't going to school, I wasn't arrested, and neither was Mum. No one could stop me from shouting and swearing at people at home, but even though I may not have had punishments in the eyes of the law, I didn't understand the huge impact my behaviour was having on my relationships, my prospects and my self-esteem. To me, the evidence supporting my invincibility was building! And this confidence didn't help me moderate my behaviour. Agreed, it was rather a simplistic way of viewing socially responsible behaviour, and I'm pleased to say that I grew out of that way of thinking a long time ago.

Having said all that, I wasn't happy with my life, and I wasn't content being the way I was. This led to internal meltdowns, which led to self-harm. For me, my self-harm consisted of cutting my arms or legs with a razor, and less frequently, of pouring boiling water over my arms. I mustn't have used extremely hot water because although it used to leave tiny blisters and red scalded skin, I never needed treatment for burns. The cuts were deeper, though, and I did sometimes need medical attention to dress them. When I was in hospital at age 11 for observation because of my behaviour and self-harm, just prior to my PDA diagnosis, I tried to strangle myself a few times with the TV cord when left unattended in the playroom. I was obviously interrupted before I could do myself any serious harm. I really wanted to get out of the hospital and was frustrated that I wasn't allowed to get dressed. I reckon they thought I would be less likely to attempt to abscond (or less successful at it) if I had pyjamas on. My mum bought me great big furry seal slippers and a huge dressing gown. I now wonder if this was so that I'd be easier to spot if I did manage to get out! I do remember trying, and occasionally succeeding, at following visitors through the locked doors when they left the ward, but I didn't get very far. Close to the end of my stay I managed to convince the hospital staff that I wouldn't run off if they let me get dressed, and I put forward a very convincing case about my self-esteem and being singled out. They fell for my bullshit, and despite my mum warning them not to, they let me get dressed. Within an hour I was off and out of the hospital. I remember making it into the town centre, which was a 15/20-minute walk away, and then trying to hitch a lift with someone. The rest, including how I got back to the hospital, is a blur, but I know I did end up back on the ward somehow.

I'm sad to say that cutting has been the hardest of these habits to kick, although at the time of writing I haven't done so for at least a year.

When I cut myself, I take a step away from the rest of my day or my life and just concentrate on the moment. I focus on watching the blood flow and can get absorbed in that. It doesn't cause me pain until much later. Then the guilt hits.

When I cut myself, it's like having a mindfulness experience, except that I'm focusing on a really unhealthy activity. Maybe in the future I can learn to change my mindfulness focus onto something less harmful.

Adult meltdowns

Generally as an adult, I tend to get more 'ratty' in my mood rather than have full-blown meltdowns. I can recognise when I have been snappy with Paul, and I apologise now. On a day when there are multiple irritations, I can have three or more mini-explosions, during which I will rant and shout about something for ten minutes or so, and then calm down. I am aware that I react much more strongly than most people I know to life's little niggles.

These niggles contribute to my fuse getting shorter and shorter. Sometimes I can feel my fuse starting to sizzle as it's lit. Usually as an adult I manage to quell it in time, helped by the right people around me, so that it doesn't turn into a big meltdown, but sometimes that's still not possible. Every now and then I reach a tipping point that takes even me by surprise. Some days it's such a delicate balance that I'm not surprised a younger me couldn't contain it.

An example of a more recent meltdown was when I had to make a train journey on my own. It was probably a bit over ambitious, with hindsight, but I don't want to avoid stretching myself even if sometimes it's hard. The section below is based on a blog I wrote at the time.

So where have I been?...

Well, I've been away in Dover for the past few days giving a talk. I had to travel by train because Paul was away at RAF Fairford working for a week so I had to fly solo, pardon the pun!

Basically, I had my first meltdown in public for a very long time. Those with PDA reading this will no doubt be able to relate to just how awful that is, but for those of you who don't have PDA I shall try and explain. It's mortifying and terrifying. We all get the extremeness of the anxiety felt by those with PDA but for me it's worse in public. I'd almost forgotten that but I've had a stark reminder over the last few days!

I left home (I was living in Devon then) for a long train journey to Dover to give a talk on PDA at a SEN Conference. I had to travel alone as Paul was away. I thought I might struggle with the journey, but I didn't dream I'd struggle as much as I did. That did take me by surprise. Also, which part of the journey I struggled with surprised me. I thought I'd struggle most with the London Underground but actually that was the least of my problems.

Anyway, I boarded the second train of the day at Exeter and BOOM it hit! I literally couldn't move! I was stuck in the 'joiny bit' between the carriages (I'm sure it has a proper name but you all know the bit I mean). Now when I say stuck I literally mean frozen. It was like my feet grew roots. So I'm like what the f*** do I do now?! Everyone pushes past me and then before I know it the train is moving and I'm still stood there in that 'joiny bit'. Now I'm there alone. My heart is racing and I'm sweating but still rooted to the spot. I lean sideways and look into one carriage. It's packed and I swear it's a mile long. I then look around the corner into the other carriage and it's just as packed and seems just as long. The aisle also appears much narrower than it should be. Like it's shrunk. I can't go in there. I'll get stuck. Trapped. By now I'm convinced everyone is looking. Judging. Of course no one actually is. There's no one else there. Just me and my anxiety. I open the window for some air. All I'm thinking is 'breathe'. My chest feels tight and it hurts. By this point I'm crying. Come on Julia, get hold of yourself!

Breathe. Just breathe. I check the time on my phone – f*** me, only ten minutes have passed! I've got another two hours of this. I don't even have the comfort and option of getting off the train at the next stop because this train is the speedy one. The stops are Exeter (where I boarded), Reading and London Paddington. Great! Reading is over an hour away. Now I'm in floods of tears.

As quickly as I wipe a tear away there's another one on its way out. I'm sure people have noticed by this point because I'm rooted near the loo and it feels like there's a queue of eyes. Some of them are bound to have noticed. It's the law of averages surely. I'm now shaking and dripping with sweat. And crying. If I don't stop crying soon I'll end up with a bright red and puffy face for ages and then everyone will definitely know I've been crying. I check my phone again. Another 20 minutes have passed.

Okay, so I'm 30 minutes into a two-hour journey. That's not too bad. It's not ideal but it could be worse. Rooted to the spot for the remainder but it's doable. It is better than the alternative of walking into one of those packed carriages.

I look at my phone screen and see that my friend has replied to a message I sent before I boarded. It felt like she was offering me a lifeline. I reply and tell her I'm stuck and that I don't know what to do. I tell her I'm scared and she listens. She gets me. She understands me. I don't need to explain or justify things. She talks to me. Tells me it will be okay. She makes me smile. A virtual hand-hold – just what I needed. She enabled me to focus and think. So I follow her advice: I look out of the window and just breathe. I'd been trying that earlier but I just couldn't. It took someone else to remind me to just breathe for me to be able to do it. In, two, three. Out, two, three. In, two, three and so on. Funny how the mind works.

After about an hour I finally get the courage up to stop the guard when he passes me. I stop him and hand him my PDA awareness card (see below) and I simply say, 'Help me'. Thankfully I'd put my train ticket in with my PDA awareness card earlier in the day, just in case.

He took my case and showed me to a seat. It was as simple as that. So that was the outbound journey. Not perfect but I made it...just.

So, what of my journey back? Well I was on that same train again and you'll never guess what?...déjà vu, but worse! I hadn't even set foot on the train before I started crying and forgetting to breathe. I thought, 'Dear god! What's wrong with me?' I forced myself on board and then froze. Here we go again! Another public meltdown. I hated myself for this part but I thought 'why me?' I really did. Why did this have to happen so publicly...and twice? Why can't I just board a train and find a seat like any other passenger? Why must I have to burst into tears in front of half of London? I also (shamefully) thought 'it's not fair'. I want to be able to do the ordinary things like get on a train. I want to be normal! I hate having those types of thoughts, the self-pitying type of thoughts. Woe is me, and all that. Normally I 'suck it up'. I deal with it. I'm tough and I can handle most things (apart from physical pain). I'm certainly not the type of person who cries because they are scared of boarding a train alone! I'm confident and bubbly, right? Well, yes and no. I am confident and bubbly if I have someone I trust with me. I can't emphasise that word enough. Trust. It can't be just anyone. It can't be a randomer on the street but it also doesn't have to be Paul or even a close friend. It can be someone I've just met, someone who looks trustworthy or whose job it is to help. By pure luck I boarded in the buffet carriage (this fact is important, but not just yet), and I headed towards coach F; I'm teary eyed and scared but I'm okay. I think I've got this nailed. The slidey doors open and I walk forward about 10 steps into the carriage, I see a sea of heads, the air is still and hot, there are bags and cases sticking out everywhere, how can a train that was completely empty a few minutes ago already be this full?! The train looks so long and narrow again, I pause to scan the carriage for a seat. Any seat alone will do. Wait, I can't sit next to a stranger. I look but can't see anything free. The train begins to move and I panic. I start backing out. I just can't. I reverse as far back as I can go and end up back in the buffet carriage. Now this is where the fact I'm in the buffet car comes in and also the young man. He saw me right away and asked me if I was okay. I just handed him my PDA awareness card and blurted out that I need help to find a seat. Straight away he told me it would be okay and asked me to follow him. He carried my case and took me through to first class. He stored my case and told me to sit down and to relax. Before my bum had even managed to warm the seat another gentleman had arrived with a refreshments trolley and he, upon seeing how upset I was, said to me that if I needed anything to just give him a shout, even if I only wanted someone to chat to.

All is well. I think, 'I'm safe!' It's almost empty in first class and the air is fresh and cool (God bless air con!). I relax. I breathe. In, two, three. Out, two, three. I'm going to be okay now. Just sit here and breathe. Simple really, when you think about it. Except all good things must come to an end! The third member of staff I met was the ticket inspector and he was something else altogether!

He saw my PDA awareness card but upon seeing my ticket announced loud enough for the rest of the carriage to hear that my ticket wasn't valid and that I'd have to move. Through tears I asked him repeatedly to speak to the young gentleman who seated me here. After about the fourth time of my repeating this, he finally relented and grabbed my ticket and PDA awareness card and stormed off to speak to him. A couple of minutes later he returned and told me that I could stay there until I'd 'pulled myself together'. As he walked away, he said that if I want to upgrade then I'd have to pay, again loud enough so that those around me could hear. I couldn't face being a spectacle for the people around me. I pretended to read my book like everything was cool. I was in fact more than happy to pay the extra, but I wasn't about to become another source of entertainment for those around me. By then I was even more upset than I was before. I'm now sat waiting knowing that at any moment he'll be back to get me to move and then I'll be back exactly where I started: seatless and scared.

A few minutes later the trolley gentleman comes past again and can see that I'm more upset than when he left me last. He sat down across the table from me and I explained what's just happened. It was at this point that he informed me that the ticket bloke was in fact the train manager. I had to stop myself from laughing through the tears at this point! That rude and grumpy man is a manager? Well now I really have seen everything! The trolley man apologised and promised me that I wouldn't have to move. I offered to pay the extra to upgrade but I was told there was no need. He was very sympathetic, and not in a patronising way. He sat with me for a good ten minutes. We just chatted about this and that, mostly how unfair it is that we can't smoke on trains any more! Boy I needed one at that point.

With massive thanks to both the buffet and trolley men my experience wasn't a complete nightmare but it was exacerbated by ticket man aka 'train manager' who interestingly enough I had spotted was wearing a Mr Grumpy pin badge!!!

What have I learned? That I'm not made of stone. I'm still vulnerable to meltdowns and that I can't always stop them. I think I already knew this, but I tried to convince myself that I was past all that. I think I've spent so much time now surrounded by the right support that I'd forgotten that without all of that I can't manage. That's scared me. I don't like that.

Could I survive without Paul? Yes, but my world would shrink massively, more so now than ever I think. He really enables me to have a life outside of the home. Without him I would hardly ever leave the house.

Paul is much more than just my partner – he's also my carer, my rock and my best friend.

Thank you, Paul.

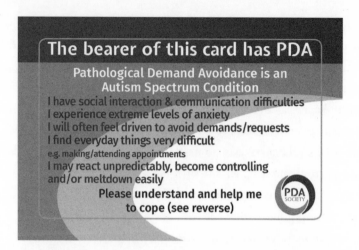

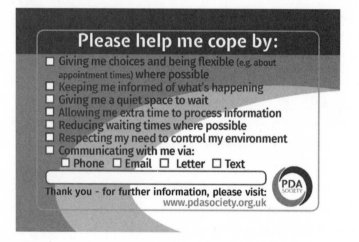

Triggers

I didn't like conforming to most things when I was younger. I definitely still resist it more than most people, but I can make adjustments and exceptions now. The problem for school-aged children is that there are so many rules for pupils, from where they sit to what they are wearing, from what they have to learn to how they are required to speak. At a time when my understanding of myself and social expectations was not great, this meant that school was full of triggers. It didn't help that I thought rules didn't or shouldn't apply to me.

At home, I really wanted to be treated the same as my brothers, and felt it was incredibly unfair that I wasn't. I didn't understand the context that my brothers were 10 and 11 years older than me. If I wanted to go to London on my own for the day, I didn't see why that was so out of the question when my brothers were allowed. Except that they were probably teenagers at the time, which would have meant that I was still in primary school.

Everyday life continues to be full of demands. Some of them I mind less than others. Some of them are almost always stressful (like medical and especially psychiatrist appointments), and some of them are just irritations. They all have a cumulative effect. It helps that as an adult I have more influence over what I can choose to do or not do. Low-level irritations include being asked if I would like to email some customer feedback on the new multi-surface cleaner I just bought. The short answer is 'NO'; the longer answer is 'It cleans multiple surfaces and smells quite nice, now go away.'

Everyday events that trigger instant 10-minute or more verbal blows include:

- Some professional questioning my diagnoses and discounting multiple previous assessments.

- Seeing a psychiatrist. Even just getting a letter from one usually guarantees a meltdown. My experience of psychiatrists has not been good, although recently I've been referred to an excellent one, at last.

- Someone confronting me aggressively or provoking me.

- Someone telling me to do something without being polite.

- Someone pushing me.

- Someone preventing me leaving a room or a space.

- Being told to 'calm down'.

- Being told 'it's nothing to worry about' – well, it's clearly worrying me. A lot!

- Waiting for a reply and not hearing back straight away, so getting anxious about waiting.

- Getting a substitution in our online grocery shopping.

- Getting an 'official' letter such as from the bank/tax office/benefits department.

- Sudden changes of plan.

- Getting lost on the way somewhere or being late for an appointment.

- Irritating people. I mean, people who dither with their shopping trolley, people who nick your parking space, people who don't ring you back after they've said they will, poor customer service and people behaving stupidly in general.

- Not having control over myself, for example, if I'm ill or in an environment where the control is with someone else, such as in hospital. Also, having a bad psychotic episode or a meltdown, which means I can't think rationally.

- Injustice. Like queue jumpers or when the 'little guy' who is trying to do their best is blocked by bureaucracy or systems. Queue jumpers. It annoys me that we're not a very fair society and some people get overlooked. Also anyone breaking the rules deliberately, e.g. one rule for 'the privileged' and one rule for the 'little guy'.

- Paul being unwell. Of course I know it's not reasonable, but it's not okay for me if he's unwell because it puts pressure on me to do things that are too hard for me. Also, it's especially hard for me to look after him if he's got a tummy bug because I'm a bit of a germophobe and I have a fear of vomiting, so in that case I need to keep such a distance that I can only bring him drinks if he's in bed by leaving them halfway up the stairs. When he gets better, every inch of the bathroom gets scrubbed, steamed and bleached (by him, following my specific instructions).

• Friends who (to my mind) carelessly let me down. To me this feels deliberate, even though I know they won't have planned to let me down. It's people who say they're coming round at 10 and then by 10.30, when they're still not there and I contact them, say they forgot the time. 'I forgot' is not a valid excuse to my mind. Don't tell me 'I forgot to look in my diary' because I would think, 'Well why have you got one then?!' There are literally dozens of ways of setting yourself reminders nowadays! I suppose to me, the 'deliberate' part means they have given an inadequate excuse. It also includes one-way friendships, for instance, when you help a friend out but in similar circumstances they don't help you. Crappy excuses aren't good enough for me, although I do understand unforeseen consequences. And I don't judge people with ASC or PDA if their plans have to change at the last minute, even though that may be tough for me to accommodate.

• Liars. I don't mind white lies to protect people and relationships. In fact, I think it would be horrible to live in a world without white lies. But I do have a problem with people who lie deliberately or to cover their bad behaviour. There's no excuse for lying for personal gain. If someone I regarded as a friend is found to be lying, they are 'deleted', regardless of history.

Managing meltdowns

Managing meltdowns follows a pattern. The pattern is used both to prevent and to recover from meltdowns. It is a repeating cycle of preparing for an activity, doing the activity, and recovering from the activity, a demand regulation cycle. Following more draining activities the recovery is slower and more delicate.

The demand regulation cycle looks like this:

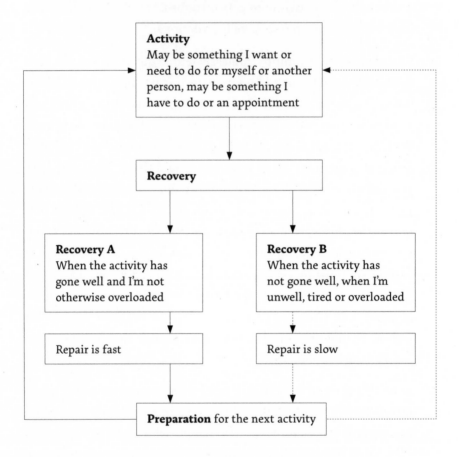

If there is considerable disruption to this cycle, it becomes increasingly hard to cope, and that makes meltdowns more likely to occur.

As it is, I feel that my life is a constant round of preparation for and recovery from everyday events. If I am not able to have sufficient recovery and repair time, I become more anxious, less well emotionally regulated, I lose engagement and I stop enjoying activities I would otherwise like.

When Ruth and I were talking about this point it was interesting to think about how often children and young people with PDA may not be able to have the preparation and recovery time that they need, before they're faced with the next activity or expectation. For a lot of children, their experience of school may feel like back-to-back expectations and activities. This will inevitably have an impact on their engagement with and enjoyment of school, and will probably affect the state they are in when they get home. The pressure of dealing with it all can mean that some children behave very differently at home than they do at school because by the time they get home they are simply unable to contain their overload.

I have learned some strategies that help, and I can use these at varying stages of the demand regulation cycle. Sometimes they are part of managing a difficult event; sometimes they are part of recovery.

My strategies for preparation and recovery include:

- Removing myself.

- Taking a short break (e.g. going outside for a cigarette).

- Watching a lot of familiar TV.

- Having a long bath (pre-new house; I can't have a bath in the new house).

- Doing something for someone else, to get me out of myself.

- Spending many hours on games involving 'candy'.

- Not going out (until the recovery cycle is complete).

- Not doing anything sociable (until the recovery cycle is complete).

- Reducing everyday expectations like not getting dressed, washed or cooking.

I love crafting. Crafting is neither a preparation nor a recovery activity.

I can only craft when I am in that rare period of having nothing to prepare for and nothing to recover from. That frustrates the hell out of me! During lockdown in 2020 (for the Coronavirus pandemic) I was able to craft so much more because I was neither preparing nor recovering – it was wonderful!

For me, as I've got older and more self-aware, it has been really empowering to understand what works for me. This means recognising what tends to trigger or build towards a meltdown as well as what helps to prevent or recover from one. I try to incorporate these strategies into my everyday life to maintain my demand regulation cycle. Compared to when I was a teenager, I'm doing brilliantly at it, but it's not without difficulty, and I know I will continue to be aware of it. I've accepted that being prone to meltdowns is one of my characteristics. The train journey example above shows me this really clearly. I try not to judge myself or other people for it, and just work around it as far as is possible, as a way of life.

Chapter 10

Events and Appointments

Coping with events and appointments when I was younger was usually rather chaotic and utterly random in terms of outcomes. Of course, as a child, it wasn't my job to plan or organise things, so this fell to Mum, who remembers,

> ...as a child, and pre-diagnosis, Julia's moods were so labile that preparation for anything was futile. That applied to a child's party, which she stopped being invited to because of the frequency of 'trouble', and also to medical appointments. Appointments had to be conducted on her terms or not at all, whatever was their original purpose.

It was a small miracle that Mum managed to get me to attend and cooperate with as many appointments as she did, to be honest, and it must have been very stressful for her not knowing what would happen from one moment to the next, even once she had got me there.

As I've described in Chapter 9, I go through repeating cycles of preparation for an activity followed by recovery from it. This applies to most activities in my everyday life, although some are obviously easier than others. The regular events and appointments (when we're not in the middle of a pandemic, as we were when I was writing this in 2020) that feature in my life include:

- **Committee and group meetings for various organisations:** four meetings a month, not necessarily one a week.

- **Social life, meeting friends or people coming over:** perhaps once a week.

- **Writing commitments with Ruth:** a booked phone call (of up to two hours) every week plus another couple of hours a week of reading and commenting on chapter drafts.

- **Medical appointments:** probably once every two months. I tend to 'store up' ailments and issues and then go to the GP to deal with them all in one visit.

- **Speaking at PDA awareness events (in person and online):** typically it's about one every two months on average, but not always spaced out like that.

Preparation and recovery for different events and appointments

Some of the activities described in the list above are easier than others to get my head around. If it's an activity that motivates me, it can help if it follows a predictable pattern, especially if it's one I know I can change to suit my needs, if necessary. If it's one that I feel is a pressure, then the predictability of it can feel too demanding. For example, Ruth and I have regular chapter review days and regular phone call days, which helps me plan my week, but it's good to know either of us could alter these if we needed to.

Committee meetings probably take me a day to prepare and one or two days to recover. Again, I can just make this part of my regular routine. One of them happens in a local pub, which is more informal and therefore easier for me. The more formal meetings are definitely the hardest, so, as you can imagine, one of the bonus features of the pandemic is that they are currently happening online, which is much better for me, although I do miss seeing people I like, especially for the craft club meetings.

Some formal meetings I attend can be as long as three hours. I participate as much as I can, although I need fairly frequent cigarette breaks. I find that it helps if I take my anti-psychotic medication before I go. Similarly, I need a day or two to prepare and at least two days to recover. I don't mind that this is what I need to do to manage, but I should think there are not many people who need to go to those lengths to attend Parish Council meetings!

Regular phone calls with Ruth about the book are dates set in my diary, but they aren't too stressful for me because they are only phone calls, which I don't mind, and I can have them at home in my pyjamas. They only require about an hour to prepare for and the same to recover from afterwards. Although we set a time to talk, I call Ruth 'around' that time rather than exactly at that time, so I have control over initiating the phone call. What helps is that I want to keep the appointments so that the book actually gets written, but I know that if I need to rearrange a date, then Ruth would be fine about it. Sometimes she even needs to rearrange a date too! It also helps that Ruth is so easy to talk to. She's a very special lady.

My social life is manageable because I can look after my own diary and choose who I want to spend time with. It's not like an organised appointment or a job, and many of my friends are on the autism spectrum or are parents of someone who is, so they understand needing to make some accommodations. Friends who don't have a personal connection to autism or PDA have learned about it through me and are understanding.

The easiest of my regular organisational events are the Women's

Institute stuff, basically because it feels like meeting up with some mates. The hardest is the Parish Council because it's formal and lengthy. It feels like a long time to have to wear my 'I'm a grown-up' hat! Anyway, I enjoy both in different ways and wouldn't want to give either up.

Managing the expectations of a schedule

Some of the earliest experiences of diary 'commitments' were going to school, which I've talked about in other chapters. School meant other events such as sports days, assemblies and tests. I wasn't a fan of any of these. I recall that we had a list of words to learn at home for our spellings tests. Needless to say, I was neither motivated to do so nor very good at it. I might have been better if we could have written the words down because I am quite a visual processer, but back in class we had to spell them out loud, which I found extremely difficult. I didn't actually care about knowing how to spell words, and in reality, if I needed a spelling I would just ask my friend, or copy from someone else, so I didn't feel I needed to trouble myself with spellings tests.

These days, I keep my own diary and I'm usually responsible for putting events and appointments in it, for me and for Paul. I am surprisingly efficient at looking after our diary, given some of my other organisational skills regarding paying bills, etc., and it works well if one person organises us both. I organise events around his work commitments because I need him to accompany me to all of my diary dates. I have a paper diary and a separate book for birthdays. I check my diary quite often, up to four times a day if I'm busy. Then, if I know we have a quiet couple of days at home, I may not look in it at all for a day or more. We have an understanding about keeping Paul's 'orange weeks' free of other non-essential commitments because these are weeks he has his work deadlines. Orange weeks have been mentioned in Chapter 8, but if there are any readers who are reading chapters in their own chosen order (I can relate to that!), let me explain. Orange weeks are so-called because they were originally marked out in orange highlighter. Having the date highlighted is less demanding than the written words. They are a clear visual reminder that these are weeks when we need to reduce other events because of Paul's work commitments. I wouldn't want to use this strategy for anything else, though, because I could get easily muddled on what the colour coding meant. Plus, it would risk being too restrictive – I can cope with the limitations of orange weeks because they are about Paul's work, which is important to him as well as to us both.

Emergency events and appointments

From time to time one of the cats has become ill and needed an emergency vet appointment. One of them is not only elderly, but is also chronically ill, so when he needs to see the emergency vet it can be really worrying. If this happens, then I will just do it. I can do it by going into auto-pilot and I deal with any recovery necessary afterwards. Paul usually needs extra recovery time afterwards too, to get over the vet bill! The reason I can cope with vet emergencies is because my concern for the cat is bigger than for myself.

It's not the same when there's a medical emergency for myself. When Paul was away recently, I developed a big abscess on my skin. It was very painful and I could tell it was getting infected, but I couldn't go to the doctor. I called the GP who said it wasn't acute enough for a home visit, although they did realise I needed antibiotics as soon as possible. I knew that too, but I still couldn't go. Fortunately, after a few phone calls, the GP prescribed me some antibiotics that the local pharmacist kindly delivered to the house. After a bumpy start I was able to take them regularly as required and got better in a few days.

During the 2020 Coronavirus pandemic, when GP appointments largely moved online, I was delighted to not have to go to the surgery. I had a phone call and sent the GP pictures of a different leg infection on an app. I also had a video appointment and on another occasion the practice nurse saw me in the car park – it all worked really well for me and I hope I can be offered these options in the future, even when life returns to 'normal'.

I have a strong dislike and specific fear of hospitals. In ranked order of worst first, what I don't like is: germs; people; heat; smells; doctors; the size of the buildings; bright lights; certain sounds. I find it incredibly hard to tolerate hospital environments, even if I'm not the patient. When Paul had a routine procedure recently, although I went with him, I had to wait outside in the snow for four hours rather than go in with him. My mum was ill in hospital once, and although I had lots of messages and phone calls with her, I wasn't able to go and visit her in hospital. Thankfully, I know she understands why and she knows it's not because I don't care. I think that if I fell down the stairs and broke my ankle, I would prefer to manage somehow rather than go to A&E. However, if someone told me the vet could treat me, I would probably be fine with that!

An unexpected event but not quite such an emergency could be if the car breaks down. We are not strangers to this happening. I suppose having experienced these situations has helped me to get used to it, and I have grown to trust the excellent breakdown services we have used. My biggest concern when the car breaks down is what I will do if I need the toilet, as I don't have very good bladder capacity and I don't get much warning when I need to go. If I can be reassured about dealing with this aspect of the situation, I can then make light of it rather than getting stressed.

If we get lost when we're driving somewhere, I do get stressed and cross, usually with Paul, even if he has just turned left because I told him to! Once I've had a little rant, I'm able to apologise to him and I'm calm again straight away when we are back on the right route.

Medical appointments

I feel like I have fairly frequent medical appointments including check-ups and reviews. I certainly seem to have a lot more than most people

I know. By far the most challenging of my medical appointments is when I need to see a psychiatrist. Sadly, this is because I have a history of unsatisfactory encounters with psychiatrists who I have felt haven't listened to me and haven't understood PDA. I also find it intensely frustrating to have to follow 'systems' that don't seem to make sense to me. For example, I have been taking methylphenidate since I was 12. It works very well for me and I have been taking it now for years. When I moved house and area, I needed to ask for a repeat prescription from a different doctor, who was unable to provide a prescription without a reassessment by an unfamiliar psychiatrist who then queried my diagnosis. It was an extremely stressful time for me, but I'm pleased to report that it's all sorted now and I've now been allocated a really nice psychiatrist who has a much better bedside manner and is much more understanding and supportive. Plus, I only have to go to one appointment a year, so I can manage that.

When I have medical procedures, it helps me if I am prepared for what will happen, what will be expected of me and how long it might take. For instance, before I had my MRI scan I Googled the noises that the machine would make. It also helped that I had Paul nearby and that I took in my own playlist to listen to. I found having lumbar punctures a very strange experience: I felt a tugging on my spine and like my legs were having the energy pulled out of them when they drained out the fluid. It was really weird.

Significant professional events

I have now been a speaker at the National Autistic Society (NAS) PDA conference a number of times. I have done these sessions with Ruth, as a conversation between the two of us, with 100 or more people listening in. We agreed broad topics to talk about before the event and Ruth asked me questions about them. Ruth guided the conversation and managed the time-keeping. We didn't take questions from delegates, although I am always happy to chat to people at other times during the day. We asked people not to clap after our session because I would have found that too awkward and I would have been uncomfortable with the attention. But I did want to know that I had done a good job, so we came up with a strategy to allow delegates to show their appreciation by leaving a selection of blank post-it notes around the room, so that instead of clapping, people could leave feedback. In fact, this has been much nicer than clapping, not only because it didn't agitate me on the day, but also because it gave us a collection of positive comments to look back on. Some of the comments have included:

> *Thank you SO MUCH Julia for your amazing talk. I found it charming, enlightening and inspiring.*

> *Thanks Julia for spending time with us, particularly now we know it takes so much out of you. I have a lot to take home to think about to help my son.*

> *Nailed it. Best one yet, Love you, Paul xxx*

Now lots of people who might be giving a presentation at a national event would need some preparation and recovery time I'm sure, but theirs may not be quite like mine.

For big events like these, I start preparing by reducing other ordinary demands about 10–14 days before the event. That means little or no getting dressed, no doing chores, not going out, etc. A few weeks before the conference I would have a meeting with Ruth to discuss what we would cover and to run over any final queries. I need a plan to take account of looking after the cats, the journey, travel arrangements, and my needs on the day, e.g. reserved seats at the front of the conference room. Paul is a great support too.

On the day itself the things on my mind causing extra stress include: having to cope with crowds; using public toilets; not knowing who will want to talk to me and what they will say; queuing (for coffee or lunch); conference facilities (will there be long overwhelming corridors? No natural daylight?); temperature (I overheat very easily so I need a desk top fan); access to my regulating strategies (when can I have a cigarette break? Can I have a nice smelly wax melt to hand? What if I need to pace or sway instead of sit down while we talk? When should I take my additional dose of medication to help me get through the session?); and leaving the venue (I prefer to hang around and to leave after most other people to avoid the crowds). Once I leave the conference I am exhausted, and when I get home I need a good fortnight to shrink all expectations once again while I recover.

It makes a huge difference having people around me who accept me and who support me in various aspects of the above.

If I have a number of events that bunch up in the diary, I can't always have the usual time allowance for preparation and recovery. In these circumstances I would try to build in accommodations where possible, such as:

- Sharing my presentation slot with Paul so we could step in for each other if necessary, in case one of us dried up.

- Working on an exhibition stand selling cards so I have a safe place, a role to play and somewhere to 'retreat' to.

- Taking my phone to the conference so I can watch a few episodes of *Murder She Wrote* or browse Facebook if I get too stressed.

Although these events are stressful, I'm extremely grateful for the opportunities they give me to stretch myself and to have my experience shared with families, professionals and other PDA-ers.

Weddings

I'm really happy for other people when they get married, but I often find their weddings difficult. It's easier if I don't know them that well because I'm not expected to go to the celebrations for as long. Family weddings are really long events, often starting with gathering to get dressed and to put make-up on together, and not finishing until the bride and groom leave at the end of the night. That amounts to so many hours! I also find weddings extremely emotional. I cry when I see the bride arrive, during the ceremony, when I hear the speeches, for the first dance, and lots more times in between. And on top of that, I'm not very good at shedding a discreet, quiet tear so I find myself full-on sobbing, which leaves me with a throbbing headache!

Parties

I don't mind parties as an adult, probably because it's easier to decide which ones to go to and how long to stay. Children don't really have the same options and choices, which means that by the time they leave, they might be overloaded and over-stimulated. If that has led to a meltdown, as it often did with me, that might end up being the reason they are leaving at that point, which can be distressing for everyone. It's much better to leave calmly, even if I leave early, than push myself until I'm not coping. I prefer parties at a venue rather than at someone's house because there's more space and it's less noticeable if we leave early. I like parties that I organise even if they are at our house, because then I can set things up in a way that will not only work for our guests but for us too.

Holidays

We hardly ever have holidays, basically because we can't afford them. Our last holiday was to Cornwall and I loved planning what we would do each day, visiting various tourist spots. One of those plans was to have a special meal out on our last night at a proper restaurant. A few days into the holiday, we stopped the car at a beauty spot to look at the view but the car wouldn't start again. After waiting for the breakdown service, we had to use much of our precious holiday funds on a new battery. We didn't want to let this spoil our holiday treats, so we did our best to work round it. I still wore the posh outfit I'd packed to eat at the fancy restaurant when we went to a supermarket to have their all day breakfast, and I'm proud to say I was the best dressed person there! Maybe it looked like we were coming back from a big night out rather than the truth, which was that this actually *was* the big celebration!

Now we tend to plan day trips instead of holidays. Not only are they cheaper but they also work better around the cats' needs. I used to go with Paul to airshows, which I enjoyed, but I haven't been with him to one for the last three years. The reason isn't because I don't want to be with him or that I don't want to go to the show. We found ways of managing them that worked for us, like arriving extremely early so there was no queuing, and standing at the front of the crowd so I didn't feel squashed amongst other people. The reason is because of the cats that are getting elderly: I don't like to ask too many favours of friends because they already help us when I go to do talks, which I greatly appreciate. If, one day, we have younger, healthier cats or even a dog we can take with us, then maybe I will start accompanying Paul again.

Coronavirus pandemic in 2020

The Coronavirus pandemic has been an event that none of us would have chosen, but it arrived uninvited into our lives all the same. For some, very sadly, it's had tragic consequences. It has presented varying degrees of worry, loss, isolation and relaxation to the rest of us. Writing this in June 2020, fortunately we have stayed well, as have our friends and family. I'm conscious that this is a very secure background in which to be thinking about the impact it's had on me and on our life. Anyway, so far, this is how it's impacted me...

I wrote in my blog mid-April, 'I know I shouldn't brag but this isolating malarkey is actually my idea of heaven... I've been practicing avoiding social gatherings for years!'

It feels like life has been paused. In the main, I'm enjoying it, but I realise for us it's been relatively calm and grief free. I'm actually starting to get concerned about the prospect of everything opening up again and having to deal with the big wide world all over again. It will be strange when what was familiar then feels so unfamiliar.

There are some aspects of lockdown that I've enjoyed hugely. I've appreciated being under less pressure and having been able to step away from the cycle of preparation for activities, followed by recovery from them. It's meant that I've been able to do more craft projects, for instance, which I've loved. We've had no uninvited visitors, and those we have had haven't come into the house, so there's less pressure about housework and hosting. I really liked having a remote GP appointment, which meant no turning up at the surgery, no waiting room, no dealing with receptionists or members of the public. I've really appreciated having Paul at home more and taking a break from having to manage invitations to go places. Even not going places we enjoy with people we like has been relaxing. I haven't missed any form of shopping or restaurant because, to be honest, we can order whatever we want online. I'm certainly not interested in queuing for half an hour just to go into a shop that allows internet orders anyway, or to pick up a drive-through meal! I would have missed friends a lot more if we didn't have alternative ways of staying in touch with them, but missing seeing them in person is balanced with the pleasures of not having to leave the house. I have missed the snooker and my craft group, and I'm gutted that Keith Urban cancelled his concert tour when I finally had tickets to see him. By the time I get to see him I might qualify for a senior citizen ticket! At least I had my long-awaited Keith Urban tattoo done this summer, despite two cancelled appointments.

Things will begin to open up again soon; in fact, they've started already, and goodness knows what will be happening by the time you are reading this. I've always been acutely aware of trying to avoid germs and getting ill. Pre-Coronavirus I would count the days between seeing someone and being well or ill. For example, if someone came to visit on a Friday, even if they were well, I would be counting the days until about Monday to decide whether or not I'd caught anything from them. Now I will have to count even longer between seeing anyone. I've always been careful about hand washing and wouldn't dream of touching anything unnecessarily in public toilets, shops or cafes.

I'm nervous about getting back into the practice of going to meetings or appointments and I'm not in a rush to go back to shops. I've avoided busy shopping times when I can for years now, as a matter of course. I would like to go back to my favourite charity shops, though, especially as I reckon people will have been clearing out some good stuff. I need to begin thinking about Christmas present shopping too. We planned a very small and carefully socially distanced outdoor birthday party for Paul's 40th. It followed health guidelines and I enjoyed planning it down to the tiny details of what people could or couldn't touch and what to do if someone needed to use the toilet.

I would love to go to the beach, but I know there will be hoards of people there on any day with half decent weather, so that's not an option for us. We would also usually use the school summer term time to go to places like a zoo while children are at school and adults at work, so that's another thing we can't do for now. I have missed doing my PDA talks, even though I also find them stressful. What I miss is the excitement of the event, meeting people and the buzz of the achievement of a job well done.

It's hard to predict how I will feel about events and appointments in the future, as life returns to the inevitably ordinary way of doing things. What I hope for, post-pandemic, is that people will become more hygienic generally; that they won't be so offended if I ask them to give me more space; that it's more acceptable to ask for the windows to be opened; and that I'm not put in the social dilemma of shaking hands or doing silly air kisses. I will miss hugging, though.

Chapter 11

Julia through Paul's Lens

It's not often that I spend time focusing on myself, so this is an unfamiliar experience for me. This chapter has been written in the same way as the rest of the book. I have had long conversations with Ruth who has then written the content for us to edit. That's worked well for me for different reasons than it worked well for Julia. For me, it's because I tend to overthink things and worry too much about what to say so it's been helpful to have someone to frame my thoughts and to share that pressure. It's also been helpful because, despite being accustomed to writing as part of my job, writing about myself feels very different. I often get asked about Julia but very rarely do people ask me about me, so I've appreciated being able to do that.

I have watched the development of Julia's book with pride and I've done all I can to support her in her project. It's been interesting to see the manuscript evolve because it has helped me to comprehend Julia in a broader context. It has explained lots of thoughts, emotions and stories about her past in a way that helps me understand her better now. I've got every admiration for the way the book has woven together the themes of her profile with a true portrait of her personality. In some ways I look upon it as having had my own Julia Manual written! I'm sure it will prove invaluable.

I first met Julia through an online dating site. She contacted me initially and I remember seeing her picture and thinking 'that's a lovely photo and she's got a sweet smile.' Very shortly after first making contact online we were on a long phone call during which she explained her various diagnoses, which I didn't know much about at the time. I went off to have a quick Google. I didn't want to keep Julia waiting (partly because I was worried what she'd think of me and partly because I was imagining how anxious she'd be if I was much longer) so I phoned her back within an hour and said it was fine by me. I remember thinking to myself, 'Well this one's going to be a bit different.' Never a truer word...but for all the right reasons in my view! We have now been together for 16 years. We met when I was 24 and I've literally just had my 40th birthday.

I noticed Julia was not the same as most other people I had known, right from the start. Having had some very keen phone calls early on, prior to us meeting, it certainly was a bit unsettling to spend our first date together with instructions not to look directly at her and to be told she would need to sit with her back to me until she was ready to turn around. I tried, though didn't quite understand what that could be about, but I went with the flow, trying to be patient and kind until something unlocked the door. Needless to say it did! I wasn't as anxious a person as I am now, so I was able to take it in my stride and didn't feel too hurt by it, just a bit surprised. Since that first connection we've not looked back.

Our first weekend together was planned to each tiny detail by Julia who got increasingly excited with every new element of the plan as the date approached. I was told the schedule so I knew in advance what we would be doing when and where. To be honest that worked in our favour: it meant that Julia had control over the timetable of our activities so she wasn't as stressed, and it lifted the pressure off me in terms of what to do with our time together. I've always been comfortable with being guided through social events so to me it was a relief to have received an itinerary so that way I wasn't worrying about what suggestions to make to try to please or impress my new date! That first weekend was wonderful and we made a precious connection that's still strong all these years later. She's the sort of person I always needed to be with.

We've always bounced off each other. We're really in tune with each other which is mostly a huge positive although it does also mean that sometimes we pass on our low mood or negative frame of mind to each other. If one of us is upset and we can't work out why, we check in with the other one to see if we've 'contaminated' each other with our feelings.

The only time it's probably not helpful that we bounce off each other is when I'm driving. Julia is very much a co-pilot, not even a back seat driver. It's interesting that she has as much advice as she does given that she isn't an experienced or licenced driver herself, and sometimes it feels like she even blames an uneven road surface on my driving! I've got used to her using the horn on our behalf if someone does something they shouldn't, and she's very reliable at spotting cats that might run out into the road. I think she's on high alert because as a passenger she's not in control, but she's an excellent navigator, in-car DJ and sweet passer!

It's hard to know why I feel more anxious than I did when I was younger. Julia jokingly says she's 'broken me', but actually I think that I always was an anxious person; it's only as I've matured that I can recognise it for what it is. Also, the older and more experienced I've become the more aware I am now of how many things could go wrong in a situation. I have a tendency to overthink things and to catastrophise. I often think 'what if it all ends badly because…happens?' I'm very good at imagining the next disaster! On the other hand, I've always been able to talk to Julia about my concerns and she has been very supportive. I do need to pick my moment wisely to talk about my problems, though, so that she has the available headspace for me. I don't like to burden her or upset her so learning to open up is something I am continuing to work on in myself. I think I'm probably a 'rescuer' by nature, which is something I need to bear in mind too. It's great that Julia and I have found each other and I'm happy to support her, but it's equally important that we find ways to look after both of us in this relationship and for me to protect my boundaries for my own wellbeing.

We moved in together after we'd been going out for six months (Julia wanted us to do so sooner but I wasn't quite ready as early as she was) and I moved from Bromley to Devon. I hadn't lived with a partner before and went straight from my family home to live with Julia so I don't have much to compare the experience with, but there were more than a couple of things that surprised me. Julia has extremely precise requirements for lots of everyday tasks. For instance, when dusting she has particular procedures to follow regarding how to dust, with what cloth, which cleaning products and most importantly, how to replace lamps or ornaments that have been lifted to allow for dusting. Although I didn't quite understand *why* the details mattered so much, I could see *that* they did and I didn't mind then, and still don't mind now, doing tasks in a way that soothes Julia. It is my way of accommodating her needs so that we have a harmonious home. From the beginning, the real clincher was that both of the cats seemed to take to me. Julia felt this was all the validation she needed that she had chosen well and we settled into a pattern of life together.

Over the years there have been arguments. Some of them have been rather spectacular and one ended with my hastily packed bag being thrown out of the house! I even once spent the night in the car but we have always got past them and loved each other through them. It helped that we had some relationship counselling to guide us in healthy ways to resolve disagreements. The way we tend to manage differing views or preferences is that I try to be extremely understanding and to react slowly. I'm not a martyr but I do need to be balanced and to contain my feelings a lot of the time. I often have to pause and ask myself 'is this worth making big waves about?' We argue a lot less now I decide more carefully what to react to and what to let go. The issues and irritants in our lives haven't really changed, but my reaction to them certainly has, and that's helped.

I need to be careful and considered an awful lot of the time. Generally, I feel that I'm not really at liberty to express my own emotions in a naturally responsive way: I need to pause and plan most things I do or say. I do wonder whether that makes me inauthentic in some measure. On the other hand, it is also an expression of my care for Julia alongside my motivation to maintain our peaceful home life. Maybe I have lost connection with my instinctive responses to situations now I've become so used to curbing my initial reactions. When I described this to Ruth she was struck by how it reminded her of what she has heard a lot of parents and teachers say about living with children or young people with PDA.

It's certainly true that Julia is affected by mood swings and she can have extreme emotional reactions. I'm not like that, so my moods are more stable and don't change as fast. It's also true that Julia's swing travels in both directions. Sometimes if I don't react to something that has irritated me because I think it could lead to a fallout, it doesn't take long before Julia has changed her mind anyway or realised that it would work better for us both to approach something in another way. If I can give Julia the space she needs to move on from something that has irritated her, the issue often blows over more quickly, or is resolved more positively than if I had challenged her directly.

Occasionally Julia might speak to me abruptly to say that she wants me to get away from her (or words to that effect!). I try not to take this personally any longer: I know she is telling me what she needs rather than rejecting me. If she speaks to me in a way that someone else may feel is rude or dismissive, I know she doesn't mean to be hurtful; it's just that her emotion is spilling out. She is very sensitive and she does reflect afterwards and apologises if she's overreacted. If I go out for a walk or a drive to give Julia some space I genuinely don't know what mood I might be walking back into. That can be exhausting and anxiety-provoking. Our relationship works because we both want to support and love each other through every day. However, it's not always straightforward. It's as though we don't only have to manage our different individual personalities but we also have to navigate Julia's conditions, like they have their own presence in our lives.

We have a pretty intense life together because we are with each other almost all the time. Julia doesn't work and I mostly work from home. We don't really have separate social lives and it's extremely rare that we even have the change of scenery of staying away from home overnight. I feel that most of my waking hours I'm 'on call' to Julia's needs. Don't get me wrong, I do so with love, but nonetheless that is my reality. Even when I'm working or if I'm upstairs when she's downstairs I'm constantly keeping an ear out for her in case she needs anything. If I'm listening to music when I'm doing the washing up I would only have one headphone in my ear so I can still hear Julia.

There are times when I slip too far into carer role and I lose sight of being a partner and an equal person in our relationship, but in the main, we have got the balance right, although we continue to refine it. It's probably the key to any successful relationship to continue to connect with each other, to communicate and to make accommodations for both individuals' needs.

Julia said to me recently that in some ways I'm like the parent in our relationship. When we were talking to Ruth about this we wondered if it could be because:

- I take the greater responsibility in some aspects of running our life, e.g. paying bills on time, putting out the bins, putting shopping away and mowing the lawn. I don't really view these jobs in terms of a division of labour, but more as these being necessary jobs, and it's just that I'm in a better position to fulfil them.

- I have a lot of responsibilities as Julia's carer. These range from cooking to helping Julia with most of her self-care.

- I accompany Julia to places she wants and needs to attend. It would be very rare for her to feel able to go out anywhere without me.

- It has become my role to 'rise above' tension so that we avoid falling out about the smaller stuff.

I have chosen to share my life with a very delicate person whose sensitivities may be triggered at any time. If our life is going to work well, I need to make accommodations for her. That's about our shared needs. I do need to be careful about what I say, when I say it and how I say it. Sometimes Julia says she thinks I'm too careful, but I don't like to upset her.

I know I can tend to hang onto my emotions too long without talking about things. I have fallen into this pattern because I am reluctant to overload Julia or to risk upsetting her, but there are occasions when I get this wrong. Julia says that I could lean on her more sometimes but I don't always know when these times are going to be so I err on the side of caution. I'm only human, and if I attempt to talk to someone close to me about something that is troubling me, I want to be heard and supported, not to be told that I need to wait until they're ready to listen. I suppose over the years that has made me reticent to talk. When I'm wrestling with a complicated situation or emotion, I can meander around the issue while I'm talking until I work out what my key point is. That can annoy or unsettle Julia because she can see that I'm worried but she can't work out what I'm concerned about. It can all become a bit circular!

We have just had a lovely afternoon tea party for my 40th, which Julia organised. She also organised a party for my 30th, which was a surprise. She told me we were going to the theatre to see a friend of ours in a musical – to be truthful, I wasn't really looking forward to it as *my* birthday outing, but I went along with it. As we were getting ready, I thought Julia had really excelled herself in her controlling behaviour when she announced I had to change my pants (I had put some on with a rather busy pattern). She wouldn't explain why but simply said, 'I need you to be in different pants!' Anyway, I duly changed and off we went. It turned out that what she had planned was a surprise 80s party, and when I was presented with my Freddie Mercury outfit complete with white trousers, the need for subtle pants became clear! Julia dressed as Madonna and we had a wonderful night.

I've been asked before how I feel about attending events and appointments with Julia to support her. Obviously, I am more than happy to attend any medical appointments, as would be any supportive partner; in fact, the local surgery is now very good at liaising with me on Julia's behalf and at her request. I don't mind going to Women's Institute or Parish Council meetings, although I probably got a few strange looks the first time I did so. If I need to say anything to explain my presence I would say that I'm Julia's partner, which puts other people at their ease. I just sit at the back of the room catching up with some work on my laptop and to be honest, for me, it's like a bit of time off. I know it's not time off in the sense of me being free to go somewhere separate from Julia, but it's nonetheless time when I feel I'm not entirely 'on call'. As it happens, I'm quite comfortable with the people we meet there and I enjoy a little chat to them myself. I don't enjoy lugging the boxes of craft materials between the house and the meeting and then back again (and I'm glad to have had a break from doing it during lockdown), but I do it to help Julia.

Every year (except for 2020, because of the pandemic) I have a full week away working at an airshow. Julia doesn't accompany me on these trips. There are lots of mixed blessings about them. I need to help Julia get organised with what she might need, e.g. internet groceries while I'm also getting myself organised for the week ahead. When I'm away my days are pretty packed and long, so I'm quite absorbed in my work. On the basis that a change is as good as a rest, it's a welcome break for me, but it's not exactly relaxing. In some ways it probably helps that the week is so full on because that protects me from dwelling too much on how Julia is doing back home. If I was having a beach holiday without her, not only would I miss her company, but I would also feel distracted by worrying about her. When I get back home after airshows it's always lovely to see Julia and the cats again, but her needs are invariably at a high level, having managed on her own for the week.

Writing this has happened mostly during the 2020 lockdown. It's not been as bad as I thought it was going to be (says the catastrophiser!). In some ways it has been very peaceful for us to have calm time at home together. Julia says I shouldn't speak too soon because she thinks I will be pining for airshows once the summer season should have begun. She's probably right. I enjoy my writing and my photography work, and aeroplanes are my passion. Having more time recently has helped me reflect on a few things. I don't necessarily have huge aspirations for my future but there are some aspects of my life that I want to develop. I think it would do me good to have some social activities separate from my life with Julia. Not in any way to be disloyal to her, but just to add to my personal interests and ways of expressing myself. I wonder about joining a photography club or a music jamming group, but I don't feel ready to take on something new yet. I also want to work on some more aviation writing and maybe one day study an Open University degree.

I'm aware that some of what I'm writing might sound a rather overwhelming way of life for other people. I do get really tired from time to time, particularly if I'm having a bad time with my IBS and chronic pain, but I love Julia and I value her not only as a person but as my partner. I don't feel overly controlled by her or that the support she needs of me is unreasonable. I get a great sense of satisfaction and peace from helping the woman I love.

If I was talking to someone else who was starting a relationship with a PDA-er partner I would say to them:

- Appreciate the differences and the new direction your life will take.

- Don't take things personally. Remember that your partner will sometimes need space; that doesn't mean they have had enough of you, just of everything at that precise moment. They will benefit from some time to refocus and de-stress.

- Be willing to have an open attitude to how you organise your home and your household chores. Be prepared to do the tasks they can't, and encourage them gently with those that they can manage.

- Be patient and give them more processing time. For example, after I've asked a question and/or made a demand, and Julia doesn't answer straightaway, I try not to heighten the demand by asking 'well, didn't you hear me?!' Instead, I might make a little noise after a while – cough or shuffle my feet – so she realises I'm there, waiting. It's subtle but effective.

- Remember that moods change. When something happens to cause a flare up it can also calm down as quickly, so try to take a step back from becoming caught up in the latest storm, partly to protect your own wellbeing and partly to navigate the situation proportionately.

- Be understanding and do what you can to sympathise with a different perspective or interpretation of what happens.

- Be flexible in your plans. Sometimes plans will need to be changed or postponed, so try to agree some fixed points (maybe related to work or important family commitments) and layer flexible arrangements around them. It's more likely to work well if you are a person who likes plenty of quiet time at home without too much of a busy social life too.

- Be grateful that there are some uncomfortable conversations that your forthright PDA-er partner may be happy to have on your behalf that can help you, e.g. complaining to customer services.

- Life may not be busy socially, but it will not be boring! You will have lots of fun, love and interesting discussions.

- Don't neglect yourself in your endeavours to support your partner.

I have covered some of the challenges of sharing my life with Julia here, but it's really important to me that anyone reading this understands that we truly have a happy life together. In many ways it's not so different to what I observe in lots of other relationships, although at the same time there are certainly some very unique aspects to it.

In Julia I have a very loving, caring, honest and supportive partner. She is loyal to the core, creative, practical, fun and a born leader! Even during the darkest moments of arguments, I've often reminded myself that I'll never find anyone who loves me more. She gives me daily support with my anxiety and forgetfulness and calms my flusters! She cheers me up if I'm feeling frustrated about having been ill or in pain so I haven't been able to be as productive as I would like to be. She helps me accept 'the practice of the possible' on the days I'm unwell or anxious. Most importantly, she's never given up on us.

I've mentioned some things that I hope for in my personal future, and it's important for me to have my distinct identity, which Julia supports. As for us as a couple, there are other things we hope for. When our dear cats finally depart (we're not being morbid, but they really are quite elderly now) we would like to have a holiday. We have talked about going away maybe to Scotland with Julia's mum, which would be a lovely treat. We would like to have a dog as our next pet – actually, we can't agree on names or breeds at the moment so we might need to have two dogs! We would like to do some home improvements (which Julia has finely planned) as and when we have the money, the inspiration and the will. And we have it in mind to get married one day, though so far that day hasn't come.

It's been really interesting and constructive writing this chapter. Even more so than I imagined, actually. It's given me an opportunity to re-evaluate how things are for me and how we go about our life together. It's felt cathartic to reflect and to be able to express my thoughts very honestly, although it's also been exhausting at times. It has helped Julia and I look at our relationship through our writing – classic PDA-friendly strategy to de-personalise an issue via an objective third party! – and that's given us more tools to strengthen our relationship for the future. Thank you, Ruth!

I am so happy to have found Julia and I love our life together. She's taught me things about myself and about PDA that have most definitely enriched my life. Ours is not necessarily the life I had predicted for myself 20 years ago, but most people would probably say that of theirs. The point is that although being in a relationship with a PDA-er does bring some challenges, it is certainly not miserable: it's loving, supportive and honest. I think I'm very lucky to share my life with someone I love who also loves me.

Chapter 12

Now and Next

This is now...

Well here we are, at the momentous point of the final chapter. Like the view from the top of a mountain, I can look behind me and see the distance I've travelled. There were times when I never imagined getting this far with writing the book – and for many of you readers, congratulations for making it to the final chapter too!

Coming to the end of writing is a bit unsettling to be honest; first, because I still have to navigate the editing and production processes (which will all be done by the time you read this). Then the book will be out there, and I don't know how it will be received. It's been quite stressful and tiring to do so much looking inwards, but it's also been a really significant experience.

Paul says that it's had a big presence in his head too. He found that writing his chapter highlighted all sorts of themes. It was lovely to see him come alive talking to Ruth about our life together and sharing stories with her, but it was also sad to hear that some aspects of our life together are so challenging for him. For the few days following phone calls with Ruth he said he felt like he had heightened awareness of me. Almost like when you return home from a holiday and you see your own house through slightly more objective eyes until it all becomes very familiar again. He said that it has been really helpful in his understanding of what makes me tick and he feels more 'at one' with me for having worked on his own chapter.

Of course, that's a lovely thing to say and a wonderful thing to hear, but I did feel a bit strange reading what he's written and facing his perspective of how our life is for him. I feel a bit sorry for him and rather guilty because living with a 'Julia' is not something I could do, and it highlighted how many accommodations he has to make for me. I've always tried to remember that he does an awful lot for me. I'm grateful for that, but sometimes it's good to be reminded. That reminder can be painful, too, as it highlights just how different I am and just how much support I need. Nothing for me is simple. I'm so pleased he contributed to the book because I really want his perspective to be heard too.

Working with Ruth has been very enjoyable too. She's an easy person to talk to and to get along with. Nothing with her is an effort and I've enjoyed talking to her once a week. Thank you, Ruth, for making this whole project possible. Not sure what I'll do now to fill my Friday mornings! Perhaps another book?!

Ruth's words to Julia

Julia, it has been a pleasure working on the book with you. It's been a long and complicated process, which makes it all the more satisfying to have completed it. Whatever will I do with my spare time now?!

It was not straightforward coming up with a way of writing that worked for us both. Initially, I set out very broad parameters, hoping they would leave you feeling under less pressure, but actually it just seemed to make it harder. You got stuck and so did I. I wasn't sure how to help us move forward together. I was worried about placing too many demands on you or being perceived as 'taking over', but without doing some degree of both of these things I could see that we were going nowhere fast.

For approaching 30 years I've worked with autistic individuals, many with PDA. I have been very privileged to have known lots of wonderful people and their families, but I am still learning. I know there will be times when I learn slowly and others when I learn by making mistakes. There will also be times when things run more smoothly and then the learning is in reflecting on why that has happened too.

As we got to know each other better I think you began to trust that I understood, accepted and liked you; that I am on your side, keen to facilitate you achieving your goal; I am comfortable being flexible – indeed, sometimes I need to shuffle things around for my own needs as well as yours; and that I am committed to finding alternative ways to continue if we hit a roadblock. So, we began to talk honestly about what else we could try, and I'm truly delighted that we found a way of working that suited us both.

Julia, I've known you since 2014 when we were introduced over a memorably delicious carrot cake (made by you). I've known Paul the same amount of time. In those years we have worked on a number of conferences together and enjoyed lots more delicious baking over cups of tea. I value spending time with you both.

Looking through the enormous box of personal documents you gave me to read dating right back to your pre-school years, it stood out that there were many of the usual pieces of work one would expect from most children. Drawings, imaginary stories and a scrapbook about your favourite pop bands. There was less of your own handiwork representing your teenage years, but what was clearly demonstrated was your humour and creativity. You had lots of interests and were eminently capable of learning and of producing work of a high standard. However, your pathway through education, both in terms of your engagement and academic achievements, told a very different story. I think that *largely reflected your needs not being recognised and understood by enough people at the right time. It astounded me, for example, to find amongst your papers a report from a professional who wrote, when you were only 11 years old:*

> *Julia is...impulsive, irresponsible, immature, self-centred, aggressive and dangerous towards others without internal controls, remorse or insight...she is a severely disturbed and disturbing child who needs very specialised care and control. She needs a package which includes social educational and therapeutic work in a context where her behaviour can be contained as well as challenged. Without this she will be unable to function appropriately as an adult.*

Well, you've certainly outdone yourself now! Reflecting on some of the detail of your earlier life, it's clear that you had some extremely positive, nurturing experiences, but sadly, many deeply distressing and unhelpful ones too. Your experience shows the importance of children like you being understood and valued for who they are. You have pre-vailed, and that's what makes the writing of this book and the life you lead now all the more remarkable. I say that without being patronising, but with the intention of celebrating what 'Being Julia' means to you.

I am very grateful to you for sharing your experiences, pretty much uncensored! I am honoured you have trusted me to tell your story and it is my wish that your readers find it both enlightening and entertaining.

And what might come next...

I feel that I have achieved a lot in my years so far (37 to date). If someone had looked at my life when I was teenager they might be surprised that, even though I don't have a job as such, I live in my own home with my partner of 16 years, that we have looked after two cats for years, that I have a friendship circle, that I have voluntary work roles as well as some paid work, that I keep our house clean(ish), that I have learned to cook and I even do some gardening!

I have had brief experiences of work in my earlier life. My first paid work was about age 12, cleaning down muddy motorbikes at a garage. It was as a favour to someone Mum knew and only lasted a couple of weeks. I then tried childcare, ranging from babysitting to my hours in daycare as part of my unfinished course. I made cards and painted glass, which I sold on a market stall, but I spent most of the proceeds on bacon sandwiches and snacks (not a great business plan!). My most successful paid work has been the public speaking events I have done in recent years. They're not particularly highly paid or frequent, but they still qualify as paid work and they represent my first successful work. I doubt I will ever have an ordinary paid job. It's not because I'm lazy or because I don't want to do something meaningful. I like to think my commitment to the various committees and voluntary work I do demonstrates that. I don't think I could hold down a job because I would find it really hard to know how to prioritise my time and attention and to know what to do first. I would find it hard to complete a task, especially if it was a bit boring or irritating, and I realise that every job has some boring bits to it. I could risk getting stuck mid-task or having a meltdown. I wouldn't take kindly to the rules/protocols/policies I may see as unreasonable or as too demanding. All in all, the thought of it leaves me feeling sick. I know all this about myself, which is one of the reasons I've tried so hard to do other meaningful things with my time.

In the future, I don't have any grandiose aspirations (although I wouldn't say no to being extremely rich one day). In many ways some of the things I hope for are probably much the same as most other people. I would like to:

- Be more financially secure (this may be rather optimistic as for a while now our costs have exceeded our income, but then there are lots of other people in our position).

- See the book do well and be useful to other people.

- Continue my happy and secure relationship with Paul.

- Keep my bedroom organised and sleep in a bed at night.

- Carry on baking and crafting.

- Have lovely Christmases (Christmas is a really important time for me and I want to have as many nice ones as I can).

- Continue with my blog and with the talks I give. I'm pleased to have been asked to deliver some input to a local council adult care team.

- And, in typically random Julia fashion, I would like everyone to know how to make decent brownies having eaten some dreadful ones in cafes all over the country. You will find my favourite recipe at the end of this chapter, so get baking!

I want to marry Paul one day. Don't worry, we've already discussed it, so this isn't the first he's heard about it! It's hard to explain why, but getting married is really important to me, although I can be patient. (Actually, I have already been patient, 16 years Paul, just saying!) I want us to make that total commitment to each other and officially be each other's next of kin. I've been working on planning my ideal wedding since I was about 5 years old, so as soon as we are ready it will be easy to swing it into action.

I don't know if many PDA-ers will read this book, but I hope that they might enjoy dipping into it from time to time. I certainly hope the people who live with them and support them will find it helpful. Personally, I hope that it will help adult care professionals to understand more about the sort of support I might need if Paul were ever not around or if I needed care when I'm old. We live in our own bubble and it works for us, but I would be in a difficult situation if the bubble popped one day for some reason.

My life now has a nice rhythm to it and it's one that I can manage and enjoy. I don't do anything illegal. I don't drink or use drugs. In fact, I've never been drunk and only tried weed once. I endeavour to be a good friend, neighbour, daughter, sister and partner, and I try not to get into conflict with people. I'm much happier now than I've been since I've learned more about PDA and about myself. I feel far more settled and it's from that position of strength and self-belief that I look forward with hope and contentment.

If I had to pick just one message from this book that I want to be heard, it would be the message of hope. Even in difficult times, things don't have to stay dark and hopeless. Yes, there may be times when darkness is all that you can see, but the light can break through again. Life is full of ups and downs – that's what helps make our journeys exciting and interesting. If all else fails, if you're doing no one any harm and you've got a lifestyle that suits you, then you can always say to yourself 'f*** 'em' – this is how it works for me! And finally, I hope that parents of children with PDA who are reading this will be encouraged by an example of a potentially independent, successful and positive life ahead for their young people.

Julia's Perfect Brownies

250g unsalted butter (NOT margarine or spread)	80g cocoa powder, sifted
	65g plain flour, sifted
200g dark chocolate broken into pieces, min 70% cocoa solids (good quality, not cheap stuff)	1 teaspoon baking powder
	360g caster sugar (seems like a lot, but trust me)
75g sour cherries (must be sour cherries, usually available online)	4 free-range large eggs, beaten

1   Preheat the oven to 180°C/350°F/Gas 4. Line a 25cm square baking tray with greaseproof paper.

2   In a large bowl over some simmering water (make sure the bottom of the bowl doesn't touch the water) melt the butter and chocolate until smooth. Stir in the cherries.

3   In a separate bowl mix together the cocoa powder, flour, baking powder and sugar, and then add this to the chocolate and cherry mixture. Stir well.

4   Whisk the eggs in a separate bowl and then add to the main mixture and stir until you have a silky consistency.

5   Pour the mixture into the baking tray and place in the oven for around 25–35 minutes. You don't want to overcook them so, unlike when you spike cakes with a skewer or knife to test they're baked through, it shouldn't come out all clean. The brownies should be slightly springy on the outside with a soft crust and still gooey in the middle.

6   Allow them to cool in the tray and then carefully tip out onto a large chopping board and cut them into chunky squares. Makes approx. 20.

7   Delicious on their own, but also nice with cream (preferably clotted cream!) or ice cream.

8   Store in an airtight container. Eat within five days.

References

APA (American Psychiatric Association) (2013) *Diagnostic and Statistical Manual of Mental Disorders*, 5th Edition (DSM-5). Arlington, VA: APA.

APPGA (All Party Parliamentary Group on Autism) (2017) *Autism and Education in England 2017: A Report by the All Party Parliamentary Group on Autism on How the Education System in England Works for Children and Young People on the Autism Spectrum*. London: National Autistic Society.

Carpenter, B., Happé, F. and Egerton, J. (2019) *Girls and Autism: Educational, Family and Personal Perspectives*. Abingdon: Routledge.

Christie, P., Duncan, M., Healy, Z. and Fidler, R. (2012) *Understanding Pathological Demand Avoidance Syndrome in Children: A Guide for Parents, Teachers and Other Professionals*. London: Jessica Kingsley Publishers.

DfE (Department for Education) and DH (Department of Health) (2014) *Children and Families Act*. London DfE/DH. Available at: www.legislation.gov.uk

Department of Health and Social Care (2018) 'Government review to improve the lives of autistic children.' Available at: https://www.gov.uk/government/news/government-review-to-improve-the-lives-of-autistic-children

Fidler, R. and Christie, P. (2019) *Collaborative Approaches to Learning for Pupils with PDA: Strategies for Education Professionals*. London: Jessica Kingsley Publishers.

Newson, E., Le Marechal, K. and David, C. (2003) 'Pathological demand avoidance syndrome: A necessary distinction within the pervasive developmental disorders.' *Archives of Diseases in Childhood 88*, 595–600.

To Llarjinder,

Enjoy the read!

I've Got a Stat For You

My Life With Autism

Andrew Edwards

DARK RIVER

An imprint of Bennion Kearny

Best Wishes
Andrew

Published in 2015 by Dark River, an imprint of Bennion Kearny Limited.

Copyright © Dark River

ISBN: 978-1-911121-00-8

Published by Dark River, an imprint of Bennion Kearny Limited
6 Woodside
Churnet View Road
Oakamoor
ST10 3AE

Acknowledgements

Firstly, I would like to thank my Ma, Hazel Davies, for fighting endlessly throughout my life, when even emotionally strong people would have given up long ago, and in her dedication and determination in making me the person I am today. Additional thanks go to Ma for keeping all the documentation from meetings, assessments and important incidents throughout my life – without which this book would not have been possible. You are a very special lady, Ma, I love you very much even though the autism sometimes doesn't always allow me to express this in the way I would like as I owe everything to you.

To my sister Melanie Beckley for being the best sister I could ever ask for and in being like a second mother to me. Your help in the writing of this book in getting out my emotions has been an asset to the book and has added enormously to it. You have also acted as my filter and your straight talking has weeded out any garbage in my head or my writing.

Thanks to my brother in-law, Billy Beckley, my nephew Louis, and niece Chloe for being the best family I could ask for.

Thanks to my godparents Jim and Shirin Nelson.

The following people, listed in no particular order, have also played a big part in my life over the years.

Kevin & Lindsay Apsley, Hayley McQueen, Michael Shaw (who must take credit for coming up with the title idea for this book), Steve O'Shaughnessy & family, Aled Rowlands, Dave Cunnah & all his family, Gary Jones, Nick Hughes & family, Stephen Parry & family, Gareth Evans, Joseph Cooper, Andrew Bode & Sophie Waterfall-Bode, "Uncle" Michael & "Auntie" Pauline King, Mark Pearson, Kasia Cooke, Magdalena Oczkowska, Stewart Gardner, David Stowell, Janette Horrigan, Andrew Dickman, Mark Sullivan, Ross Wyllie, Jamie Shepherd (for passing on my details to Bennion Kearny), Jimmy Hunter, Mai Rees-Moulton (for the foreword), Maxine Pittaway MBE, and Mark Powell

Thanks also go to Katie Inman & John Humphrys from BBC Radio Four's *Today Programme* as the interview I gave to their show during Easter 2015 began a chain of events that led to the publication of this memoir.

And lastly, but by no means least, thanks to my publisher and editor James Lumsden-Cook from Bennion Kearny who approached me after listening to my interview on the *Today Programme* on Easter Saturday 2015. This was one of the few times in my life that anyone had approached me rather than my Ma or me getting in touch with them over anything. I didn't make it easy for James as I don't have any social media presence, I deleted my account on Facebook in early 2009 as I believed it wasn't compatible with my autism, and I am not even on Linkedin. I am very easily contactable on my mobile and email, though. Thank you James for being so persistent in pursuing me, having the belief in the book, and helping me achieve my long-held ambition.

Foreword

I carried out therapeutic sessions on a weekly basis for many years with Andrew. The aim of the sessions was to educate him about puberty and the appropriateness of behaviours; also to work around emotional regulation and behaviour.

Andrew showed a lot of resistance to the sessions initially with displays of aggression and inappropriate comments. Andrew tried to shock me in many ways. He showed his anxieties by engaging in obsessive conversations mainly around sport and simulating sporting moves, e.g. playing cricket or bowling. With set parameters, Andrew used the first five minutes of the sessions to settle by talking about his own topics, these topics were then reserved for the last 10 minutes of the session when he could talk about his chosen subjects. The session was then structured and Andrew responded well to this, often bringing questions that he would store up to ask me rather than ask inappropriate questions in other settings; these were usually about sexual acts or words.

The sessions took place at a time when Andrew was trying to make sense of the world around him, often talking to me about incidents that had happened at school, or at home, where he had not been able to regulate his behaviour. We eventually forged a strong relationship, which has lasted over 20 years – some 15 years after I stopped working with Andrew because he entered adult services. The friendship is very much a two-way process and we meet up regularly for a coffee and a catch up.

Andrew's relationship with his mother has always been very strong and Hazel fought with every ounce of energy she had to provide Andrew with the best possible service and education. She forged a strong network with family members supporting Andrew and scrutinized anybody else that worked with Andrew to ensure he received a safe and supportive package of care. Hazel has always been straight talking and a force to be reckoned with! She is also very kind-hearted, honest and warm.

Hazel is strict with Andrew and has instilled very high morals and standards. His autism was never allowed to stop him from being polite and respectful.

Andrew has matured into a very mindful adult. He is self-aware and with support can reflect on his actions and make changes. Andrew has been a very talented public speaker and an advocate for autism awareness. His knowledge of sport and his ability to retain information, scores, dates, facts and figures has been used to gain employment and given him opportunities to enter the world of sport in a very proactive way, where he has made many friends. He continues to be supported by his family. This provides a very safe environment for Andrew where his anxieties are reduced, allowing him to engage in life in a very positive way. Without this support, I feel the future would have been very different for Andrew.

Andrew is a very intelligent man who has worked with his autism and used sport to regulate his emotions and behaviour. I am very proud to have been part of Andrew's life and to have witnessed the power of love and determination from his family.

Mai Rees

Nyrs Cymuned / Community Learning Disability Nurse

Prologue

Chambers Dictionary defines autism as "An inability to relate to other people and the outside world". Although I can relate to people in many situations and have, to a great extent, started to show empathy, I can't always cry when I am upset. Living with this disability has moulded me into the person I am today.

According to statistics from The National Autistic Society, around 700,000 people may have autism in the United Kingdom. Five times as many males as females are diagnosed with autism. In addition to this, an estimated 2.8 million peoples' lives are "touched" by autism, a figure I believe to be much higher if you include everyone who comes into contact with someone with autism.

One thing I hope the reader will learn from this book is that there is no stereotypical autistic person like the portrayals of the condition in feature films like *Rain Man* and *Mercury Rising*. One person could suffer from the disorder completely and, in footballing terms, could be likened to a player at the lowest level of Sunday League. Other sufferers not only appear "normal", but can gain qualifications at a high level and pass in a crowd on the street with nothing apparently to set them apart. These individuals could be likened to the clubs in the latter stages of the European Champions League.

Most of all, I want to show parents who have just had a diagnosis of autism for their son or daughter that there is light at the end of the tunnel (and it isn't an "oncoming train" to use a Half Man Half Biscuit song title from their 2002 LP *Cammell Laird Social Club*) and also to those who have had similar experiences to my family and me. Yes, there will be very stressful days and times, but it is worth being persistent. Trust me, as my family and I know better than anyone. Don't take the word of so-called "professionals", who think they know better than you. They usually don't have to live with autism 24/7, 365 days a year. In our experiences, you must fight them until you basically have to use every single sinew in your entire being, like my Ma has. If you don't, it will be to the detriment of your autistic child. They don't know your autistic child like you do. In my opinion, some of them are just following the advice of the Government who control their budgets while protecting their positions and are not giving you the advice that they would do if they were in your position. Obviously, some professionals are good, just, in our experience, they are unfortunately few and far between.

At the end of the day, we all have autistic tendencies in our everyday behaviour. Whether you place objects in a certain order, do your house chores in a certain order, have a set routine in the morning, hoard or collect things like gig tickets, football programmes, CD's, vinyl, DVD's, videos or just papers from meetings – these behaviours are in just about all of us. The difference being that it affects or consumes someone with an autistic spectrum disorder infinitely more greatly than someone without; it would matter greatly if you changed their routine or their collection slightly.

In fact, I believe that a lot of musicians of all genres, comedians, thespians and top athletes must have autism or similar conditions, many more than has been publicly acknowledged even by themselves. This is due to the sheer dedication, almost beyond obsessional levels, that it takes to reach the top of their chosen professions – much more than most people are willing to give.

Many musicians must have ridiculously large music collections to learn their influences, along with the obsessional levels of practice it takes to reach the height of their skills. As well as musicians, athletes must work at their conditioning, mentality, and skill levels to way beyond what would normally be deemed obsessional.

In many ways, someone with autism would be a prime candidate for professions like this. To further enhance my point of view, journalist and former New Zealand cricketer and seam bowler Iain O' Brien made the following observation:

"If you went around the dressing room, you could pick someone out who was suffering from Obsessive Compulsive Disorder, you could pick someone with an Autistic Spectrum Disorder and (then) there's those affected by depression. There would be a small minority, who would be actually quite "normal".

Nonetheless, a lot of autism sufferers have non-sporting or cultural skills which can be utilised in a regular working environment. Unfortunately, many aren't lucky enough to have the requisite social skills or help to thrive, like I have been fortunate to have from my family and at M.U.T.V., where I worked for over a decade.

Every story is different. This is mine and I hope you can take something from it even if you don't have autism in your family, be it in your workplace, neighbourhood or a mate with it. I won't lie… my story has had its ups and downs, but I believe I am a much stronger person from the experiences, which I hope you can gauge from reading my words.

I have had plans to write my memoirs periodically since the age of 14, but either didn't have the inclination, motivation and, on occasions, the ability, for one reason or another, to execute my long held plan. Everyone, no matter how good or incompetent, has plans to succeed and prosper but due to infinite factors cannot execute their plans. Everyone has plans, but it is those who successfully adapt and adjust them that have the best chance of executing said plans.

Fortunately, a change in my life circumstances when I was made redundant from my long-serving job at M.U.T.V. gave me the ability and time required to write my memoirs, which I hitherto didn't have. Despite my autism, I have learned to be unafraid to tinker with long-term plans, which hasn't always been easy, in fact far from it. Usually, people with autism find it nigh on impossible to adapt or tinker with their plans. Aided by my family, I have been able to do this in my life when needs must.

At exactly a year to the hour from when I was made redundant from my position at M.U.T.V. on Monday 20th April 2015, in a coffee shop in Chester City Centre, I met a man for the very first time who I didn't know, except for two phone conversations in the previous week. This can be very stressful for so-called "normal" people, but it is far more so for someone with autism. I needn't have worried as within fifteen minutes of first meeting this man he made my long awaited, previously unexecuted plan to have my memoirs published come true.

At the end of the day, as you will find out in the course of reading this book, life may not have always been easy, but it could have been worse. As my sister, Melanie, always says to me: "worse can always get worse!"

Finally, if any of you are wondering where I got the titles of the fourteen chapters… they are song titles from my music collection that best suit what each chapter describes.

I hope you enjoy the book.

Andrew

Chapter 1
Born of Frustration

I am autistic.

I know I will always be autistic.

I was born on Tuesday 20ᵗʰ November 1984, in Wrexham Maelor Hospital. It was a sunlit day with the hanging sun closing in towards its inevitable lowest point of the Winter Solstice four-and-a-half weeks hence. It was the type of day when you would willingly take a walk with your footwear crunching the fallen foliage on the ground from the trees above. This is exactly what my Ma did on the day I was born as she made her way to the local post office in Gwersyllt to collect her weekly family allowance. Little did she know that by 2.35pm that afternoon she would have given birth three weeks prematurely at Wrexham Maelor Hospital to the baby boy she was expecting. The first male of her now three children after her two daughters. The baby weighed 7lbs 3oz, which is quite large considering the premature birth. The baby was named Andrew Michael James Edwards.

I claim unsuccessfully that the Michael was after "King of Pop" Michael Jackson, as I was born just a year after the worldwide success of his sixth studio album, *Thriller*, and almost a decade before any of the allegations levelled at him. Subsequently, there have been stories that Michael Jackson may have been autistic. However, the name Michael was after my estranged father, and the James, which is an epithet I more proudly hold, is after my godfather James Nelson, who ran his own double-glazing firm near to The Racecourse Ground, the world's longest serving international football ground and home of Wrexham F.C.

Stories in the news on 20ᵗʰ November 1984 included 2,282 miners returning to work during the long-drawn-out, bloody saga – which even divided families in some areas – of the miners' strike, Marie Osmond fleeing from her marriage to basketball star Stephen Craig, although they subsequently remarried in 2011, and, last but by no means least, a clairvoyant predicted that Queen Elizabeth II would appear in Dynasty! Probably, in our house, like many in Britain at the time, the first story took precedence over the other two as my Taid (grandfather), Samuel Davies, was a retired miner of 51 years. On Friday 22nd September 1934, my Taid swapped his shift at Gresford Colliery to attend choir practice and to watch Wrexham play Tranmere Rovers, the area of his birth, in a Football League Third Division North encounter at The Racecourse. It was fortunate he took the day off, for him and for five generations of family later – as 266 miners were killed on shift, with survivors in single figures.

The day I was born, Taid went around the neighbourhood merrily drunk on whisky as he was celebrating my arrival. Unfortunately, he informed whatever people he encountered that my Ma had had a baby boy named "David"!

My only personal memories of Taid are of him having his meals-on-wheels delivered, his black leather sofa, and his best mate "Ossie", who would be in his flat at 9pm – on the dot – every evening with both men waiting for the clock to strike to signal the beginning of the 22nd hour of the day.

When I was born, Taid had nothing to bequeath me. So he went to Wrexham Town Centre and bought a grandfather clock. He also carried the clock all the way home, and I still proudly have the clock in our front room although it unfortunately no longer ticks over.

My first word was "aubergine" when I was three years old. My logic behind this was that the word reminded me of the end titles of the Channel Four soap *Brookside*. After this, every question that was posed to me I answered with the word "aubergine", including everyday pleasantries such as "What are you watching on TV, Andrew?" or "How are you feeling today, Andrew?" Why did I do this? I do not know.

*

At three months old, I had required mouth-to-mouth resuscitation from my parents after a reaction to a colic medicine, and when I was 12 days old, I was admitted to hospital with a serious saliva gland infection. The prognosis was not good. The canon from the family church was summoned to the Maelor Hospital by my future godparents' daughter Rebecca. Obviously, I survived. In between these two eventful experiences for my family, I was the first baby in my diocese to be christened during a mass at St. Mary's Roman Catholic Cathedral on Sunday 23rd December 1984. Shirin Nelson was named alongside her husband James as my godparents.

Despite only being a town, Wrexham boasts both a cathedral and a university named Glyndwr University after Owain Glyndwr, who led the Welsh Revolt against Henry IV at the turn of the 15th Century. Wrexham has failed to obtain City status on two occasions during the 21st Century, in 2002 and 2012. In the latter instance, Chelmsford, where Essex County Cricket Club have their headquarters, and St. Asaph, in Denbighshire, were awarded City status.

As time advanced after my illnesses, it became clear that I was not progressing at the usual speed. My mother noticed that whereas other children fixed their gaze on their mothers I withdrew mine. I was not making progress as regards to sitting up and crawling. As well as problems such as walking and delayed speech, I required nappies for bedtime until age six as I would wet the bed. Unfortunately, even later on, I would have an occasional overnight accident if I had drunk too much juice the night before. Other difficulties I had included not being able to sit up, getting undressed as soon as I got home from an outing, and failing to differentiate between hot and cold water. I also flapped my hands. Ma tried to find excuses for my lack of progress. After all, she had reared two girls before me, and girls develop more quickly than boys, don't they? There was nothing wrong with her son; there mustn't be.

There was a playgroup in Wrexham – and along we went. The room was full of toddlers happily making their sandcastles, painting, crayoning, reading, and attempting puzzles. A calm, domesticated scene prevailed with smiling mothers looking on fondly. Within a few minutes of my arrival, I managed to create complete mayhem. Sand was thrown, paint was splashed over the floor, books were torn and games were broken. Shocked mothers gathered up their screaming and distressed infants, and my mother beat a swift retreat. The whole episode lasted around half an hour. Once back in my pushchair, clutching my toy cars, I was quite content with my 'performance'. Not so my Ma who cried all the way home.

I remained trapped in my own little world with kicking, screaming, scratching and biting being my only forms of communication with

3

the rest of the family. The only person who could control these tantrums was Ma, who would get down on the floor beside the screaming, flailing child and hold him to her as he would rock gently until the storm was over and calm was restored.

Visiting the local shops and remaining in my pushchair was not too much of a problem. However, a weekly visit to the supermarket in Wrexham on a Friday was a nightmare as I struggled with the bright lights. Due to this, it was not only a nightmare for Ma but also for the other shoppers and the supermarket staff. I usually chose a crowded aisle to display my tantrum, sweeping goods off the shelves using both feet and hands with much more strength than was the norm for a three-year-old. People commented, "I would smack him if he was my child." Such words were unhelpful to my Ma and they hurt her deeply.

As well as this, when I was about four or five I used to be impatient in shop queues whilst shouting "I'm autistic and hyper-bloody-active!" This was without knowing the meaning of what I was saying. If I had to wait in a queue, I would rock back and forth whilst repeatedly flicking my fingertips like a footballer from the 1970s celebrating a goal. I got better with this with the help of the couple who ran the grocery store in Aberystwyth where we went every year on holiday. They would make sure I was polite, said thank you and stayed in the queue. They also used to keep toy cars behind in the shop for me.

*

When I was three, it was obvious to my Ma that there was a very serious problem stunting my progress. The paediatrician at Wrexham Maelor Hospital had previously called me "spoilt" because I had two much older sisters and was given more attention. It was now clear that this was not the overriding problem. My Ma was at the end of her tether trying to find out what was wrong with me. She wanted guidance, support and, most of all, answers, but this was again not forthcoming. It is sometimes easier to cope when you have a 'label' to attach to the symptoms as then you can start to tackle the issue and find coping mechanisms to deal with it. But even this did not appear to be available.

Appointment after appointment ensued, with professionals claiming invariably that I was spoilt or levelling other discouraging comments at me. In a 9am appointment on Monday 3rd April 1989, at Wrexham Maelor Hospital, I was eventually diagnosed as severely autistic. The consultant's only words of 'advice' to Ma were, "to go home and watch Rain Man. It is likely your son will be institutionalised."

Ma left the hospital in a daze as she took me in my pushchair out into the mild, mid-spring weather. After taking a couple of days to gather her thoughts, Ma was determined to prove the consultant wrong. I would talk. I would walk. I would mix in society and be the same as my sister, Melanie.

Ma went to seek help, which, to this day – more than a quarter of a century later – is seldom forthcoming. I was referred to the Wrexham Home Pre-School Advisory Service for Children with Learning Disabilities. This service covered provision for autistic children: there was no separate organisation to deal with autistic children. The service ran a playground in Wrexham. Nevertheless, Ma felt I was inappropriately placed within this group as it contained children that were severely disabled and couldn't speak. Ma believed that I would copy the actions of the other children with my autism, and I would not be able to progress like she wanted me to. The placement was discontinued for this reason.

One morning, I made my debut appearance at the mainstream Pre-School that the professionals recommended, accompanied by my mother. However, this was not so much an appearance as an explosion in the quiet school filled with mothers and toddlers. I shot around the room like a bullet, small children fleeing and toys flying in every direction. Mothers hastily snatched their little ones away from my path of devastation. Eventually, my Ma managed to regain control of me and calm me down, but the harm had been done and I was never to return.

*

My Ma observed that I had an interest in cars. I would line my toy cars up in sequence on the lounge floor while noticing if any had been moved. When walking around the neighbourhood, Ma recited the names of the models of the cars that were parked near and would get me to regurgitate them. This was a very long process that brought about a very gradual improvement over a sustained period of time. I would also do this with numbers.

In addition to having an interest in cars, I was infatuated with the police. I remember that I had a Ladybird book giving a potted history of the force. I always recall the first couple of pages were about Sir Robert Peel who formed the first police force, which was known as the "Peelers". For my fifth birthday, in November 1989, Ma and Mel came with me to Wrexham Police Station for a tour of the facilities by a WPC. We got to see the cells, the control room; I got to sit in a police car and I was also allowed to wear a helmet. At the time, this day was one of the best of my short life, and I was very excited and thoroughly enjoyed the experience.

In September 1989, I briefly attended a special school. Ma went in a taxi with me, and the taxi driver had a beard and his name was Ian. I found the journey very long, but I remember to this day that *Ride on Time* by Black Box, which was number one for six weeks in the UK Singles Chart around this time, and was the biggest selling single of 1989, was on the radio every day I went to school. I also remember a lad in the playground, who would roam around aimlessly talking about a "moo cow". Except for him, no other pupil could talk, apart from me. My classroom had a big ascending ramp to the door, with wooden rails on either side.

I love cricket and thinking about this ramp reminds me, although I am not sure why, of the 385-run partnership between Australian batsmen Steve Waugh and Greg Blewett at The Wanderers, Johannesburg, in the first Test against South Africa as they batted throughout the entirety of day three of the match on 2nd March 1997. In addition to this, certain episodes of the long-running U.S. sitcom *Married With Children* come to mind. On the day of that Test, Manchester United also beat Coventry City 3-1 at Old Trafford with the Sky Blues netting two own goals as I was at Flex Gym on Wrexham Industrial Estate.

During the school day, Ma stayed with me – apart from one time when she was reluctantly persuaded to have a bit of a break. When she returned, she saw me tied up. The school claimed that this was to "control me", which, needless to say, we disputed. Understandably, after this incident, Ma decided to keep me at home and educate me herself despite having no formal educational training. I would get changed for P.E. while she would take me around the locality on nature walks as part of another lesson.

As you can imagine, after that previous incident, Ma wanted to make sure I was safe from harm and, at this time, it would take some convincing for me to go back to school. So, she started to educate me herself at home. She taught me to count, although I regurgitated the numbers like a parrot with no real understanding of the actual numbers. This was just a stop-gap solution and I would eventually find a school. But the fight was not finished. It was not the end, only the beginning.

Chapter 2
Family Affair

My mother has always been there for me, along with my sister Melanie. Inevitably, meeting after meeting regarding my wellbeing, as well as running a loving home, takes its toll but the day she loses her "get up and go" will be the day that I call the undertakers.

She is undoubtedly a matriarch and since I was first diagnosed as autistic, she has shown such determination in raising me that emotionally weaker people would have thrown in the towel years ago. In saying that, though, she has brought up Melanie and me in exactly the same fashion. Although she hasn't been a career woman, she is one of the strongest people I have ever met. She has done this while being easy-going.

When I was young, as one Doctor explained, "She (Ma) showed remarkable insight into his condition and intuitively handled him well; i.e. forcing eye contact, cuddling him, talking to him constantly."

*

My mother Hazel Davies was born on 2nd February 1943 and for all but one year of her life has lived in the village of Gwersyllt in Wrexham. She is the youngest of three children and got married in February 1967 to my estranged father. Hitherto, in her teens and early twenties, she had been a decorated Latin American ballroom dancer, even dancing in an international competition at the Royal Albert Hall, London, in 1966.

Over the years, her trophies have unfortunately been either misplaced or broken. In 2013, for her main Christmas present, I got in touch with the relevant arm of British Ballroom Dancing, who had a record of Ma's successes, and they sent us copies of the trophies. I got the relevant information engraved on them for Ma. Hopefully, Ma can look back happily on her dancing days with a version of her trophies now back in her possession.

Away from dancing, Ma's day job was as a lifeguard and swimming instructor at the baths on Tuttle Street in Wrexham. She was known for giving short shrift to anyone who messed around in the pool, including her future long-standing next-door neighbour, Michael King, who I have always referred to as Uncle Mike. When the baths moved to its current location – what is now known as Waterworld – Ma was offered the job as the bath's assistant manager. She rejected the position as she was pregnant at the time. I think, from what she has told me subsequently, that she regrets this decision as, according to Ma, the manager really wanted her to be his second in command.

As well as raising me, she had to struggle to keep our house after her divorce. Only her single mindedness kept us from losing it. I dread to think what would have happened if my Ma wasn't the strong character she is.

Although life has, at times, been trying for Ma – like for most people – funny events do happen to her. A typical instance of this occurred during the Easter holidays of 1992 whilst I was innocently watching *The High Chaparral* on television. A leak started to drip into the toilet's wash basin, and as we were preparing to go on holiday the next day, Ma decided she would sort the leak out herself. While attempting to fix it, Ma's arm got trapped while placing putty behind the sink. Requiring help, Ma called out to me, but I was more interested in the television. Eventually, after several pleas for assistance from Ma, I went to get help. Unfortunately, the paperboy was passing and I got waylaid talking about Manchester United's run-in to the 1991-92 First Division season and their attempts at trying to win a First League title in a quarter of a century. After a long time, I eventually got help and the fire brigade was summoned. Ma needed a sling after this rather sorry, comedic affair.

*

Melanie is my older sister – born on Saturday 29th July 1972. From day one, Mel has been like a second mother to me. Twelve years my elder, she was at St. Joseph's Roman Catholic High School in Wrexham when I was born. Her teacher even used to bring her home at lunchtime to visit me. She was smitten from day one and has never been jealous or envious of me.

Although we often argue, we are probably as close as a brother and sister can be. She has always been there to support me, Ma and the rest of the family. She gave up her nurse training to look after our great aunt, who I used to call Nanna Nell, and Mel even helped us financially by sharing her nurse's bursary when we had little money after Ma had got divorced. My close mate, Andrew Bode, once pointed out, "your sister hasn't had the time for a career as she is looking after her family."

Mel met her husband Billy Beckley at a christening on Sunday 15th May 1994. They were engaged within a matter of weeks after Bill proposed to her in the Plas Coch car park. They got married at Gwersyllt Church on Saturday 3rd February 1996, the same day Manchester United won 4-2 at Selhurst Park against Wimbledon. She was given away by her godfather and I was best man, aged just 11.

Billy is a quiet, easy-going man. Mel is more assertive when it comes to dealing with matters that may arise, but Billy is very reliable and has his strengths in other ways. Until May 2014, Billy was my support worker for 17 years. He is extremely dependable, genuine, and would do anything for the family. Mel became my support worker in St. Christopher's – the school I attended between the ages of 13 and 18 – after it was determined that I needed a "two to one".

It was even Billy's idea to give their son – Louis – the middle name Andrew when he was born on Friday 21st June 1996. On the same day, Jack Russell hit his second and last Test hundred for England against India at Lord's in what was also legendary umpire Harold "Dickie" Bird's last Test Match before retirement. That match also saw a debut hundred for Sourav Ganguly and 95 for fellow debutant Rahul "The Wall" Dravid, who is the best Indian batsman of his generation, in my opinion, bar none.

Billy and I had a relationship that suited my routine and which was comfortable for me due to difficulties in the past with trusting people. We had difficulties at times, of course, with Billy not always being assertive enough in certain situations. Nonetheless, I wouldn't have wanted anyone else. I always trusted Billy. Looking back now, it would have been even better with Billy if he could have received the support of his superiors and received more training.

Over the years, we loved watching cricket together, especially watching Lancashire in the County Championship. He would take me where I needed to go at little notice, for which I will always be grateful. I think it always helped with him being a family member as Mel didn't mind him being out with me. I was able to go to gigs, sporting events, and meet up with mates. Some of my other support workers, over the years, were very poor – with one being drunk, another not having road tax, and one that fell asleep while working. Having Billy took the stress off Ma as she knew he would be there to work with me.

Louis and me are like brothers and close mates rather than uncle and nephew. Louis has willingly taken on many of my interests like cricket, football and music gigs. I have never pushed him into my activities… he just shares them with me. He is a deeply educated, mature, sensible lad who I even go on the train with on my own. I hope I have helped him by adding a little bit of culture in his formative years with the comedy and music gigs that most young kids wouldn't even think of attending with me! He left the family home, which is next door to Ma and me, in September 2014, to go to The University of Manchester to study Law.

Louis' younger sister Chloe was born on Thursday 9th May 2002. Chloe was a very quick birth as Billy and I were at Marchwiel and Wrexham Cricket Club training until two hours before her birth. In her early years, I was extremely biased towards Louis and rather hard on Chloe. Eventually, we bonded around the time that England regained the Ashes after 18 years in September 2005 when I looked after her when Mel and Billy were putting laminated flooring in the conservatory.

When Chloe was younger, Mel had to go through the same rigmarole of finding answers as Ma did with me – as Chloe struggled with her physical development at pre-school age and had grave difficulty in getting a night's sleep. At times, Mel was running entirely on fumes during this period and there was no way she could have had a job with Chloe's appointments and her lack of sleep. Chloe was diagnosed with dyspraxia – which affects her physical coordination as well as her sensitivity to textures in food, alongside difficulty with certain clothes, disrupted sleep patterns, aches and high stress levels – when she was five. The lack of help out there for autism in the mid-1980s, when I was diagnosed, was, unfortunately, apparent with Chloe in the late 2000s. We have been determined and caring as a family. There is no support out there.

Fortunately, Chloe overcomes her difficulties by having a quick-witted, funny, caring, articulate personality and is, at times, a bit of a "mini-me" and has a quip to make about most things. She is the polar opposite to Louis, and I see a few similarities between some of her difficulties and mine in that her condition has several of the same traits as autism, but she is far better than me – socially and emotionally – at the same age and has relatively few problems in mainstream school.

*

Without my godmother Shirin Nelson I would have no qualifications. She helped me obtain four G.C.S.E.s, including History in six months, and also taught Mel at St. Joseph's R.C. High School in Wrexham in the 1980s. Ma met Auntie Shirin during this time while she was on the PTA and they became firm friends quickly. Auntie Shirin was Deputy Head during this time and Head of History and was known for her lack of stature. She was only 4'11", but is now just 4'8", and wears four inch high heel shoes.

The pupils gave her the nickname "Little Hitler" and quipped that she was thrown out of the Gestapo for cruelty. I can vouch that she is strict, but is most certainly fair and only had the pupils' best interests at heart as she is a very caring person who always turns the other cheek and attends the Catholic Cathedral, where I was baptised, every Sunday. I am sure Auntie Shirin would like me to join her, but I am an atheist, who believes a Frenchman who wore a red number seven on his back between 26th November 1992 and 18th May 1997 is the messiah.

My godfather, Uncle Jim, is her husband of over half a century. Like I previously wrote, he owned his own double glazing firm – imaginatively titled Nelson Glass – until he retired due to ill health in the late 1990s. Previously, he worked for a double glazing firm on Merseyside and was once accosted by legendary footballing hard man of the 1960s and 1970s Tommy Smith over a delivery of double glazing that the defender claimed he had not received.

Seriously though, Uncle Jim is tough. He has beaten cancer at least twice and suffered a heart attack following tics which used to shake his whole body. He has lived at least a decade more than I thought he would. I even joke with him about it.

As I explained in the previous chapter, I get my middle name James off my Uncle Jim. All in all, he is a lovely bloke, although opinionated like Victor Meldrew as he argues with John Humphrys every morning while listening to BBC Radio Four's *Today* programme. A typical case of his opinionated and principled streak occurred when he was driving his work van over Gwersyllt Railway Bridge and saw that sheep were being mistreated. Obviously, he respected that they needed to be slaughtered, but he gave the workers a piece of his mind as he felt they were not doing their jobs sufficiently humanely. He also tells eccentric stories to Chloe, who calls him Granddad Jim as she laps up his wonderfully long-winded anecdotes.

My Nanna Nell was actually the sister of my "real" Nanna, who passed away on 5th December 1977; however, I still called her Nanna as she had no children of her own. Although my Nanna Nell passed away when I was eight, I have many other happy memories of her. She used to cook me pancakes on Shrove Tuesday, too many in fact, and made the thickest, loveliest gravy I have ever tasted; again, this was very unhealthy. I used to go behind her back while she was sitting on her green springy chair and pretend I was the pilot of a jet that I called "Nanna Jet". I even watched Shane Warne's "Ball of the Century" at Old Trafford on Friday 4th June 1993 on her television.

I vividly remember the day she passed away over twenty years ago on Wednesday 1st September 1993. I bought a Magnum ice cream, but fell over in the process of purchasing it. Ma, knowing that Nanna Nell was passing away, got some relatives to take me to their house. Ma rang them later that afternoon and I knew she has passed, but the relative sugar-coated it. When Mel told me that Nanna Nell had passed away, it broke my heart. I was devastated and sat on my toy panda bear in my bedroom.

Her passing affected me greatly in school and I didn't attend that much in the first six weeks or so of the 1993-94 school year as I was grieving and felt devastated that she was no longer here. I needed to be weaned back into school briefly after this. Obviously, now – over twenty years later – I think of the happy memories and am not upset at her passing.

In later formative years, I became close to Nanna Nell's brother, Uncle Herb, and his wife Auntie Vera, who were married 52 years. "Death do them part".

Uncle Herb passed away on Sunday 18th November 2001, the day after United beat Leicester City 2-0 in the Premier League and Druids beat Ruthin Town 2-1 in the Welsh Cup Third Round, and two days before my 17th birthday. I still think about him often, especially while walking Ellie past Royal Court, where he lived. I was very sad when he passed as he never got to meet Chloe, who Mel was pregnant with at the time. Nevertheless, he predicted she would have a girl. Unfortunately, he never got to meet her.

As well as human members of our family, we have had three dogs that have made an enormous impression on all of us. They are two Yorkshire Terriers named Tara and Ellie and, most importantly, a Great Dane name Beauty.

Tara was very much a lady who hated walks or exercise of any description, but would find any resemblance of sun in the garden and lie there contentedly. Mel bought Tara for £125 in February 1992 as a pet for me as I was only seven at the time. She would lick the tears off our faces if we had been upset and would come on any family holidays in my youth to places like Aberystwyth, Prestatyn or Talacre.

Ellie was born on Monday 6th March 2006 and has helped Chloe tremendously with her dyspraxia and her difficulty with wearing different clothes. They absolutely adore each other. In fact, Ellie pines after Chloe when she is in school and, strangely enough, is aware when it is time to pick her up and informs us accordingly by howling. She is infinitely more energetic than Tara and loves walks around the neighbourhood. She also sneaks into the lounge as soon as the door opens, even though, at times, she is forbidden from going in there.

Last, but certainly by no means least, was Beauty. She had a terrible start in life and was set to be put down by her breeders. Ma went to get Beauty with Bill on the day United last played Nottingham Forest on Saturday 6th February 1999 at The City Ground. United famously defeated "The Tricky Trees" 8-1 with Ole Gunnar Solskjaer, who came off the bench with just a quarter of an hour left in the match, scoring four goals. My Forest-supporting close mate Michael Shaw ("Shawbles"), who attended the match, still has nightmares about the game over a decade and a half later!

Mel named Beauty after the Lassie Collie she had in her childhood and after the T.V. show *Black Beauty*. Beauty, after her poor start in life, lived longer, according to our vet, than any other Great Dane he had come across in the Wrexham area. She was 13 and a half years old when she passed away. The average for a Great Dane is said to be only six to eight years old. I don't think I will ever come across a dog that had such expressive facial features as Beauty. It was, at times, as if she was speaking back to us by moving her mouth.

When she was put to sleep on Tuesday 20th March 2012, which was pre-planned with the vet a week before, Billy and I couldn't face coming home that night and arranged with Shawbles to go to the Great Northern Cinema in Central Manchester. The movie we went to watch was the Oscar-winning *The Descendants* starring George Clooney. It was bloody awful. However, I was extremely thankful for Shawbles' friendship that evening. Even Billy had a cry when he said goodbye to Beauty for the last time that morning. All in all, Beauty was the favourite of the three dogs I have owned.

My relationships with the dogs have altered as I have got older, like they tend to with humans. They had a calming effect on me when I was upset. If I was having a "turn", Ma would say you are scaring and upsetting the dog. At this point, I immediately stopped and either stroked Ellie or, when I was younger, held Tara. At this point, I would feel becalmed. Beauty, on the other hand, was always utilised to get me up off the settee at night when I had fallen asleep and was refusing to go to bed. This was due to her size. When she got on the settee, I would immediately get off and go to bed. Beauty also helped me get over my fear of big dogs.

It has taken longer to build up a relationship with Ellie in my adult years. She calms me, but it's a smaller part as I now talk and express my emotions to friends and family.

Although we aren't massively endowed in numbers as far as biological family is concerned, we are a close-knit unit. The six of us in our immediate family live next door to each other and we don't even have to go outside to visit each other's homes. When all is said and done, I would rather have just a few of us as close as we are rather than several dozen, who are distanced from one another.

Chapter 3
School of Seven Bells

In Wrexham, there was a school called The Special Education Centre (SEC) situated on Park Avenue, not far from the town's police station, which would have pleased me greatly at the time due to my fascination with the people in blue. The school was initially a pupil assessment centre for the short term but became a special school in itself as there were few provisions at the time for special needs children of infant school age.

I started at the centre in the Easter of 1990 and was to spend four happy years there. Initially, I attended on a part-time basis for a few hours every morning. This meant I got home in time for *Rosie & Jim* or *The Riddlers* on television. Coincidentally, I can still easily recite the theme tune to *Rosie & Jim*. When I watched the show, it was John Cunliffe, who also wrote *Postman Pat*, steering the boat. However, after my time, Neil Brewer – out of 1970s progressive rock band Druid – steered "the old Ragdoll", named after the production company that made the show. Druid also included Andrew McCrorie-Shand, who wrote the *Teletubbies* theme tune, in their line-up, releasing two albums in 1975 and 1976. I personally thank BBC 6 Music's *Radcliffe & Maconie* for this piece of music trivia.

One funny incident occurred after I got home from school to watch *Rosie & Jim* one day in 1991. During a visit to the downstairs' toilet, I trapped my willy in my trouser zip and a neighbour came round and helped me to remain seated in my rather compromising predicament. I went in an ambulance to the Accident & Emergency Department at the Maelor Hospital. On the way, I rattled off stats on Manchester United's history to the paramedics, and although only six years of age, I knew all my details like my full address and date of birth off the top of my head. Although this story seems rather humorous, looking back almost a quarter of a century later, it did have repercussions for me as for years afterwards I couldn't wear a zip on my trousers and required velcro to be fitted by a long-standing neighbour, who had been a tailor.

Whilst I was at SEC, the headmaster was an opinionated but very likeable man named George Derby. I was a frequent visitor to his office due to my difficulties. It was not unknown for me to steer the conversation away from my indiscretions to ask him about his weekend, or more impertinently, his wife; or, more often than not, rattle off historical statistics for Manchester United. More often than not, these distraction tactics worked well with George and seemed to amuse him; he promptly forgot the reason why I was standing against his office wall. I was so cheeky with George (the staff were referred to by their Christian names at SEC) that I even used to sing the nursery rhyme "Georgie Porgie" to him. This was an activity I indulged in frequently, much to George's annoyance and the amusement of the other pupils, who even started to sing the song. This prompted the school to prohibit the song.

When there was a fete at SEC on Saturday 21st September 1991, the day that United beat Luton Town 5-0 in the Barclays First Division at Old Trafford, George went into the gallows to have the pupils throw wet sponges at his face. Needless to say, I didn't hesitate to step up to attempt to soak him and I didn't even wait for my turn – proceeding to repeatedly put the wet sponge in his face directly. I even had my picture in the local paper as, to quote the *Evening Leader*'s article, I "threatened to steal the show". The fete raised around £1,000 to help the school's funds. I remember going to Saunders Opticians, who are currently my opticians, with Ma and Melanie after the fete.

At SEC, I participated in various activities, including trips to Chester Zoo, The Museum of Science and Industry in Deansgate, Manchester, an outdoor activity centre, and concerts put on for our families. In one of these plays, I was the King. I even vaguely remember one of the songs about the King and Queen living long ago and coming back to life a century later.

I was so comfortable at SEC that even big issues, which arose, were dealt with effectively. For example, I was briefly bullied by a fellow pupil but this was dealt with efficiently and effectively as the pupil was transferred to another class, away from me, to prevent further disruption.

Nevertheless, one unfortunate incident involving a nursery nurse allegedly pulling my hair saw them suspended from duty. I never saw the nursery nurse in the school again, and whilst I very vaguely remember the incident happening, I can't remember any emotions that well, from the time it happened, as I couldn't express any hurt or pain I had at the time.

On days when I was ill, I used to make every effort to attend school as, due to my autism, it was the routine and the norm. I became uncomfortable (and still do) when routines got disrupted. On one occasion when I was under the weather, SEC phoned Ma to tell them that I wouldn't go home until the end of the school day as it was the routine to stay there 9am-3.15pm, Monday to Friday. So, Elspeth Nicholls, my teacher, very kindly made me a bed in the classroom until home time. On another occasion, I was distraught that my Ma had forgotten to give me a Valentine's Day card and Elspeth called Ma to explain that I was upset about this. Ma told Elspeth she had one and was going to give it me when I arrived home.

Unfortunately, however, I wasn't always well-behaved in her class. I once kicked Elspeth in the shin and was suspended for two days from SEC. I don't know why I did it, but I do remember that I felt annoyed at myself for the two days I was excluded and felt deeply ashamed. I don't think I got dressed on at least one of those days. On the first day I was suspended, Goran Ivanisevic defeated Stefan Edberg, who was my favourite tennis player, in five sets in the 1992 Wimbledon quarter-final. Ivanisevic eventually lost in the final to Andre Agassi, also in five sets.

Despite some shows of aggressive behaviour, I would greet fellow pupils at SEC affectionately by trying to hug them. To prevent this, and due to my tall build, the school taught the other children to put a hand in front so that they could shake hands instead. Later on, I used to attempt a sharpshooter greeting, which was the finishing move of Canadian wrestling legend Bret "Hitman" Hart, who was my favourite wrestler. With a sharpshooter, you twist your opponent's legs around yours, turn them so they are lying on the ground, facing the floor, and then sit on them. I never successfully orchestrated the manoeuvre, but repeatedly threatened to do so.

To raise funds for SEC, as the school always struggled for funding, I correctly answered all twenty questions on the history of Manchester United at The Black Horse Pub in Summerhill in July 1992, aged seven. Ex-Liverpool European Cup winner Joey Jones was the quizmaster. My answering of the questions was energetic – to say the least – and I still have a copy on DVD, converted from VHS, of this evening. During the quiz, I accosted members of the crowd when I thought they laughed about a question regarding the air crash of 1958. However, the real reason was that they found it amusing that a child so young had the ability to correctly answer questions of this ilk. I have, in recent times, given the footage of this to close mates as a present for birthdays and Christmases. I wonder if they could see any of what I am like now compared to the seven-year-old me.

After the quiz, I told a Wrexham player that he was "on the dole" after he had been released, which is something I would only think about now but would blurt out without any resemblance of tact as a seven-year-old. In addition, a young Robbie Savage, who is from the same village as me, was present in the pub. Just weeks before, he was part of the famous "Class of '92", which included the likes of David Beckham, Paul Scholes, Gary Neville and Nicky Butt, that had beaten Crystal Palace 6-3 on aggregate over two legs in the F.A. Youth Cup Final.

While at SEC, I had shown a great aptitude for mathematics. Ma taught me my multiplication table on Sunday 29th March 1992 while I was watching *Little House on the Prairie* on Channel Four. I learnt all the tables in the space of no more than a couple of hours and they still stick in my head to this day. I remember that United won 3-1 at Carrow Road against Norwich City in the Barclays First Division two days later.

Due to my maths abilities, SEC sent for someone from the county headquarters of Shire Hall in Mold to look at my high mathematical capabilities. It slightly baffles me that children of high achievement struggle to learn and memorise all their timetables even towards the end of primary school. Perhaps, it came naturally to me at the time due to the autism. Unfortunately, with disrupted schooling in the years after this, my mathematical abilities diminished significantly, although the timetables have pretty much stuck.

*

Towards the end of the 1991/92 school year, it appeared I would potentially have to attend a new school in the September of 1992. At this juncture, SEC catered for children of infant school age. In an article in the *Evening Leader* on Monday 8th June 1992, Ma and I were interviewed with a photographer coming to the house. My mathematical abilities were heavily mentioned in the write-up. Fortunately, SEC extended the 1992/93 school year to include pupils of year three, but it was becoming apparent that in the near future, I would have to attend a new school, which worried Ma and Melanie greatly.

An educational psychologist's report from Monday 18th January 1993, the day United won 3-1 at Loftus Road against Queen's Park Rangers in the Premier League, discussed my move to another school from SEC in September 1993 and underlined many of the issues regarding the likely change. Her recommendations included the following:

- *Very gradual sessions, initially with the support of his class teacher from SEC. Initial sessions for football may be a "way in".*

- *It would be useful for another adult to take over from his teacher for support sessions but to be additional to the unit teacher. Possibly supervision from this extra adult might need to extend to playtimes.*

- *The unit class teacher would need to have some experience of children who have behavioural difficulties.*

- *There would need to be very close liaison between SEC and the receiving school; back-up support in the event of a serious outburst would need to be operational in minutes if necessary.*

- *The unit teacher would need to handle Andrew fairly and firmly, but also to show him warmth and understanding; Andrew needs access to a setting which provides opportunities for him to "loosen up" and talk about his feelings when he wants to.*

- *The integration period needs to be trialled over a considerable number of months to give it a fair chance and mother's support will be the most essential feature.*

- *A review after an agreed period of time to ascertain whether or not the integration needs to be extended or whether recommendation 3 is the more appropriate.*

- *Good liaison between all professionals and Ms Davies, for information sharing and support whenever necessary.*

Despite the several recommendations, only the first one was taken on board. This made little difference as the other suggestions needed to be implemented to have any chance of me surviving in a mainstream school. The rest were either ignored or lost in translation somewhere along the line. The mainstream school that was selected for me to go to was a primary school in Wrexham. Due to the strategies not being in place to deal with my condition, the teachers lacked the expertise and experience to deal with autism. If the teachers lacked the ability to cope, then the pupils stood no chance of understanding my difficulties.

Therefore, I was bullied repeatedly on a daily basis due to this lack of understanding of my behaviour. For example, I was once allowed to read the County Championship cricket scores in assembly. However, the following break time, I was hit by a fellow pupil, who stated: "you can't score 400 goals in a football match." This could have been dealt with by the staff if they had taken the time to explain to the other pupils, but they were completely out of their depth. In turn, this affected my self-esteem and confidence. In one instance, I locked myself in a cupboard when my taxi arrived to take me home and I wouldn't leave due to the bullying I had endured. I hated school at this time, so much so that at the end-of-year school football tournament, I deliberately scored an own goal as no one would pass the ball to me. I was a complete outsider.

Nevertheless, due to my autism, it was the routine to attend school every day, even if I was unhappy in the environment. I also found it very difficult to talk about my feelings at this particular time. I wasn't happy but couldn't express this to my family. I knew inside that I wasn't happy as the other pupils were nasty to me, but I struggled to get it out. I have often struggled to express my feelings as I believe they may, at times, be too trivial to discuss. Unfortunately, at times like these, my way of dealing with matters has been aggression towards other people, which made the situations worse. Sadly, at the time, I didn't know of any other way to deal with it. Fortunately, as the years have gone by, I have become able to express my feelings to my family better. Nonetheless, I can even struggle now to express feelings when I am tired or worried. If I do not prompt people, it is up to them to pick up a change in my demeanour.

The inevitable end of my time in mainstream school came when I was asked to bring "my ball in" from the schoolyard, rather than "the ball" in. If it had been "the ball", the nine-year-old me would have obligingly brought the football in. I was adamant that it wasn't "my ball". So, after being told off, I kicked the dinner lady and was suspended from school. This little vignette epitomised my time in the school. It was a time when there was a lack of understanding from the pupils, and no staff training.

I went to see the Principal Clinical Psychologist on Friday 30th September 1994, just after leaving the mainstream school, and it was clear that I had been affected intellectually and emotionally by the bad experiences. In Intelligence Quotient tests of my verbal and performance ability, I scored significantly lower than I had just over 18 months prior. According to the psychologist, the deterioration in the scores "possibly had a connection to the school placement". In the assessment itself, it was apparent that I would talk about the factual details of the mainstream school, but was very reticent in talking about the feelings and attitudes I held towards my time there. The most detail that I provided regarding this was that the "teachers say I am telling tales, but I am not" and "the boys use bad language".

After the bad experiences of the mainstream school, I was petrified to go back to school. I rarely went out at this time. I didn't want to return to education as the bullying put me off associating with my peers. I felt the mainstream school I attended contained pupils that were extremely foul-mouthed and "rough and ready", which scared me greatly. I had never experienced the language spouted by the pupils, some of whom were no older than seven, and even now it was the sort of swearing that gets used in my social, professional and home life only when I am very annoyed.

Despite this developed fear, I did visit a couple of schools in the Merseyside area in the autumn of 1994. I remember one of them had a pool table. Nonetheless, the fear of school prevented me attending any school for nine months, in which time I comfort ate and piled on the pounds!

A meeting was held in Wrexham, which Ma attended, on Thursday 8th December 1994, with the purpose being "to identify Andrew's educational needs and how best these can be met". At this time, there were increasing concerns about the length of time I had been out of school, with the mainstream placement ending two-and-a-half months earlier on Wednesday 21ˢᵗ September. This was the day United, or "Fergie's Fledglings", as they were dubbed, famously beat Port Vale 2-1 at Vale Park in the League Cup second round, first leg with Paul Scholes netting twice on his debut.

The concerns arising from the minutes of the meeting included:

- *My behaviour at home, with Ma struggling to cope on a daily basis as I was giving her little respite*

- *It was a big effort to get me to leave the house*

- *While out, I was fearful and frightened of people*

- *I would suddenly sit down in the road and shops*

- *I had developed a phobia of school*

Recommendations that were made included:

- *For myself to be placed in a residential school*

- *In the short term, an option to return to SEC*

- *A formal referral to be made to a residential school as a day pupil*

- *The looking into of establishing a local unit to accommodate my requirements*

- *Returning to the school I was tied up in*

Looking at some of these "recommendations" over two decades later, it goes to show that Ma is a very strong personality to basically stand up to the system that was in place for people with any sort of disability. The sheer chutzpah for someone to suggest a return to the school I was tied up in is quite frankly laughable, and grossly inappropriate. It is scary that a professional, supposedly intelligent, articulate person would consider it.

For several years following this, the first recommendation – that of residential education or respite care – was thrown at Ma on many occasions. However, she repeatedly showed the will, determination, single mindedness and love for her son to constantly turn it down with little thought. Ma queried why I should have gone to a residential school or into respite when Mel went to a day school, came home every day and stayed at home. She was not going to rear me any differently to Mel, despite my disability and difficulties.

I did go back to SEC in June 1995, initially for a couple of hours a day, two or three times a week. This was with much cajoling and coaxing. I even remember crying when Ma went back to the taxi and I saw the car pulling out of the car park from the window. When the new school year began in September 1995, I recall Ma ringing up at lunchtime to say Mel had a "migraine" to keep me in class for the rest of the day. I settled in after this and subsequently attended full time until Christmas 1995.

Nevertheless, SEC was only going to be a short-term placement as I was approaching secondary education age. The next school I attended would make a permanent emotional mark on my family, but especially on me.

Chapter 4
Little in the Way of Sunshine

Upon my leaving SEC for the second and final time at Christmas 1995, a day pupil place was secured – by the local Education Department – at an out-of-county school as it was felt this establishment could provide for my autistic needs.

I had visited the school in early December 1995 and it was agreed that I start my placement after it reopened following the Christmas and New Year break.

My taxi would arrive at 8am every weekday, along with my escort, to take me to school. They were rather long days as, after the forty-minute journey to get to the school on time for an 8.45am start, the school day didn't finish until 3.45pm. I was usually quite tired when I got home. On Mondays, it was even longer as there was a swimming lesson for the day pupils after the finish of the normal school day.

At this point of my life, I was petrified of water and I only went in the shallow end. One Monday, after a few months with a pathological fear of water, and no prior experience of the deep end, I was taken into the far end of the pool. I was extremely scared and this really was against my own volition. Somehow, I made it home that night, but I was stressed and Ma was furious as she would never have put someone in this position when she was an instructor at Tuttle Street Baths. Due to this incident, I held a fear of water well into adulthood. Writing this now, it makes me really angry that I was put in this very vulnerable position which could have got to the stage where, since I wasn't able to swim, my life could have been endangered.

One teacher I had was very helpful and was the only one I really learnt anything off. She taught me not to comment if someone was scruffily dressed and I also found out what the word tangent meant. She explained this to me clearly and articulately by drawing a crooked line on a piece of paper. This was the first time I had heard this word. With my autism, I will go off on a tangent at some point during the day, even now in my early thirties.

Another teacher that taught me was far from helpful, or in my opinion, had little feeling whatsoever for the pupils or her job. I recall how she used to make rather sarcastic remarks to the pupils. Some were slightly demeaning to the vulnerable youngsters, including myself. She also made them towards the severely handicapped. In addition to this, I also used to overhear other members of staff talking about pupils in, what I felt, was a very negative fashion, even commenting on the parents' status and financial situation. Due to my autism, I would memorise such instances occurring.

However, these perceived inappropriate comments would pale into insignificance compared to the life-affecting day of Tuesday 12th November 1996. When I left for school in my taxi that morning, not for one second would I have believed what the day held in store for the entire family. This day was to change the whole course of not only my life, but that of my entire family.

*

Up until lunchtime on Tuesday 12th November 1996, things had gone normally. Even after a fellow pupil and I got into a physical disagreement over me dropping a glass of water, what the day held in store could not be predicted.

After the disagreement, I was taken to see a member of staff in the school's garden. At this stage, the member of staff approached me in a rather aggressive fashion as if preparing for a prize fight. I then felt what I believed to be a punch to the jaw, and was held around the neck in what was subsequently claimed to be a move of restraint. I also received red marks around my left arm, a hand mark on my back, and my uniform was torn. All this was to "teach me a lesson of how it felt to be on the receiving end". I cowered away as I thought I was about to be kicked.

As well as the physical nature of what I suffered, I was also subjected to offensive comments about my Welsh nationality, and a remark about how former undisputed World Heavyweight champion Mike Tyson would box.

During this incident, I asked another teacher for help, but it wasn't forthcoming. After asking the teacher for help, I was dragged away by the back of the collar, receiving scratches and red marks.

Once alone, later on, I left the school grounds in order to escape. I planned to walk home. I got as far as the end of the road before turning round as I was scared that if I went from school I would get lost and never return home to see Ma and my family. Once I returned to the school and the incident had finally subsided, I received an apology from the member of staff. I was so confused by this that I gave a hug to the outstretched arms before me.

In between the incident and me returning home, Ma claimed that she received a call from the member of staff informing her of an incident when they had intervened with an "over the top" approach being taken.

My lessons continued for the rest of the day, but I really wanted the day to end as soon as possible so that I could return home to my family. I was due to go to Mel and Bill's house round the corner after school finished, for tea, as Ma had a pre-arranged meeting at home. When I got into my taxi to return home that evening, I didn't even inform my driver and escort of what had happened as I just wanted to get home as soon as was humanly possible.

As my taxi arrived outside Mel's, she was waiting inside excitedly for me to have tea with her and Louis, who was newly born. I clicked open her front door as Mel hurried to see me and greet me. Unfortunately, the sight of me in her doorway, in my dishevelled state with my uniform scuffed and torn, caused her to stop short – astonished at what I looked like.

Mel's first thought was that I had been in a playground fight, which was just a small part of what had happened. At this juncture, I ran into Mel's arms, trembling all over whilst crying uncontrollably. Although Ma had received the phone call regarding the incident, Ma and Mel weren't prepared for the severity of what had occurred that day. Despite what had happened, I told her that I wanted to go to school the next day as, in my autistic way of thinking, it was the routine to attend school regardless of what had previously occurred. In my autistic mind, I thought it would be a punishment to stay at home for something I did not do. The autism was telling me to return to school, but I was terrified to do so in case something happened again. Of course, I was never to return to the school after the incident.

Mel immediately took me to Ma's, which was around the corner from her house, while the visitors who were present in the house on an unrelated matter arranged for a doctor to come and examine my injuries. At the time, I hated being touched infinitely more than I do now and the examination was not pursued as I became extremely distressed.

The following day on Wednesday 13th November 1996, the medical examination took place as I was calmer and it was decided that I go to the Wrexham Maelor Hospital for x-rays to be taken. Later, a police photographer visited the house to take pictures for the investigation.

According to the Senior Community Paediatrician's report, I had hand marks on my back, and grip marks on my neck. I had been hit with some force on both sides of the face, whilst knuckle marks were also visible. According to the report, the injuries sustained were "extensive and severe". In the Community Senior Paediatrician's professional opinion, "the injuries were not self-inflicted" and "were caused by that of an adult".

On Thursday 14th November 1996, I was interviewed by video by the police. I told them that the incident had occurred after I had spilled a glass of water in the school dining room. I then told them that I got a mop to clean up the water while another child teased me. I admitted reacting to this by punching the boy. I then recounted the full story. I then informed the police officer that I wanted to tell Ma, so I ran out of the front of the school. After this, I told the police officer that I was brought back into class to resume my lessons.

Later on, I also gave a written statement where it was noticeable from my handwriting just how distressed I was. It began as neat and tidy. By the end, it was the handwriting of a small child; prior to finishing the account I broke down in tears to Ma in the kitchen.

Due to the incident, a Case Conference was convened on Tuesday 26th November 1996, where it was noted, exactly two weeks after the incident, that "some staff members at the school have been seen by police but the member of staff has not yet been interviewed". In addition to this, Mel, who was the first person to see me after arriving from school, was never interviewed – along with the two visitors that attended the meeting at Ma's, and Ma herself.

A follow-up Case Conference took place on 28th January 1997, where we learnt that the police had decided not to take any further action against the member of staff because, in all likelihood and according to the police representative, there were no other witnesses to the alleged incident. This was despite the medical professionals stating that the "substantial and significant injuries" I sustained could not have been self-inflicted.

In February 1997, we were informed that the school's Governing Body unanimously recommended that no further action be taken against the member of staff.

Needless to say, my family were appalled by the various decisions and the trauma of the incident caused me great difficulty in coping in life. Ma was very sympathetic and supportive towards me. I experienced many subsequent problems, including a disturbed sleep pattern. Medication was prescribed in an attempt to alleviate the situation, which I am still on to this day.

*

After the events of Tuesday 12th November 1996, I remained at home for 15 months, with no educational placement. For much of this time, my feelings would have prevented me from being able to take up a school place.

To this day, I still find it hard to believe that the school wasn't willing to offer any semblance of an explanation regarding what occurred on Tuesday 12th November 1996, and whether or not the member of staff or, for that matter, anyone else present at the school on the day was responsible. How could a child go to school on the morning in question, fit and healthy with no injuries, then return home that evening with what was described as quite severe and significant injuries?

As an aside, after the incident, one teacher at the school posted a video of the 1996 F.A. Cup final between United and Liverpool to me for my twelfth birthday, which was eight days after the incident, on November 20th. I felt that maybe they wanted me to go back to the school. As the years have passed, I realise this is something they will have to live with, not me. I was just an innocent child – although, admittedly, I had got into a scuffle with a fellow pupil – who was not deserving of the injuries suffered.

*

Understandably, after the incident and all that it entailed, as a twelve-year-old with autism I wasn't coping very well. I was very bitter at what happened. I believed that somebody had committed a wrong to me, but no one was punished for what had occurred. In my black and white autistic view, I just couldn't understand why nobody was suffering for what they did, except myself and my family – who were wholly innocent parties.

It was arranged for me to go and see a social worker – a specialist in children's mental health – who focused on counselling children who had had to deal with a traumatic time or incident in their short lives. My first appointment was on Wednesday 12th March 1997 in Wrexham. However, the counselling was just short term as I was discharged in December 1997. Nonetheless, the hurt, the nightmares, the bitterness and the feeling of being wronged remain to this day. I still have the occasional nightmare regarding the incident which places me in the grounds of the school.

After the police investigation, Ma applied for compensation to the Criminal Injuries Compensation Authority. We were rejected twice – first in January 1998. We appealed the initial decision, and our solicitor received another rejection letter on Monday 3rd August 1998 from the CICA.

On Friday 28th August 1998, Ma notified the CICA via our solicitor that she requested an oral hearing, which was granted and arranged for the afternoon of Wednesday 26th May 1999, at the Moat House Hotel in Liverpool City Centre. Ma also decided to call upon the services of my Consultant Psychiatrist to give a written psychiatric report for the CICA to consider. The report detailed how I was presenting in a marked state of anxiety with an escalation in challenging behaviour, tearfulness, and refusal to go out. I subsequently displayed quite marked aggressive behaviours.

It was the Consultant Psychiatrist's professional opinion that the incidents that occurred in November 1996 had severely traumatised me, had a major impact and influence on my psychological wellbeing in the short term, medium term and long term, and there were clear signs of post-traumatic disorder. The event had a major impact on my ability to cope with stressful situations. I had started to demonstrate an increased social avoidance and, at that time, remained extremely hesitant in crowded situations. "Don't hit me, don't hit me," I was noted to have said when approached by adults.

Ma represented herself at the Criminal Injuries Compensation Board Appeal Panel's hearing on Wednesday 26th May 1999 as solicitors' costs were not covered by the CICA and if we lost the case we would be looking at a substantial bill that we could not afford to pay. The member of staff had also been invited to give their input and their side of events.

We went to Liverpool as a family, including myself, who had taken a half day's holiday from my new school. I remember that when Ma had to go before the CICA Appeals Panel how Bill, Mel, Louis and I went around Liverpool. I remember to this day that I was wearing my school uniform whilst also having Manchester United socks on. After all, this was the day that United created footballing history by winning the last leg of an unprecedented Treble by scoring two goals to come from behind against Bayern Munich at the Nou Camp, Barcelona. I was petrified what would happen if I got rumbled wearing my United socks in "enemy territory". However, when I saw a gentleman proudly wearing a United 1996 to 1998 home shirt, my nerves were settled.

More seriously, Ma, on the other hand, did not have nerves. She was in the waiting room at the Moat House Hotel, very confident, fired up and ready for a battle. Ma felt that she had all the proof that she required to win the CICA Appeal Hearing.

Just prior to commencement of the CICA hearing, a gentleman came into the room to inform her that the member of staff had phoned ahead to say they would not be present at the hearing and "would you please come this way to the Hearing Room".

Ma was then taken into a large room where a number of men sat around a very large oak table. These men were all professionals and experts in their chosen field with just little old 5'3" Ma. She was asked if she wanted a cup of tea. Ma's terse and brusque riposte was, "No, I have come for a fight, not refreshments." The large table and men were quite daunting, but Ma let it show how she felt in this manner.

Ma took her notes out of her handbag and started to tell our side of the story. Whilst reciting our story Ma was quite abrupt and stern. The Appeals Board, however, explained that they were ready to give their verdict. Ma thought this to be strange as she hadn't really started to give our side of the story. She had come for a fight as no one had believed us for two-and-a-half years and we didn't believe anyone was likely to suddenly believe us now. Ma was asked to put her notes away. "We believe you," she was told. However – quite understandably, given our trials, travails and tribulations over the previous two-and-a-half years – Ma was quite taken aback by this statement. She continued to plead our case.

One of the professional men got up out of his seat, went to Ma and put his hand on her shoulder in a caring manner to further inform her of our success. What was happening was still not sinking in and Ma told the gentleman to "Get off", again rather abruptly. She was then asked in a louder, more authoritative tone to "Calm down. We believe you, Ms Davies; you have won your case. We decided before you entered the room, after reading all the information."

Ma, again not fully believing what was happening, said, "Do you really believe me? I have fought for so long. Thank you so much."

One professional on the other side of the table explained, "I understand how you feel. I admire you for the love of your son that you have displayed, as well as your fire and determination. Today lets you know that a crime of violence took place that day."

Ma replied again, rather disbelievingly, "Have I really won?"

The professional said, "We would not have made the compensation award to you if we didn't find that a crime of violence had taken place."

Ma came out of the room to the front reception of the Moat House Hotel on cloud nine. It had taken her so long to get even this small piece of closure. It was now her job to inform me, Mel and Bill, waiting outside, of the successful outcome.

Throughout the time waiting for Ma to come out of the CICA Appeals Panel Hearing, I was extremely nervous. Like Ma, I didn't really expect a positive result after all the negative outcomes that had come our way over the previous two-and-a-half years, from the Crown Prosecution Service deciding not to take our case to court, to the two prior rejections from the CICA.

But now, as I saw Ma make her way to the foyer of the Moat House Hotel at 4.30pm on Wednesday 26th May 1999, I saw her facial reaction was one of jubilation. She had done it! Finally, somebody believed us. I had received financial compensation for the incident that had occurred on Tuesday 12th November 1996.

The CICA compensation award felt like vindication to us. Along with United's dramatic victory in Catalonia that evening, Wednesday 26th May 1999 went down as the best day of my life until my 21st birthday party on Saturday 19th November 2005.

*

Ma, despite all her successful persistence in fighting for me and gaining some closure on Wednesday 26th May 1999, is riddled with guilt for not being there for me at the time of the incident. But shouldn't a child be safe whilst in the care of the staff at the school they attend?

In my eyes, Ma has nothing to feel guilty about as she has been the best mother I could ever ask for. Her sheer single-mindedness, fight and determination to get some piece of closure are proof alone to me. I hope the publication of this book gives me, but especially Ma, total closure.

Chapter 5
So Long St. Christopher's

After the previous trauma of what had happened, Ma attempted tirelessly to gain funding for a place at St. Christopher's Special Needs School in Wrexham. Although she was very reticent in allowing me to attend any school after what had happened, she realised it was for the best.

I had been out of school for 15 months and my autism had worsened as it was not normal to be at home for this length of time, and my routine was initially all over the place. Along with the stress of what had happened previously, Ma had the stress of me being home every day and what appeared to be futile attempts at getting me a school placement.

To attempt to gain funding for a place at St. Christopher's, which, strangely, had seemed a lot easier when I was attending a school outside the county just over two years prior, Ma went (unannounced) to the Director of Education to state my case as the local authority had shown a resistance to me becoming a pupil there. Ma was determined for this to change.

After asking the receptionist if the Director of Education was in his office and getting a negative response, Ma subsequently noticed someone ask the same question and get the opposite answer. At this point, she observed an employee punching in the door code on a security keypad and, at the same time, Ma memorised it. When the coast was clear, she put in the door code and got through to the Director of Education's office. Needless to say, he was a little taken aback by my Ma's presence in his office. After a little persuasion, Ma got me my placement at St. Christopher's.

To confirm Ma's triumph, we received a letter from the Director of Education dated Tuesday 6th January 1998. It explained that I would initially attend school with my home tutor and a suitable support worker but that my integration at the school would be kept to a complete minimum initially. When appropriate, I would be integrated into a carefully planned peer group. It was recognised that Bill was the most suitable support worker for me.

Despite the success of getting me a school placement, especially one in Wrexham, I was petrified at the mere thought of returning to school as I had to learn to trust again. Would they treat me in a similar manner to what had happened previously? Or would I find a school that was kind, considerate and nice? I was scared of how I might behave since my behaviour had deteriorated and I no longer trusted anyone, apart from the family. Even then, I had become aggressive towards my family when the situation went even slightly against me.

In addition to my lack of trust, it would take time for the family, as a whole, to trust anyone in authority as it had become the norm for us to feel let down. Understandably, Ma was very protective and cautious of me going back to school, even though Bill was my support worker. Due to my time out of education, my routines had slowly become more set in stone, including my meal times. For example, lunch had to be at noon, tea had to be at 4pm, and supper had to be at 7pm. I would get awkward if this wasn't adhered to.

I was initially introduced to St. Christopher's outside the classroom environment by visiting the town centre just prior to the end of the post-Christmas term, and I went to a fast food restaurant with my new teacher, who was called David Mount, along with several of the Behavioural Support Unit, which was headed by Mr Mark Powell. I was placed in the Unit due to the aggression I had shown at home although, in time, I would attend the Autistic Unit.

Prior to the town visit, I was present at a Christmas lunch and I also went to the school one day. On this occasion, I was given some work to do by the Deputy Head, Mr Chris Pittaway. I was to find out in the future that Mr Pittaway was a bit of a gentle giant and an utter gentleman, who loved gardening and Rugby Union, including watching England internationals at Twickenham.

In fact, his green-fingered skills and infectious enthusiasm towards gardening inspired a big portion of the pupils to help overhaul the grounds of the school, which became award-winning. Unfortunately, he passed away, suddenly, in early December 2007. I was dumbfounded when I was informed as he seemed active and always seemed to be in the school's garden. He even played Seniors' Rugby Union for Shrewsbury Rugby Union Football Club.

I was eventually integrated into the Autistic Unit, although I was in a class with just one other autistic pupil. Nonetheless, we had very differing obsessions (he obsessed over feathered birds) and difficulties. He also had his own support worker and there wasn't much interaction between us. Although I was in the Unit, I could only be around pupils for short periods of time as some would wind me up. Nonetheless, in my formative years this just proved that I was more comfortable around adults than I ever was with my peer group.

My school day consisted of me undertaking my schoolwork in the morning, but in the afternoon, as my concentration didn't last all day, I undertook activities like snooker, going to the cinema, or watching a video. As well as playing snooker in the afternoon, I went to play after school – on many occasions – at Coedpoeth Library near Wrexham. One day, during a school holiday, I played snooker for an hour in the morning, an hour in the afternoon, and an hour in the evening. I vowed never to do this again as my concentration was shot. I don't know how the top professionals can dedicate so much time to practising as I certainly couldn't.

Around this time, I also developed an obsession with going to the cinema. Like I said earlier, I also went to the cinema in my afternoon activity time at St. Christopher's. After a while, I got bored of watching all the movies; it had just become a habit and I wasn't enjoying all of them. I was going for the sake of it.

Another time out activity was going to the school's Environmental Centre to help me calm down and chill. I'd even undertake work there when my concentration allowed. I really enjoyed going there as it helped with my stress levels and also introduced me to using the internet on their computers. Well, it was the turn of the millennium. For these activities, I went with my staff and seldom with other pupils.

I'll always remember that Mr Mount used to wear an orange fleece most days for school. For BBC 6 Music listeners, Mr Mount's fleece was as infamous as Shaun Keaveny's red cagoule as he wore it that often. He would also dip his toast into a Cup-A-Soup, which he tended to have most days for lunch, and he would also do an excellent impression of Sean Connery. These are my abiding memories of Mr Mount, who eventually emigrated to live in Canada. For a while afterwards, I missed him.

However, one stressful moment I vividly recall during my activity time occurred when returning from a trip to the National Exhibition Centre in Birmingham to attend the Car Show on Friday 23rd October 1998, the day before United drew 1-1 at Pride Park against Derby County.

When we got to Shrewsbury, we were involved in a "knock for knock" car accident, which wrote off Mr Mount's car. I was worried and very cold on the way home in an AA Truck. I wanted to get home for *The Simpsons*. I was quite shaken after this, although in the grand scheme of things it was a relatively minor accident. I felt slightly ill and cold throughout the weekend as I was worried about the next time I had to step into a car on the following Monday. If I went to Birmingham now, I would go on the train as it is just as easy as a car, but it would be more comfortable.

I also played squash during the afternoons with Mr Mount and Bill. It was something I really enjoyed, although I was absolutely useless at first. Not long after taking up squash, Bill got an eye injury whilst playing and was briefly an out-patient as he recovered. However, this did little to prevent me from continuing to play. I would play squash for many years after leaving St. Christopher's.

One funny story during my time at St. Christopher's occurred in the first week of 1999, when I noticed a mouse's backside appearing in a crack in the wall. As someone who has always had a pathological fear of rodents, I ran straight out into the cold air of the winter. I refused to return as I was that petrified. Mr Mount and Bill had to bring me my coat as in my fearful state I had neglected to take it with me.

After much cajoling, I came indoors.

After the mouse's backside incident, it was decided that it was best for Mr Mount to teach me at Mel and Bill's house for the rest of the week while the mice situation was being sorted. I still remember that on the Saturday of this week, I made my short walk down the road to Uncle Herb's flat and there was a mouse on the pavement that I was walking on… motionless in the torrential winter rain. I came to the conclusion after this that there must have been more mice around than normal. Or maybe it was just a simple coincidence.

After some time at St. Christopher's, it was becoming apparent that I was starting to trust again. To illustrate this, Mrs Pittaway, then named Grant, overheard me telling a prospective pupil that "The teachers are nice here. They don't hit you." I used to visit her office of my own volition every morning, I might add. This was partly due to her being such a lovely and heroic person, and partly due to it being the routine. Without fail, she used to offer a sweet to all the pupils who visited her.

Mrs Pittaway is a mother to all the youngsters that come through her doors at St. Christopher's, and after dedicating her life to the job since being appointed Head in 1993 (becoming the school's third Head Teacher after Mona Edwards and Derek S. Williams since it opened in 1960) she was rightly awarded an MBE in the 2012 Queen's New Year's Honours List for her tireless work for the school. Although I don't normally believe in a lot of the accolades that come the way of well-known personalities in the twice-yearly list, I believe Mrs Pittaway's was thoroughly deserved and think more people like her deserve awards, rather than the usual suspects who dominate the headlines when the Honours List is announced.

Mr Powell is Mrs Pittaway's son, and is extremely dedicated to his job; tirelessly, he tries to make even a small difference to the youngsters that he encounters. He is extremely down-to-earth and easy to get on with. He realised that my routines had to be kept in place to keep disruption to a minimum, including having my own parking space at the school (which Bill would park in) which everyone else was discouraged from using.

Nonetheless, I will readily admit that my behaviour during some of my time at St. Christopher's was not always up to scratch. There were many instances where I displayed quite challenging behaviour, to say the least. This misbehaviour stemmed, in my opinion, from what I had suffered when I was younger and was the aftermath of the lack of trust that I displayed when I first came to St. Christopher's.

Over time, my misdemeanours included breaking several televisions, putting my fist through the window of my classroom, hitting out at fellow pupils and once, rather ashamedly, throwing a cue ball through the window of the school's café after being told that break time had finished. I was asked to write a letter of apology, but refused after I paid for the new glass out of my bank account. Mrs Pittaway was reluctant to accept the money, but Ma was insistent as I had to learn.

Despite situations like this, Mr Powell would always try to make a positive out of a situation. His motto was "Always leave on a positive. Whatever has happened, leave on a positive and you can look forward to the weekend and start it on a positive." On many occasions, he used to climb the stairs to my classroom in a way that was very reminiscent of the early stages of the evolution of man. He would start all hunched over and slowly extend his body to an upright position; he used to do this to lighten the mood somewhat if I was stressed or generally obnoxious.

I feel utterly ashamed of my actions, but they are, unfortunately, a part of my difficult formative years. After a number of my misdemeanours, regardless of Mr Powell taking positives out of a situation, I was faced with either expulsion or having two support workers. At this point in early September 1999, when I was 14 years old, Mel became my extra support worker to stave off the threat of losing my school place.

However, there were some flare-ups of my bad behaviour when Mel first started working with me, including me being suspended for one day on 15th March 2000, after I punched her in the eye. Writing that now, I am extremely ashamed to even admit my actions, but in the long run it signalled the beginning of an enormous improvement in my behaviour. Mel's presence helped calm me down in situations greatly and aided my progression to the next chapter of my time at St. Christopher's. This would see the school moving across Wrexham to make way for an Asda Superstore, and a new teacher joining me.

On Sunday 30th June 2002, five of St. Christopher's minibuses were totally destroyed by arsonists, with only three of the school's eight buses surviving the attack. One of the three was actually off-site at the time of the attack. I was appalled by this act of spiteful, cruel criminality and was determined to help Mrs Pittaway and the school. The school was in the midst of a bad year as, in addition to the arson on the buses, flooding had taken place in January 2002, which meant pupils, including myself, had to be taught elsewhere.

To help raise some money for new minibuses, I took it upon myself to write off to any major national or local company I could think of. I wrote to about half a dozen Premier League clubs, the England & Wales Cricket Board, Lancashire County Cricket Club and other companies I could think of, some of whom were based in Wrexham. The response I received was, on the whole, very helpful and supportive, with companies on the Industrial Estates in Wrexham – like Brother – donating equipment for a fundraising raffle. Asda gave a donation, as well as England's two longest serving top flight clubs donating pennants. Lancashire County Cricket Club sent some signed goodies. I also ran a Sponsored Mile run in aid of the minibus appeal, making over £200. At the time, a mile for the Sponsored Run was an achievement for me as I was grossly overweight compared to today.

I hope all this fundraising and initiative, in some way, repaid Mrs Pittaway and Mr Powell's faith in me despite my past indifferent behaviour. It was my way of repaying Mrs Pittaway for being the best Head Teacher I ever had. She is just like an auntie figure to me. I still use Mr Powell's advice to this day, especially when accentuating the positives in a bad situation, as Dr John would say.

The sponsors on the form I made for the run included a very prominent name. The name was a certain Andrew "Freddie" Flintoff, who kindly sponsored £10 while coming out of the Old Trafford nets prior to the One Day International against Sri Lanka on Sunday 7th July 2002. I took my form to the game on the off chance one of the England players would sponsor me, not expecting anyone to actually do so. Upon asking Flintoff, he said, "I'll sponsor you. You fill in the rest and come for the money later."

I went for the money at the end of the Sri Lanka innings and asked a steward outside the England dressing room if Mr Flintoff had remembered the money. The steward said in a very friendly tone, "He has, mate. Here is your sponsor money." Flintoff hadn't forgotten. It may not have seemed much to "Freddie", but I was buzzing after this and couldn't wait to tell Mrs Pittaway the next day at school.

Many other events raised funds for the minibuses, including a reception at the Welsh Assembly in Cardiff Bay – an event for prominent South Walian businesspeople on Wednesday 17th July 2002. Eventually, enough money was raised for some new replacement buses. I know that after I left, the school received a Lord's Taverners green bus.

When I turned 16 in late 2000, I was studying for my G.C.S.E. History qualification. However, the school admitted that the new teacher (following Mr Mount's emigration to Canada) would need experience of teaching the subject at that level. So Ma decided to get in touch with Auntie Shirin, who took on the role of teaching me instead. Due to the varied difficulties of the pupils at St. Christopher's, not that many are able to take G.C.S.E.s or any academic qualification, but the school is more than willing to do anything it can if a pupil has the ability to achieve. In turn, the school caters fantastically well if pupils take an interest in a trade like gardening or car mechanics.

Auntie Shirin, I will readily admit, was the best teacher I ever had, as her long-standing experience of teaching the subject got me through. In just six months of Auntie Shirin's teaching, I memorised and absorbed many facts that I didn't previously know, but still remember to this day.

As well as teaching me the G.C.S.E. syllabus, she taught me things that some would have believed to have been peripheral to the subject. She got me learning academic historical facts that I wasn't previously aware of, or had shown little interest in, and got me involved in learning that did not involve sport or quotations off *The Simpsons*.

She really gave me a zest for history and got me to knuckle down. I always had the ability, but due to my difficulties it hadn't always been possible to teach me new things. Auntie Shirin channelled my academic energies into getting the qualifications that I would surely have lacked without her teaching.

When the results were released on Thursday 23rd August 2001, which was the first day of the final Ashes Test at The Oval, I had achieved a "B" grade. It would have been unthinkable without Auntie Shirin's dedication and infectious love of teaching that shone through to the pupils she taught. I was even on the front page of the *Wrexham Evening Leader* that evening – proudly holding my result.

After my G.C.S.E. History success, it was decided that Auntie Shirin would teach me English Language and English Literature G.C.S.E.s for the next two years. Again, the love of her work, her intelligence, and the way she could articulate a point greatly enthused me. With Auntie Shirin's teaching, however, I found out that my skills in the subject weren't anywhere near as good as I thought they were at this juncture of my life.

Even though it has been more than a decade since I left school, Auntie Shirin's teaching of English grammar has stayed with me. With Auntie Shirin's teaching, my grammar improved immensely and this has given me a love of being someone who looks out for pedantic grammatical mistakes to this day.

She taught me Shakespeare, and I can still remember a big chunk of *Macbeth*. In fact, I have been known to quote lines of it at times when the situation arises, including rain-soaked foul-weathered days. In addition to her teaching of English Language and Shakespeare, I read novels for the first time in my life rather than sports books. To this day, some of the classic books I read rank amongst my favourites, including: *A Christmas Carol* by Charles Dickens, *Animal Farm* by George Orwell, *Of Mice And Men* by John Steinbeck and *The Thirty-Nine Steps* by John Buchan.

I loved reading and learning about the satirical and allegorical comments that Orwell makes in *Animal Farm*. I especially adore the ending, which is an allegory on a meeting between Churchill, Roosevelt and Stalin at The Tehran Conference between 28th November and 1st December 1943 that seemed to establish "the best possible relations between the USSR and the West" (i.e. pigs and humans).

As an added piece of trivia, the latter novel of the four I named is where John Motson gleaned his famous piece of commentary from, at the end of the 1977 F.A. Cup Final between United and treble-chasing Liverpool. This was Motson's first ever F.A. Cup Final as a main commentator, as David Coleman was in a contractual dispute with the BBC. He found out whilst researching the final, in the lead-up to the big game, that there were 39 steps leading to the Royal Box where the F.A. Cup was presented at the Old Wembley Stadium. This was significant owing to the fact that United's triumphant captain was Martin Buchan. The famous quote went as follows:

How appropriate that a man named Buchan should climb the 39 steps [of Wembley] to receive the [F.A. Cup] trophy.

Auntie Shirin's teaching brought these classic novels to life for me and her lessons stay with me even now. I eventually received a "C" grade in both English subjects, which was realistically the highest I could get as Auntie Shirin put me on the lower tier (she wanted to take out any possibility of having an unclassified mark). On the higher tier, at the time, you needed to get a "B" grade or higher, otherwise it would result in an unclassified.

In July 2003, I was about to leave St. Christopher's and go to college. There was a meeting to discuss what future plans and challenges lay ahead. Mr Powell outlined the following during the meeting:

- I would require a "time out" area in college where I could move to, when I needed it, especially when I was stressed or anxious.

- Where Bill was to park the car with my disabled badge.

- Where I was to have my lunch, but not in the crowded canteen.

- That I also knew where the toilet facilities were, rather than struggling to find out once I had started.

Mr Powell really knew me and my requirements.

*

Recently, I visited St. Christopher's for the first time in over a decade, on Friday 3rd October 2014, and spoke to Mr Powell and his mum, Mrs Pittaway, in the Head's office for about an hour. It was like I had seen both of them the week before. They still knew me so well. Mr Powell recognised instantaneously that I would seldom download music and preferred the physical product when the subject of music arose. After such turmoil in my school life prior to St. Christopher's, it was a relief to have had such a caring Head, as well as a teacher like Mr Powell, and to have eventually felt so comfortable in the educational environment. I will always have the utmost respect for Mrs Pittaway and Mr Powell, both of whom hold a special place in my heart.

When the right people come into your life, people who take the time and effort to understand your condition and how it affects you – it can be a magical and life changing experience – as for the first time in my life, outside of home, I felt a piece of acceptance and wasn't ostracised due to my autism.

Chapter 6
The Ancient

For most of my childhood, I never had any mates and all my spare time was spent with my family. I struggled striking up even medium-term friendships with my peer group despite my outgoing nature. It is possible that being unusually knowledgeable on certain subjects, such as sporting statistics, seemed to put some off. It isn't the norm for children to rattle off stats like I could. As mentioned in the last chapter, a lack of friends continued to be the case when I started attending St. Christopher's, where I got on better with Mr Powell and Mr Mount than with any other pupil.

However, when I asked Mr Powell about a support worker from another part of the school, named Rene Bruce-Pinard, who played semi-professional football for the club then named Flexsys Cefn Druids, he asked him to come to my classroom one lunchtime in early November 1999. I got on well straightaway with Rene and admired him almost immediately. After a week or so of Rene, who was born in Abidjan in the Ivory Coast but grew up on the Swiss-French border, coming to my classroom I decided to go and watch him play on Saturday 13th November 1999.

Druids were at home to Newtown at Plaskynaston Lane, Cefn Mawr. The Ancients, to give them their nickname, had just been promoted to the Welsh Premier (named the League of Wales at the time). In achieving promotion, Druids became the first, and still only, club from North Wales' largest location to play in Wales' top division. I must have been a lucky omen as Druids, who were in the relegation zone after just two wins in the early months of the season, won 2-1 with a certain Mr Bruce-Pinard netting the deciding goal. In another football match played on the same day, two goals from Paul Scholes gave England a 2-0 win at Hampden Park against Scotland in the first leg of their Euro 2000 play-off.

Within a matter of weeks, towards the end of 1999, I started to go to Druids training. This was not for my conditioning and footballing skills, I might add – as I was a fat bastard in this era – but just as a fan. In the first couple of months of my time following Druids, I also wrote the match reports in the *Wrexham Evening Leader*. I even got a small payment for this, which I donated to St. Christopher's.

In the closing months of the 1999-00 season, apart from Rene, I was starting to really enjoy being around the Druids lads – one of whom was Aled Rowlands, who is still one of my best mates to this day. Aled is an extremely educated man who is a solicitor and I love having intelligent conversations with him. During this time, I was starting to feel accepted for the first time in my life by people outside the family. The relationship with the Druids lads flourished – possibly due to me feeling more comfortable in the company of my elders.

Even though I was starting to feel more and more acceptance, there were still times – with my autism – that I failed to understand certain jokes and statements of a non-serious nature. One instance was during the warm-up in a pre-season friendly at Plaskynaston against Shrewsbury Town. One of the lads commented that rather than coming on the pitch in a pair of trainers, I should get myself a pair of football boots. I thought he was being awkward rather than helpful. I felt hurt and slighted, while it also troubled me for most of the next day. In those days, I used to keep hold of my feelings infinitely more. Over time, I try never to keep anything bottled in, except at times when a little diplomacy and tact are required. But, like I have previously said, this unfortunately doesn't happen one hundred percent of the time.

As the 2000-01 season began, I was starting to get more enthralled going to the Druids games as well as the training sessions and it started to take over most of my conversation. The training sessions on a Tuesday and a Thursday had firmly become part of my routine. If I was ill, I would still make every effort to attend the sessions. As well as going to matches at Plaskynaston, I attended my first proper away game in the Welsh League Cup against Oswestry Town at Park Hall Stadium on Tuesday 19th September 2000. Oswestry Town were managed by a man – Steve O'Shaughnessy – who I would get to know very well.

Rather memorably, the Oswestry Town match took place on a wet autumnal night. At one point, I went to collect the ball from an embankment near the athletic track that ran adjacent to the pitch in order to throw it back into play. Unfortunately for me, I slipped on my backside in front of a crowd of around 350 people. My rebuttal to this was to shout rather inarticulately at the top of my voice, "Fuck off, you farmers".

Ten days after this game, Rene required a pair of boots on the night of the home game against defending League champions Total Network Solutions Llansantffraid. Rene, Bill and I went to Broughton Retail Park to get him a pair. In the game itself, in front of the S4C cameras for *Sgorio*, Rene scored the winner in a 2-1 win for Druids. He celebrated by doing a little jig. The 2000-01 season turned out to be Rene's last at Druids as he left in the summer of 2001 when Gareth Powell resigned as manager after a second successive 13th place finish in Wales' top flight. An eight-game losing streak from late February to April had seen the Druids slip from 6th in the table.

I was worried, at this point, that any new managerial team wouldn't want a supporter to join in the training sessions when appropriate, as Gareth Powell had allowed. Steve O'Shaughnessy (who had just parted company with Oswestry Town) was appointed as the new manager and, happily, he saw no reason for me not to watch and join in training when appropriate. Nevertheless, Ma and Mel wanted confirmation for themselves face to face. So, we went to Alyn Waters, Llay on the first day of pre-season training on Saturday 7th July 2001.

I can vividly recall the first words I exchanged with the man I now class as my best mate and call "Shaughssa". They were "I remember when you were player-manager of Oswestry last season, Mr O'Shaughnessy. You were such a good organiser." His riposte, delivered with the velocity of an exocet missile, was, "If I was such a good organiser, why was I sacked?" This put the fear of "Eric" into a 16-year-old and Ma worried it wouldn't end well. Shortly afterwards, I would realise that responses like this were just Shaughssa being himself. Initially, I was petrified of his abruptness when I was younger, and I even used to have to pluck up the courage to ring him. But over time, maturity helped me understand different characters and adult humour.

Prior to being appointed as Druids boss, Shaughssa made 201 Football League appearances, scoring 18 goals in a career encompassing Leeds United, Bradford City, Rochdale, Exeter City and Darlington. He was top scorer for Rochdale during the 1989-90 season when "Dale" reached the F.A. Cup Fifth Round for the first time in their history before narrowly losing to eventual finalists Crystal Palace, who were three divisions higher. I later found out from a club sponsor who happened to be a butcher that Shaughssa missed out on receiving a large supply of meat by just one goal against his club target of ten League goals.

Shaughssa's assistant manager was Nick "Jacksie" Hughes. I remember thinking, "Who is this cocky bastard who is strutting around like he owns the place?" In actuality, Jacksie is the complete opposite of this and is a very caring, laidback and confident individual. The first team coach was Jimmy Hunter, whom I knew from when he worked at Flex Gym on Wrexham Industrial Estate. One of Shaughssa's first signings for Druids was Dave Cunnah, who joined from local club Lex XI, who were in the Cymru Alliance for 20 years before the restructuring of the Welsh footballing pyramid in 2010.

It took a while to get to know the likes of Shaughssa, Jacksie and Cunnah, and I even find it hard meeting new people nowadays as bad experiences with people have, at times, made me feel wary of them. I worry what these people will be like several months in the future. Will I see them in a different light from how I did when we first became mates? Will I see them for what they really are? Obviously, with Shaughssa, Jacksie, Jimmy and Cunnah, I sincerely doubt that will ever be the case.

As Shaughssa's first season in charge developed, two cup runs were interspersed with a relegation battle. Ironically, safety was secured with a 6-0 defeat to champions Barry Town. One of the cup runs saw Druids reach their first Welsh Cup semi-final since 1904, when they won their eighth Welsh Cup. Disappointingly, Druids were beaten 5-0 against Bangor City at Belle Vue, Rhyl.

During the back end of the season, I had started to write a column in the Druids' match day programme. At the start of the 2002-03, this was expanded substantially to me being involved in most of the content. Looking back with hindsight, I don't know what the club were thinking giving a 17-year-old with autism – who, at the time, had infinitely less tact than now – that responsibility. I struggled an awful lot to show diplomacy at this time and didn't have much of a filter over my opinions, a number of which were not appropriate for a club publication.

As it turned out, I made a comment about a referee along the lines of him being relegated from the Welsh Premier list, which was inappropriate. Considering future events, with my nephew Louis being a referee, I now have more respect for the men in the middle. At the time, I would get wound up at Druids matches as I aggressively questioned referees' decisions from my usual match day position near the Druids' dugout.

The first instance of me doing anything out of hand was against Barry Town on Saturday 3rd March 2001 at Plaskynaston. With Druids trailing 2-1 in the second half against ten men after the Barry goalkeeper was sent off, I lashed out at a Barry Town player from the side as he went to take a throw-in. Instantaneously, I felt deeply ashamed at my actions. I still remember thinking that Aled, who stood next to me as he was suspended, would never bother with me again. Fortunately, well over a decade later we are still good friends, but I sure have made it complicated at times for him and the rest of my mates over the years.

As soon as I got home, I typed a letter to Barry Town F.C. addressed to their home ground of Jenner Park. Ma and I also rang then Druids manager Gareth Powell the next afternoon to apologise. I will always remember him saying, "If you learn from this mistake, it will be worth making." Subsequently, whenever I have been to a game at Welsh or non-league level, I have always stepped away if a player is taking a throw-in near where I am standing. Although there was nothing in it, I remember reading the match report of the game in the *Evening Leader* thinking it would feature in the write-up.

Nonetheless, I didn't learn from this incident initially as autistic people can repeat the same behaviour over and over again despite the consequences. That part of the brain is affected, and I struggle with this on a daily basis. Even though people guide me and give me excellent advice I can still make the same mistake. This is where I need a lot of support. Some professionals don't seem to understand this and believe I should learn from my mistakes regardless of the consequences. Unfortunately, autistic people very often don't.

I was becoming more boisterous at matches, even after Shaughssa took over as manager in June 2001. I used to repeatedly abuse referees and was vitriolic in my verbal slurs as I castigated the poor man in the middle. Although I was behaving indifferently at times near the dugout, the situation would reach boiling point in a game against Rhyl on 2nd September 2003 in a League Cup Second Round, First Leg encounter, at Plaskynaston Lane. As Druids were reduced to ten men on the pitch and Jacksie was given his marching orders from the dugout, I insanely and unacceptably invaded the technical area, shouting to the referee: "Do you want a piece of me?" I felt deeply ashamed, but this had been on the cards for quite some time, as my overly boisterous support was starting to get out of control.

At training, two days after the match, Shaughssa had to inform me that I was not allowed near the dugout for a month. Now, with hindsight over a decade later, I can see I was lucky not to be banned entirely from the ground. Nonetheless, I shouted at Shaughssa and told him to "fuck off". When I got home, I rang Shaughssa to apologise and told him I wasn't going to my first day at Yale College the next morning. I was upset and felt that if I had disappointed Shaughssa, what was the point – according to my autistic logic – in furthering my education as I thought so much of him (and still do). He convinced me to go and told me that education was important. I subsequently found out from Jacksie that Shaughssa had never spoken to some people again over much less than my childish outburst.

After another Welsh Cup run to the quarter-finals in 2003-04, disappointingly losing 1-0 against ten-man Port Talbot Town at Plaskynaston Lane on Saturday 6th March 2004, Shaughssa was set to lead Druids to a very respectable finish of 11th or 12th. This was with a very young squad with around half a dozen teenagers and the vast majority of the rest of the squad under 25.

During this time, and like many Welsh clubs, Druids found themselves in difficult financial waters, and it prompted me to come up with a couple of fundraising events that I organised myself. I undertook a small sponsored run around Alyn Waters in Gwersyllt on Monday 14th April 2003. Shaughssa kindly agreed to accompany me on the run, but went to the Alyn Waters in the neighbouring village of Llay. After the confusion, we ran the mile and had a laugh about it. I think I raised around £250 for this run.

Later on in 2003, some eleven years after the first one, I again organised a quiz on the history of Manchester United. After an ambitious attempt to lure the then Wales manager and local hero Mark Hughes to ask the questions failed, I again got Joey Jones to be the quizmaster and raised over £400. Although the second fundraising event was just as successful in the money it raised, there was a poor turnout on the night at Cefn Druids Social Club. I had booked the room for the night over the telephone and had had to pluck up the courage to do so.

Despite using my phone regularly to phone my mates, when I was younger, I used to panic going on the phone if it wasn't someone I spoke to regularly or to any business or organisation. I did not overcome this fully until I was 23, in the summer of 2008, when I rang the Manchester United Club Historian, Cliff Butler, regarding a fact I couldn't find in books or on the internet. His helpful intonation on the phone thankfully solved this issue for me.

As well as raising funds for Druids, I nominated the playing and coaching squad for the National Autistic Society's Inclusion Awards in late 2003. I received a letter back informing me that the club had been one of the Nominated Winners in the "Mainstream/Non Autism Specific Groups for Young Adults/Adults Category". For this, the club was mentioned in the final report. I had nominated the lads as a small token of appreciation of how good they had been with me over the previous four years and how they had given me a purpose at this stage of my life.

In just under three seasons, Shaughssa and the lads achieved a Welsh Cup semi-final, a quarter-final, a League Cup quarter-final and what was set to be two top twelve finishes. Nevertheless, the club board, some of whom had joined during the previous year, obviously didn't see their accomplishments this way. Shaughssa and Jacksie were sacked the evening after a 1-0 win over Barry Town at Jenner Park, a result which saw the Welsh champions from seven of the previous eight seasons relegated. After this, I vowed never to support the club again after what I deemed to be the shabby treatment of Shaughssa and Jacksie.

Because of this stance, I had to buy a new wardrobe with Mel as all my clothes had Druids emblazoned on them; they were all I would wear for the previous two years. This was part of my obsession. I binned everything in disgust. I will always remember coming home from the last training session when Shaughssa said his goodbyes, with Louis in tears, and reassuring him that "This is not the end, only the beginning", not necessarily believing what I was saying. Even though a couple of the lads rang me attempting to persuade me to watch just the final two games of the season, I stuck to my word as I couldn't face it and declined the offer.

In the time after I stopped going to watch Druids, I still ring a few of them as I worry if they will one day wake up and never want to speak to me again. I struggled without the weekly routine of attending Druids training. I attempted to replace this with going to watch United instead and I missed only five matches in all competitions at Old Trafford during 2004-05. However, this became expensive and became a routine based on attendance rather than enjoyment.

The following season, in 2004-05, Druids finished in the relegation zone. Due to this, I felt a sense of closure. Although, in the end, they weren't actually relegated to the Cymru Alliance, as Buckley Town rejected the opportunity for promotion, this closed the book on it for me. Or not quite. With Shaughssa, I went to four matches at Plaskynaston in 2008-09, and two at The Rock in 2010-11, Druids' new home.

However, by this time I was very much a 'groundhopper', who would go to attend a match I liked the look of, rather than having any emotional feeling towards the football, and was quite happy to feel objective, relaxed and removed. Nonetheless, as I said to Louis, it was to be "just the beginning, not the end".

Chapter 7
These are my friends

After I decided to stop going to watch Druids matches in mid-April 2004, I got to know some of the lads much better in many different environments. For instance, Jacksie was a different character outside football. Rather than obnoxious (as he could be towards officials), I got to know him as the laidback, easy-going man he actually is. Lynn, our mutual friend, who cuts our hair and has known Jacksie even longer than I have, always said that only driving and football wind him up.

After most of us left Druids, I was deeply unsure if my friendships with the lads would last. In the months that followed, and in my insecurity, I would routinely ring my mates every day as I believed they would forget me or we would lose touch. Looking back now, I would have seen my mates more often than I do currently, but my friendships are infinitely more developed now and I feel more settled on the whole. Nonetheless, I struggled greatly with the ringing and texting part of friendships with some close mates early on and felt insecure when people did not text and ring back. It has been something which has dogged me for most of the time since.

In the summer of 2004, I went to watch several of the ex-Druids lads in pre-season friendlies with their respective new clubs, but I was merely a "groundhopper" and things didn't have the same feel or attachment. I felt slightly isolated that summer – mainly due to the big change of me not attending Druids.

A flashpoint with the insecurity and change around friendships occurred on Friday 21st August 2004, when I went to watch Connah's Quay Nomads against Welshpool Town, which consisted of several of the old Druids lads, at Deeside Stadium with Shaughssa and Jacksie. Quite a few managers of other Welsh Premier clubs were in attendance at this game, including Peter Davenport, then manager of Bangor City and United's top scorer from Alex Ferguson's first season of 1986-87. I vividly recall calling him to his face "Hello, Mr Poor Man's Mark Hughes". I also made an embarrassing comment to my mate Aled, who was briefly Druids assistant manager in the aftermath of Shaughssa's sacking. I told him and his manager that "he was not as good as Shaughssa".

As I write these statements here, I cringe at the lack of tact and my borderline stupidity – although, at the time, I felt such behaviour was acceptable as I wanted to support Shaughssa, who hadn't found a senior managerial role after Druids. At the time of his Druids sacking, I sent an impassioned composition to the local paper in what was, what I now see as, a crusade to support my best mate.

Following the Connah's Quay Nomads match, we went into the bar adjacent to Deeside Stadium, where Shaughssa quietly, calmly and subtly took me to a quiet area of the bar and had a word with me about my "performance". After this, I was under no illusion that this kind of behaviour wasn't acceptable and I have not made the exact same mistake in Shaughssa's company in the decade since. On rare occasions since, I have made a couple of similar errors when I was struggling with stress but in significantly more difficult situations than this particular night.

I really look up to Shaughssa like a big brother and a father figure. When I first met him, like I explained earlier, he had an abrupt, "man's man" hard façade – when, in fact, he is a bit of a softie.

A prime example of this occurred on Christmas Day 2003, when he turned up unannounced on our doorstep with his family, with a Christmas present of a CD for me. Although I don't particularly like Justin Hawkins or The Darkness, I will forever treasure that gift due to the thought put into it. Coming round that day started a Christmas tradition that still takes place over a decade later with Shaughssa coming round during Christmas week, a lot of the time on Christmas Eve after he finishes work.

All my close mates have given titbits of advice like Shaughssa did at Deeside Stadium. For instance, Jacksie advised me it was silly to rank my mates at Cunnah's son's christening on Sunday 10th August 2008. I had got into a bad habit in the previous 18 months and even gave friends their respective rankings to their faces. I also did this with female co-workers at this stage of my life. Not only was it deeply inappropriate, it was sexist, immature and just plain embarrassing. After Jacksie's words of wisdom I never resorted or stooped to this again. However, at times, I struggled to differentiate work behaviour from social conduct; I did not realise that football craic with the lads wasn't appropriate for day-to-day life in an office.

I have very seldom seen some of my mates drunk as they have always protected me from drunken environments. I am really appreciative of why they do this as I wouldn't cope in this sort of situation and would be freaked out. I am teetotal as I take medication for my autism.

*

Coming into my late teenage years, I was always very uncomfortable around women who weren't members of my family, or who were older than me. In my mind, at this time, men and women couldn't be mates in the platonic sense, only lovers. I believed that if a girl of a similar age to me engaged in conversation with me, she wanted a relationship rather than being cordial or seeking a future friendship. My beliefs, due to my autism, were exacerbated by stereotypical portrayals of male-female relationships on television and movies, where characters of the opposite sex would jump into bed with each other without, it seemed to me, any hesitation. Magazines and newspapers fuelled this view.

I have always had a great friendship with my sister Melanie, but I would, when I was in my early teens, sometimes see women in a slightly sexist fashion. For example, I thought it unusual for men to help out around the home (even though I was never brought up in this fashion by Ma and Melanie). Rather than the tabloid newspapers, I should have really listened to Homer Simpson's speech at the end of the season one (1989-90) episode "Homer's Night Out", where he tells us that we should treat women correctly rather than sexualising them, as "they are our wives, girlfriends, sisters, mothers, grandmothers, aunts and nieces", which positively jogs the minds of the rest of the characters in the scene about their female relatives.

Coincidentally, Homer had been caught out with a pole dancer earlier in the episode before having his eureka moment, but in my opinion it is good social commentary. However, there was far too much on television that cancelled this scene out in my mind when I was younger. Perversely, I was petrified of approaching girls of a similar age until my late teens, even when I was following Druids.

What helped reduce my fear was my friendship with Cunnah. After I had got to know him well, Cunnah would take me to his home where he lived with his wife Niki. At times, I would arrive early after being dropped off by Billy, and Cunnah would not have arrived home from work or would be elsewhere.

On these occasions, Niki would always make me welcome in their home and because of this I started to overcome my reticence towards having female platonic friendship. With the help of Niki, I was able to have conversations without feeling embarrassed or coming across as weird to a lady who was not a family member. In the summer, Cunnah and Niki would have a barbecue at their home and I would always be invited. In fact, I was the only person present who wasn't related to either of them biologically or through marriage. I felt accepted and touched by their kind gestures in allowing me to not only visit their home, but partake in a family event like a barbecue.

Although I didn't know Cunnah very well in the three years he played for Druids, over the decade or so since, he has become one of my best mates. It all started when I was given his number in the aftermath of our departures from Druids following Shaughssa's sacking. He is a great lad who tries to please everybody, including myself. He worked really hard at a complete change of direction in his working life to become a driving instructor in the mid-2000s. I was really proud of him for achieving this.

Cunnah would also take me to his Mum and Dad's house. At first, I found this slightly daunting as I didn't go to other people's homes without Ma and Mel. I needn't have worried as Cunnah's parents, June and Bryan, would always make me feel welcome as soon as I walked through their door by offering me drinks and snacks. Now, in addition to being mates with Cunnah and Niki, I have also got to know the rest of his family, including his sister Trudy, who also works at my optician's in Wrexham. Trudy would be at these barbecues and, over time, I have become mates with her and her husband Stewart. We have even been to a few United matches together. I also feel very comfortable going to the optician's!

As well as the lads I met at Druids, two other long-standing mates from home have helped me tremendously. They are Kevin "The Beast" Apsley and Stephen "Pazman" Parry. I met these two when I was 15 and they became my support workers when I required a "two to one" outside school.

The Beast is like my brother – as we comically bicker all the time, then five seconds later we give each other a hug and all is forgotten. He is like an extra member of the family and Mel even sees him as a bit of a brother figure.

I first met Pazman on Sunday 3rd July 2000. He is very easy-going and tries to use my autistic "powers", as he calls them, to find him a decent parking space. Unfortunately, I am not programmed to do this, much to his disappointment.

I have always liked to plan social events well in advance. However, some of my close mates won't commit too far in advance as they have families, whilst others are more "last minute" kind of people. I now try really hard not to ask too far in advance as I have to respect different people's personalities. I hope I am getting better with this as I am making efforts with it.

Light-hearted comments from some close mates amuse me when I ask them too far ahead to meet up. A typical riposte might be "I might be run over by a bus by then!" Pazman jokes I will be asking to meet up with him in the year 2025 next. Occasionally, rather than sitting back and enjoying the moment, I am planning for the next time I am meeting up. I had to stop doing this with my mate Aled a few years ago as I was bombarding him with future dates and not sitting back and enjoying the time I was spending with him.

Due to situations like this, I can come across as demanding and domineering with my mates, as well as my family. As you have guessed with that sentence, I am not in the slightest bit easy-going and can be intense, but I have found recently that if I am not like this in the house I won't take it with me elsewhere. Mel told me for years about this and I didn't take much notice. Despite all things, I am told that I can be wonderful, intelligent, good humoured, articulate company to be with!

When I was growing up, people of my own age appeared intimidated by my big personality, not realising that behind the façade was often a very nervous, worried little boy, who expressed his feelings in ways they would find bizarre. By reciting stats or spouting big words. However, I only did this as an ice breaker to make friends, but it had the opposite effect as kids would back away from me. My mates see past this. They see past the autism and can see that underneath I am a caring person, but can't always express it in the right way because I don't always know how to.

*

I always pay great care and attention to what my family and mates would like for birthdays and Christmases. I remember little bits in conversations when topics of a CD, vinyl, books, DVD or other interests arise. My mates and family always tell me not to spend so much on them, but they are worth every penny. Besides, their real attitudes soon get rumbled as I pass over their gifts!

Being mates with the lads from home has enabled me to have the social skills to cope in a working environment as well as different situations that have arisen over the years. They have also helped me to take jokes, but I do struggle at times. I ask Mel and Ma to explain things and they give me a lot of reassurance.

Whilst my family built the foundations for me to cope in social scenarios, the lads at home have completed the building of the wall for dealing with social situations in a working environment and in day-to-day life. I still worry tremendously, though, if my close mates don't reply to my texts, when the reality is that they are just busy with work, family, or simply out and about at the time.

In addition, I have worried in the past – incessantly – that all my close mates would wake up one day, get fed up with me and never ever want to bother with me again. I now know this is ridiculous as they have had many opportunities to break ties over the years and haven't done so. So, I'd hope they are not going to do this now. Nonetheless, trying to live the life I lead with my friendships is, at times, difficult when some of the thought processes I display are typical autism.

I believe that I don't show too many traits that would alienate me from my mates or "stick out" from the expected norms in company or society. This is testament to Ma and Mel, and to my mates, for understanding more than many professionals with specialised training in the condition of autism.

When all is said and done, I don't really know how I would have coped without my mates over the last 15 years or so. I wouldn't have swapped my time with them for anything. I love them so much and I can't envisage life without them.

Chapter 8
Mr Manchester United

As you might have gathered, by the odd reference in the book, I am a Manchester United fan.

I first became a fan of the club when I was five – after being impressed by Leslie Mark Hughes, a player who was Wrexham born and bred. I was hooked following United's run to the 1990 F.A. Cup final, their first trophy under Alex Ferguson and the Red Devils' first success in five seasons. For many people now, it must be hard to believe that United went five years without a trophy. Then again, big clubs like Arsenal (2005-2014) and Liverpool (2006-2012) have gone longer in the recent past.

By the way, I will correct anyone who calls Manchester United "The Reds", as that is not the club's nickname. It is for many other clubs, but not United. According to some reports, the "Red Devils" nickname was said to be lifted from Salford RFLC just after World War II – which, in the years either side of the Busby Babes, ironically might be considered one of the more angelic periods in the club's history.

My interest in Manchester United grew further with their run to winning the 1991 European Cup Winners' Cup, which included victories over the 'might' of Pecsi Munkas in Round One and my hometown club Wrexham in Round Two. Montpellier Herault, which included future United defender Laurent Blanc and Columbian star Carlos Valderrama, were dispatched in the last eight, and Legia Warsaw in the semi-final.

The final saw United take on a more fearsome foe in Johan Cruyff's Barcelona at the De Kuip Stadium in Rotterdam, home of Feyenoord. My then hero, Mark Hughes, was up against his former employers. He proved that their decision to let him leave was an injudicious one, with two goals in the final. The first goal was pinched off Steve Bruce and the second was a great drive from a very acute angle past goalkeeper Carles Busquets, father of the current

Barca and Spain midfielder Sergio, who played against United at Wembley in the 2011 Champions League final.

In November of 1991, as a present for my seventh birthday, I received *The Official History of Manchester United*, narrated by John Motson, on VHS. From the video, my interest in the history of the club was further developed. Needless to say, I absorbed what seemed like every second of Motson's 90-minute narration – from the club beginnings with railway workers on the Lancashire-Yorkshire line, who founded the club in 1878 as Newton Heath LYR, to the very end of the film in summer 1988. This was when Mark Hughes returned to United from his spells at Barcelona and Bayern Munich. I memorised the video up until that point and I could probably recall many parts of it to this day. After this, there was no turning back – I was to be a United fan.

Another vivid memory of being a young autistic United fan was when they lost out on a first League title in a quarter of a century on Sunday 26th April 1992 after a 2-0 defeat at Anfield. As a seven-year-old, I attempted to kick the T.V. in – while I was shedding tears, distraught. Although I believe it to be pathetic for adults to cry regarding sporting outcomes, I was only seven years of age at the end of the day.

If United lost, it would really affect my weekend and my mood. I would be miserable and angry if United lost, but delighted if they won. I would sometimes stay in my room for hours on end if United had lost that weekend. I would also go to school on the Monday and be affected either way by the weekend's result. I couldn't wait for the next game so they could get back to winning ways in the event of a defeat. If the game was on television, I would walk back and forth on my tiptoes for the whole 90 minutes of the match. Maybe this is why I have muscular calves or "Mark Hughes Legs", as some people used to refer to them when I was a kid.

This continued unabated into my teenage years and I could even get very aggressive if a result didn't go United's way, like when Paul Ince scored a late equaliser for Liverpool v United at Anfield on 5th May 1999. The aggression came as I felt aggrieved at referee David Elleray's sending off of Denis Irwin for a second booking. This prompted me, I am rather ashamed to admit, to go next door to Mel and Bill's and punch a hole in their lounge door as, in my mind at this time, it was Bill's fault for being a Liverpool fan and, of course, Paul Ince's for scoring the goal.

My interest in United quickly turned into an obsession. I was deeply immersed into anything United. My bedroom was decorated with posters and newspaper cuttings of United players (even players on the fringe of the first team), pictures of Old Trafford and match reports; and I must have had several posters of the same team picture that is taken at the start of every season. I also made scrap books on Manchester United, filling them with even more newspaper cuttings.

When I was at the Special Education Centre, I used to type up old random results of United – all wins, I might add – on their old BBC computers. I was hooked. I would regurgitate United's historical results and statistics to people who I had just met. I didn't know how to communicate any other way with new people so it served as a coping mechanism. At this time of my life, I was oblivious if people weren't interested as, with my autism, rattling off United's stats was all that mattered to me. Due to this, I would miss blatant verbal cues and people's body language expressing their disinterest, confusion and lack of understanding at what I was talking about.

I felt isolated, lonely and confused at times in school, as fellow pupils didn't share my obsessional love of Manchester United. Occasionally, this caused me to suffer bullying, which made me feel more of an outsider. The other pupils couldn't comprehend my love of Manchester United statistics and this made me stand out even more. Other children, even at home, would back away from me as they didn't have the faintest idea about Manchester United beating Bristol City in the 1909 F.A. Cup final at Crystal Palace. I had no mates when I was growing up due to this, and it still has an effect on me to this day. Then, unlike now, I believed the entire world should support Manchester United. If anyone supported another club and criticised United, I would get wound up and argue with them. I would defend United to the hilt.

I was forced to reconsider my entrenched stance regarding people supporting other clubs – apart from United – when Mel started to go out with Bill in June 1994. Bill, coming from Liverpool, supported the Red half of Merseyside. Initially, I found this difficult, but Bill helped me realise that I could associate with people that supported other clubs. Nowadays, I will not bad mouth other rival clubs in a petty manner, other than in jest; football is the world's most popular sport but also, unfortunately, attracts the biggest number of small-minded individuals. Most of my mates support clubs other than United. I would now find it very boring if people all liked the same sports, clubs and cultural figures.

At the end of the day, barring extreme circumstances in certain nations, it is only a football match. Much worse things happen to all of us over the course of our lives than a club we support losing to our arch rivals.

*

United did finally win the title, after Aston Villa lost at home to a 29th minute Nick Henry goal for relegation-threatened Oldham Athletic, on Sunday 2nd May 1993. United had won the League title for the first time in 26 years! When a graphic appeared on Ceefax stating "Manchester United are Champions", I remember to this day that I ran up my street celebrating and shouting joyfully. I was unaware of anyone else's existence in the vicinity at this time.

During the next season, on Sunday 20th March 1994, I finally met Mark Hughes. He was starting a charity run in Wrexham, near what is now called Glyndwr University and the Racecourse Ground. Before leaving home, I watched an episode of *Rugrats* on Nickelodeon. As we were leaving the house, the fourth day of the second Test between West Indies and England was about to come on television. This match is best remembered for being 19-year-old Shivnarine Chanderpaul's debut on his home ground of Bourda in Guyana. As I write, Chanderpaul is still playing Test cricket into his forties, averaging over fifty with the bat. A final sign of his longevity is that his son is now playing first class cricket.

Sunday 20th March 1994 was overcast, with a blowy wind interspersed with intermittent light, and unpleasant showers in what was now early spring. Ma, Ma's brother Uncle Peter, Mel and I set off in Uncle Peter's sky blue Peugeot 309 to meet my hero. I remember being extremely excited and nervous waiting for "Sparky" as I adored him. He eventually arrived in a privately registered Range Rover to start the race. I was awestruck by his mere presence as I had only seen him on television. Although there were other people around him, I was determined that I got his attention.

I remember talking with him about whether the F.A. Cup semi-final should be held at Wembley. I seem to recall he didn't agree with it at the time. He signed my Patrick trainers, which I wore in school before the signature wore off, and my 1993 version of United's Newton Heath away kit. People say you should never meet your heroes, but fortunately – be they Ian Brown, Tim Burgess, Gruff Rhys, Eric Cantona, Sir Alex Ferguson, Phil "The Power" Taylor or various cricketers – I can't recall being disappointed many times. I was in complete awe of him and I stood there as if I couldn't believe I was actually in his company.

Whilst I was speaking to my hero, then Wrexham striker Gary Bennett asked me to put his Lucozade bottle in the bin, to which I retorted, "Do it yourself." I guess he wasn't used to nine-year-olds in Wrexham giving him this sort of treatment at the time.

After meeting "Sparky" Hughes, I adored him all the more. However, when he left United for Chelsea on Friday 22nd June 1995 for £2m, I was distraught and didn't get dressed all weekend. I felt hurt that he had the utter chutzpah to leave United. I didn't realise that players come and go from clubs all the time – unless you are Ryan Giggs, Gary Neville or Paul Scholes, of course. I remember Mel got me Ross Kelly's autograph off GMTV around this time when she was on holiday in Spain. I didn't want it as I felt it was a replacement for Mark Hughes.

*

On Thursday 16th November 1995, which was four days before my 11th birthday, I was told school was closed due to a staff shortage and we were going "to a golf course in Wigan" instead. I did not want to go as the routine was for me to go to school. Imagine my surprise when Bill, in his maroon 1987 E-Registration Ford Sierra Sapphire, pulled up at the famous Cliff Training Ground of Manchester United in Higher Broughton, Salford.

After a short while, we followed the players to Littleton Road, where the first team were training that day instead of at The Cliff, the club's base since WWII. I watched training and can still remember how cold I was in the overcast, chilly late autumn weather. I remember that the players and Alex Ferguson filmed a piece for Coronation

Street's 35th anniversary (broadcast the following month) while we were there watching.

I had my picture with "Le Dieu" (Eric Cantona), who politely said in his broad Marseille accent, "You must get off the pitch", after I ran after him onto the pitch. He still posed for pictures and signed autographs for everyone while leaving out no one – which, I am told, he did every day. Is it any wonder that for reasons like this, almost two decades after his retirement, his name is chanted at every home match at Old Trafford. I still treasure that picture with Le Dieu. I also had my picture taken with Alex Ferguson, who didn't receive his knighthood until the Queen's Birthday Honours in 1999. I still also have this picture hanging up in our lounge.

After watching the training session, we went to a local café and I didn't eat my lunch of cheeseburger, cress and chips, a rare event that should be put alongside the Pope resigning his post in March 2013! I was so cold that day, and I was also so excited. In the afternoon, we went on a tour of Old Trafford and had a kind gentleman, of what seemed like retirement age, as our guide. It was fantastic going on the tour; the stadium was under construction as it was being extended at the time, but it still felt enormous to someone of only ten years of age.

Due to my autism, an unease of big crowds and noise, and a lack of money, my first United match was against Swindon Town in the Football League Cup Third Round on Wednesday 23rd October 1996. Mel and Bill bought the tickets the day before the match as an early 12th birthday present for me. They would also be taking me to the game.

I remember we left the house at around 5.35pm with *Moesha* showing at the time on Nickelodeon. As we neared what I would now identify as the road that takes you to West Didsbury if you head straight on, I recall seeing what I thought was the Swindon Town team coach passing by, although more than likely it was a supporters' club coach ferrying United fans from all corners of Britain, Ireland and beyond. We arrived in our seats in the lower tier of what is now unimaginatively titled the North Stand, but which previously was the United Road Stand as it was on the road bearing that moniker, at around 7.15pm for an 8pm kick-off.

I recall the crowds converging on Sir Matt Busby Way for the long walk down to their seats. The aroma of the burger vans and fast food restaurants on the adjacent Chester Road was overpowering as was the cool, fresh autumnal air that you smell on someone when they enter a room from outside in the colder months.

Once in the ground, I remember radio adverts and jingles playing loudly on the public address system for United's now defunct eponymously titled match day radio station. Whilst taking in the vast scenery of Old Trafford on a match night, I was impressed by the newly-built third tier of the stand formerly known as the United Road Stand. It appeared so distant and high that, to me as an eleven-year-old, it resembled the top of a skyscraper in a modern day metropolis.

Once the match began, I remember being petrified at the crowd chanting "You Scouse bastard" to Mark Walters, who was playing for the Robins and actually has the middle name Everton, and the Swindon Town manager Steve McMahon. I briefly thought the whole of Old Trafford had realised that Bill was from Liverpool and the crowd were insulting my brother-in-law. It sounds rather far-fetched now, but I was completely overawed by the sheer enormity of the ground and the crowd atmosphere as the difference between watching a match in person and on television seemed rather immense.

In the match itself, Czech Republic Euro' 96 star Karel Poborsky, signed from Slavia Prague that summer, put United in front in the 20th minute to give the Red Devils a half time lead against the First Division side. In the 52nd minute, Peter Thorne equalised for the Wiltshire side before Paul Scholes netted the winner on 72 minutes to seal a 2-1 win and a fourth round tie against eventual winners Leicester City at Filbert Street.

I still vividly remember the match attendance was 49,305. I also recall at the end of the game a seat snapped not far away from us as a lad accidentally broke it while stepping over it. At the time, in my mind, I rather foolishly thought it was the beginnings of a riot.

I still have my match ticket and programme from that night in my bedroom drawer, which is unusual for me as I don't normally keep football programmes or tickets from sporting events or gigs I attend.

As a final memory of my first United game, I remember that Winsford-born substitute Simon Davies, a one-cap wonder for Wales against Switzerland at Lugano on 24th April 1996, missed a couple of gilt-edged opportunities, late on, to extend United's lead.

*

Shortly after my first match, I was out of school for 15 months after the incident detailed in chapter 4. To try to cheer me up during this extremely difficult time in my life, probably the worst time of my life, Mel and Bill telephoned United to take me again to The Cliff on Tuesday 4th March 1997. This was the day before the Champions League quarter-final, first leg against F.C. Porto at Old Trafford. We were assured it would be fine to watch the team train, so we made the journey to Higher Broughton, near Salford.

Unfortunately, when we arrived there, we were turned away and informed it was a behind-closed-doors session. Disappointed, slightly annoyed, and upset that we had not been told the training session was private, Mel, Bill and I decided to go to Old Trafford. On the way there, a Mercedes Benz passed us and, as we pulled up on the Old Trafford forecourt, we could see the driver getting out of the car. It was none other than Alex Ferguson.

Determined, and disappointed for me as she had promised to get me to see the players train, Mel went up to Mr Ferguson to inform him of our predicament. He told us we could watch training tomorrow, before quickly shouting back in his Govan brogue, "Melanie, it's the game tomorrow. Come on Thursday to my office." Now, I am sure many a hard man footballer has dreaded an identical sentence being uttered but we were ecstatic.

We went to The Cliff two days later, after a 4-0 drubbing of the highly fancied Portuguese Champions, and were allowed into Mr Ferguson's office. Funnily enough, he was about to run a bath, but kindly allowed us in and, fortunately, remembered us. Mum and Louis, who was a babe in arms, were with us as well. Mum, who is only 5'3", even managed to bump into the 6'4" defender Gary Pallister and got a big fright as the former most expensive defender in Britain approached.

I even got a sneak peek into the 16-man squad for that Saturday's match against Peter Reid's Sunderland, in what was United's last ever visit to Roker Park before the "Black Cats" moved ground that summer. The players on the treatment table included Ole Gunnar Solskjaer, Roy Keane and Gary Pallister, who were either on the bench or completely ruled out of the Sunderland game. However, Pallister and Solskjaer were in the starting XI the previous evening. This was probably the first season that Alex Ferguson had utilised a squad of players rather than just a starting XI after making five new signings in the summer of 1996.

I remember, to this day, speaking for ages to Ole Gunnar Solskjaer in The Cliff car park. As has been well documented, he was an absolute gentleman with no hint of the pretension that is quite prevalent in many footballers. He was extremely modest and was very polite. He treated a 12-year-old me, who was going through a very rough time, as an equal. He probably won't remember this or think that he acted any differently than he would with anyone else, but at the time it meant the world to me. For reasons like this, Ole is highly regarded by Manchester United supporters worldwide, including myself, not just for his on-pitch achievements, but for how he conducts himself off it.

During the whole of 1997, while I was out of school, I decided to try to write about the history of Manchester United at the local library in Wrexham. After several months of writing, I put it away, unfinished, until the back end of 1999 before completing it in the summer of 2000. Looking back at my writing, I could tell that the style, grammar and use of language was never really good enough to be published properly.

Nonetheless, St. Christopher's made it into a book of sorts, and sold it from the school and shared the proceeds with myself. I got a real thrill from St. Christopher's doing this. It made me feel fantastic, gave me self-worth and confidence. I remember selling a few copies, including one to a vicar, a teacher in Louis' school, and I personally delivered one to an elderly local lady, who I think was purchasing it for a relative.

To 'publicise' my book, I even rang up Bower & Crerand of *Extra Time* on M.U.T.V. on Monday 6th November 2000. Paddy remarked that I sounded rather nervous on the line, which I undoubtedly was. Happily though, I also won the best caller prize of a United away shirt. This phone call started a chain of events that would, as you will find out, shape my life to this day. Thanks to the people buying a copy from the school I was able to buy my first mobile phone on Saturday 12th May 2001. This was the same day as the F.A. Cup final between Arsenal and Liverpool at the Millennium Stadium, Cardiff.

When I went to St. Christopher's, they soon recognised my love of United and I was, rather kindly, allowed to decorate the walls of my classroom with painted United shirts with squad numbers on. For instance, "Silvestre 27" or "Solskjaer 20" in red and white paint, along with the rest of the United first team squad of the early millennium. I thought it was perfectly normal at the time for United shirts to be painted on my classroom wall, but looking back now I appreciate how accommodating Mrs Pittaway and Mr Powell were to me. In fact, Mel and Bill painted them for me on a Saturday as a surprise. They were even re-painted when the school moved premises in September 2000.

To further the point of how accommodating St. Christopher's were to my love of United, Mrs Pittaway even invited Sir Alex Ferguson to open St. Christopher's new premises on Friday 6th April 2001. On the day that Sir Alex visited St. Christopher's, a very fat me was interviewed by Mandy Henry from M.U.T.V., whom, as it turned out, I ended up working with for over a decade; I was interviewed by BBC Radio Wales, and articles appeared in local and regional papers, with me being the pupil that everyone seemed to be interested in. I was told in early 2013 by my old Community Nurse, Mai Rees-Moulton, who now works at the school, that the pictures of myself, a lot fatter and in infinitely worse shape than now, still adorned St. Christopher's reception walls until quite recently.

On the day itself, I remember the build up to him arriving at 2pm vividly. I was so nervous with every second feeling like a minute and every minute like an hour. To keep calm and kill time, I watched an episode of the PBS ten-part documentary series *The West* narrated by the late Jason Robards, which was shown on BBC2 during the festive period of 2000. I studied this video intently for months in the run-up to my G.C.S.E. History exam, but on Friday 6th April 2001, I was far too excited to take in the programme which I had absorbed over the past four months as I couldn't wait to see "The Great Man". He finally pulled up outside the school in his Mercedes at around 2.10pm with sons Darren, who was playing for Wrexham at the time, and Jason, who was then his agent.

During the ceremony for the official opening, there were songs and other pupils presenting Sir Alex with keepsakes and mementos of his visit to St. Christopher's. He then stepped up to the podium and wittily said, "That's a better reception than I got on Tuesday night (when United lost 1-0 to Bayern Munich in the Champions League quarter-final, first leg at Old Trafford)." Then the time had arrived for me to walk up to meet him. As I made my way to the front of the hall, he put out his arms to give me a hug, which I gratefully accepted from someone who is still, to this day, one of my heroes. I presented him with the book I had written on the history of United. I cried when he hugged me. It meant so much that the "Great Man" would show me this gesture of emotion and thanks. Childish as it may seem now, I sometimes wished at this juncture of my adolescence that Sir Alex was my father. I admired him that much.

I still remember to this day, and have it in Ma's archives, a video of Mrs Pittaway saying to me in a crowded canteen, "You're a star now, Andrew." I was delighted to make her so happy and I was ecstatic with her for getting Sir Alex to the school. I don't think that any other Head teacher would have attempted so kind a gesture for her pupils as this. She even persuaded the local Educational Authority to give St. Christopher's special permission to open on the day Sir Alex visited, as it was supposed to be a training day before the Easter break. This is why Mrs Pittaway has her MBE and, even without my disrupted schooling, would be the best Head teacher anyone could ever have asked for.

A slightly amusing, yet quite sad adjunct to the day occurred when we asked Louis, who was four at the time and off school due to the training day, if he enjoyed seeing Sir Alex. He said, "I couldn't see, Uncle Andrew. I wasn't tall enough."

When I passed my G.C.S.E. History, the school wrote to Carrington to see if Sir Alex could present me with my certificate. The reply to St. Christopher's School was as follows.

Further to your letter of Wednesday 28ᵗʰ November 2001 regarding Andrew Edwards.

It will not be possible for Andrew to actually take part in a training session, but he is more than welcome to watch training after Sir Alex has presented him with his certificate.

We would suggest Thursday 21ˢᵗ February 2002 at 10am for Andrew to come to the training ground and we would be grateful if you could confirm that he is able to attend on this date. Find enclosed directions to the Training Ground for your information.

The morning we went to Carrington was after the previous evening's 1-1 draw away to Nantes Atlantiques in the Champions League Second Group Stage. Along with me, Mrs Pittaway, Ma and Bill were also invited to Carrington.

United had left their previous training base of The Cliff in January 2000 and now supporters had to be specially invited as the sessions were behind closed-doors. Carrington is in the middle of nowhere, compared to the residential area of Higher Broughton in Salford, where The Cliff was based.

Whilst at Carrington, I was interviewed again by M.U.T.V. while Sir Alex presented me with my G.C.S.E. Andrew Kerr was the interviewer and he seemed deeply impressed that I could reel off all 14 League titles (now a record 20 titles) that United had won in their history. I felt honoured that Sir Alex wanted to present me with my G.C.S.E. certificate; not many school pupils in the whole of Britain would have been lucky enough to have this accolade.

After being presented with my certificate by Sir Alex, I was allowed to go and watch the players train. Whilst watching training, Ruud van Nistelrooy came near me and passed the ball to me. Upon receiving the pass from the prolific Dutchman, who scored exactly 150 goals for United in five seasons at Old Trafford, I trapped the ball underneath my foot with my Kickers boot and whilst returning the pass I lost my balance and fell flat on my back on the grass. At this point, van Nistelrooy looked a bit concerned for my wellbeing, but I was fine, although my pride was dented. I even have a picture in an album – of me on the floor after this event.

The United starting XI from the previous evening, including van Nistelrooy, then went for a jog around the complex. Upon returning from this little loosener, Captain Roy Keane almost keeled over in laughter as he enquired of my Ma "if he (referring to me) enjoyed his trip." Needless to say, for months afterwards I dined out on the telling of this rather amusing story.

*

During the course of the same 2001-02 season as the visit to Carrington, I had been involved in a football quiz on the now defunct ITV Digital Sport Channel. The show was called *Do I Not Know That*, which was a play on a famous Graham Taylor quote from October 1993 regarding the colour of the Dutch National team's shirts. The show was presented by Simon O'Brien, who played Damon Grant on Brookside and who has, more recently, appeared on property programmes on daytime TV. Mr O'Brien was very nice, approachable, and told a few funny stories to the contestants. I found him very likeable. In fact, when she was approaching her teenage years, Mel admitted to me that she had fancied him when he was on Brookside!

On the first day of filming at Granada Studios, I was taken aback when I realised I had my own dressing room. There was water and a lot of mints on a table. On subsequent visits throughout the year, I wasn't afforded this luxury. I think *Stars In Their Eyes* was also being filmed that day, which had millions of viewers at the time. As for *Do I Not Know That* itself, it featured supporters from all 92 Premier and Football League clubs, several Conference clubs and 16 from the Scottish Premier and First Division. I was on United's team, which reached the last nine, or semi-final, as each show had three teams on it.

I had two specialist subjects on the show over the course of the season, which were Mark Hughes (club and country) and United's 2000-01 title winning season. I was nervous before the Mark Hughes round and, in all honesty, underestimated the subject matter and felt disappointed with myself. The 2000-01 season was a far more straightforward proposition. I felt I achieved far better.

Unfortunately, I pulled out just prior to the last filming day. It was a tough decision, but I had started to feel too nervous and was stressed about it. Nevertheless, I found the production staff members were absolutely fantastic, hospitable and really friendly.

The production staff later even, kindly, posted me a big Welsh flag they had as a prop in the green room. I felt honoured and touched

79

that they gave me this. I had it on my bedroom wall for a decade afterwards.

I took a lot of encouragement from being on *Do I Not Know That* and knew I would be better prepared if I ever undertook another quiz show appearance, preferably on United. In fact, I only had a matter of months to wait as in January 2003, M.U.T.V. were looking for contestants for a quiz show of their own called *Redheads*. I applied and, luckily, was accepted onto the show. I was delighted as I had a chance to prove myself on what was my main specialist subject at the time!

After a tiebreak defeat in round one, I went into a lucky loser's draw. I was gutted and surprised not to win my heat, but it was the kick up the backside I required. I won the lucky loser quarter-final and then the semi-final by 26 points, amassing more points than the other two contestants put together. I had practised for the buzzer round, which was my Achilles heel in round one, by using an electronic farting machine. It proved a successful approach. In the final, I won after my specialist subject was the 1992-93 Championship winning season. I got one question incorrect and about 15 or 16 correct.

Since I had started supporting United at the age of five, I felt – and hoped – that a day would come when I would win a quiz show on the history of Manchester United. I felt the whole time that I had memorised the stats and was now seeing the fruits of my labour. I was delighted, overjoyed and ecstatic, and I have a picture of myself with the trophy in the bath at home – on the day I filmed the final – mimicking winners of the F.A. Cup in years gone by.

After winning the *Redheads* quiz, I was again invited to Carrington and interviewed – this time by M.U.T.V.'s Mark Sullivan, who would become, and still is, one of my closest mates. The trophy was officially presented to me by 1990 F.A. Cup winner, Lee Martin, who, strangely enough, ended up playing for Druids alongside my mate Aled after I stopped going to watch.

Just prior to, and after, winning *Redheads*, doors were opening for me that would have been unthinkable less than two years before. They were enabling me to continue my 'education' on Manchester United and, in the process, embark upon a future that would shape the rest of my life to the present day. It was the fulfilment of all my hopes and dreams as an autistic youngster.

Chapter 9
There's Only One United

When it came time for a work placement from St. Christopher's, all I really wanted to do was something to do with football, preferably historical, but the seemingly impossible dream involved United.

I wasn't aware of many options for a footballing or a general sporting statto, so I went to the Wrexham County Museum for six Tuesdays in late 2001 to research a Welsh Football History project. Although I enjoyed this, it wasn't quite what I was looking for.

As an occasional interviewee, regular viewer, and, at the time, caller to phone-ins on Manchester United TV, St. Christopher's wrote on my behalf to the station on the off-chance of a work placement. They received a rejection letter stating that, at the time, M.U.T.V. only took university undergraduates on work placement. Nevertheless, yet again, Mum was not to be put off and took it upon herself to ring the channel up to explain my case. After several phone calls, M.U.T.V. agreed to give me one day's placement. I was informed of the placement in May 2002, but had to wait through the summer months before I started.

When the day finally arrived, I was very nervous. Bill and I got lost on our way there but did finally find the offices, having passed it several times previously. Fortunately, as is usually the case with me, we were early.

As I got inside the reception, I met the man who was to be my mentor and boss. He cut a rather imposing figure due to his 6'4" build and broad Yorkshire brogue. I had spoken to him on the phone previously when he was working on a show with 1968 European Cup winner Paddy Crerand in early May 2001. They were having technical issues on the lines and he came onto the phone and said something along the lines of, "Now then, don't worry, Andrew, you will be on air soon." I probably exaggerated the first two words, but I was to find out my boss would say that phrase more times than I say "I've got a stat for you" or "mate". And that is an awful lot. I enjoyed being there from near enough the moment I walked through the door and I remember ringing Mum at lunchtime, saying, "This is not like a job. It is where I want to work. I am living the dream."

I was kept on after my first day and went to M.U.T.V. once a month for the first year.

Around the same time as starting at M.U.T.V., I began to attend college. There were many issues from the very beginning. Initially, the college wanted me to use one of their support workers rather than Billy and in my opinion, looking back with hindsight, they seemed ill-equipped for someone with my difficulties, but academic and social ability. The course I initially enrolled in was a GNVQ Media course. My tutor was a lovely gentleman named Tony. He dealt with my autism well and in an understanding manner. If I went too far off-piste, he would calmly bring me back to the subject at hand.

Tony was a nice guy and I enjoyed being on his course, although I was only studying one Friday afternoon a week. I achieved a distinction with the digital story I made on my life with autism. I really enjoyed making the film, which was made up of a voiceover with matching stills. I even got Ma to help me as I wanted a piece of music – "I Am The Resurrection", my favourite track when I was 19 – to accompany my film, which required copyright clearance. Ma got in touch with the record label and it was cleared.

I felt a bit lazy during this time as M.U.T.V. and college only took up a day and a half of my week and I struggled to fill my days in the year after leaving St. Christopher's. I also gained weight as I had a left knee injury at the time.

*

The following year, it was decided that I should attend college more often and I enrolled on a BTec in Multimedia. The course leader was a man named Dave. Along with Tony, he was the only other lecturer that really tried to understand my condition. I even invited both of them to my 21st birthday party after I left college, which they both attended.

Although I got on well with Tony and Dave, a lot of the students and some lecturers didn't seem to comprehend my autism at all. College was not as structured as school, and I struggled with other students messing around and behaving in what I deemed a childish manner whilst the lecturer wasn't around. I wanted to attend college to learn and get my qualifications. I couldn't understand why people would attend college if they wanted to mess about or even skip lectures. I took it all very seriously and literally.

As the second year progressed, I started to feel unwanted as some of the students took a dislike to me. I felt unwanted, and it knocked my confidence greatly. I felt I stood out and it was becoming apparent that some of the other students couldn't stand me, through little fault of my own, while some lecturers didn't deal with the situation. The college didn't seem to take my condition into account. I couldn't help being autistic, but support didn't seem forthcoming.

I went from being around understanding adults at St. Christopher's, in a classroom on my own, to a classroom of young students who didn't have any understanding of autism or didn't want to.

Nonetheless, it seemed a scenario similar to the one I found myself in at the mainstream school I attended just over a decade earlier. I remember the feeling of getting up for college feeling sick and unable to eat my meals due to the stress and worry brought on through the situation.

It was a shame that no one acted on the concerns voiced by Ma and Mel prior to me joining college and during my time there, especially the second year. The writing was starting to be splashed onto the wall when a student made a complaint against me. I deemed this to be very petty for what I thought was a throwaway comment that I made during a T.V. production I had directed and written on Sir Alex Ferguson's milestone of 1,000 games in charge of Manchester United. It was a line that would be used every day of the week at M.U.T.V. in the same situation, or anywhere else, judging from what my mates tell me about other jobs they've worked at.

The final straw (and this sticks with me even today) was when one lecturer made a deeply offensive remark to me about my experience detailed in Chapter 4, following a little argument in his class. I felt the lecturer's comment was deeply unprofessional and hurtful, and he was on extremely sticky ground. With my unhappiness reaching a crescendo, I decided college was untenable and unworkable and decided to leave. At the end of the day, the students were young and immature but if they meet, or have subsequently met, someone with autism, I hope they will treat them with a little more understanding and empathy than what they showed me.

Fortunately, shortly afterwards, my work mentor at M.U.T.V. called me into a meeting room and decided that I could work three days a week after what had happened in college. He was so annoyed about how I came to leave college that he was going to phone them up and complain, until I told him to relent. In all honesty, I found the whole experience in college pretty dreadful and disconcerting. When I went three days a week, my job entailed doing stats on all First Team matches, F.A. Premier Reserve League North games, and F.A. Youth Cup games. I also did general stats for other shows like documentaries and topical weekly shows.

I never would have dreamt of all this at age 16. It would have been so fantastical that Joanne Rowling or John Tolkien may have had difficulty imagining it. At M.U.T.V. the office was one of the most amiable and understanding atmospheres you are likely to encounter in a workplace. The day would fly by and seldom dragged. I met several of my close mates at M.U.T.V.

My autism was never an issue, and colleagues always tried extremely hard to help and understand the condition, which is very complex to fathom. They treated me as "Andrew", even at times when I found things challenging, and forgave me for indiscretions. The job wasn't a job for me at all. I believed that it was a calling.

I felt like Charlie Bucket at the end of *Willy Wonka and the Chocolate Factory* when Wonka decides to hand over his factory to Charlie. Most people are fortunate if they could get near having the proverbial golden ticket in life, but I believed I had that plus the chocolate factory. Working at M.U.T.V. was all I ever wanted in life.

Eventually, I developed friendships at M.U.T.V., although these took time due to my lack of years and a feeling that I did not want to replace my mates at home. In time, I realised I could have mates at both home and at work. Due to this, it took a good three and a half years to socialise with people outside of work. As I allowed people in, and realised I could have work friendships, the first person I socialised with was my boss and mentor. He helped me tremendously to cope with situations that were alien to me at the time.

I started to become mates with Mark Sullivan and Andrew "Humble" Bode, and am still close to them to this day. I remember the first day I met "Sully" as I provided him with a stat on Gordon Strachan, who was Southampton manager at this time, as United were playing them at Old Trafford the next day, on 2nd November 2002. This was the game when Diego Forlan scored a late winner and couldn't get his shirt back on in the midst of the celebration and had to track back to defend topless.

Sully had been extremely understanding of my autism since we first met. I always wondered why he was especially perceptive towards me and my ways. After several years, I found out in conversation with him that he had worked with children with disabilities after leaving university.

Meanwhile, Humble and I have found a shared love of several genres of music, including hip hop, rap, soul, funk, intelligent dance music (yes, that is an actual musical genre/style!) and electro. On many occasions, we have had long conversations about music, which I have enjoyed tremendously and gained a lot of trivial titbits that have stuck in my head. We also have very strong opinions, which I like quite a lot as you always know where you stand with a particular person.

Another close mate of mine from M.U.T.V. is Hayley McQueen. I was first aware of her from her appearances on Sky Sports and, of course, I was also aware that her dad had played for United and Leeds United, and captained Scotland. On the first day we met, I approached "Lightning", as in the red car from the Disney movie, excitedly and asked her, "Do you know when your dad scored his last goal for United?"

Needless to say that I had looked it up and it was against Bournemouth in a 3-0 win in the F.A. Cup third round on Saturday 5th January 1985. This was retribution for United after a shock defeat to Harry Redknapp's "Cherries" at the same stage a year before at Dean Court when United were F.A. Cup holders.

Some people are taken aback when I do things like this when I first meet them, which, as I have explained, is my coping mechanism around new people. However, Lightning seemed to take it in her stride. On the Friday 17th August 2007 edition of *C2KO*, Lightning

87

used the stat I asked her when her father was the guest. When he didn't know the answer, Lightning recited what I said in a very convincing impression of me! We still keep in touch to this day and meet up whenever we can.

I also had other understanding mates from my time at M.U.T.V. including Mike "Shawbles" Shaw, Joe Cooper, Magdalena Oczkowska, Sophie Waterfall-Bode, who is Humble's wife, David Stowell, Kasia Cooke, Ross Wyllie and Stewart Gardner. They have all been very considerate of my autism.

I was only too happy and obliging to help any of my co-workers and mates, even on my days off if they emailed, rang or texted me for stats. I used to research the stats with a number of books, along with the internet and visits to the Manchester Central Library, and loved carrying my two big bags of books from home up four flights of stairs three days a week. My job, or "calling", gave me a great sense of achievement.

As an added bonus, if such a thing was possible at this time, Billy, like me, was always accepted and seen as a part of the M.U.T.V. furniture. Billy accompanied me to work, and some people I worked with for years didn't realise that Billy's paymasters weren't Manchester United. I say this as a massive compliment to M.U.T.V., as not every workplace or educational institution would have allowed me to have my Support Worker with me, nor prove so understanding. When United reached Cup finals at Wembley or Champions League finals, along with me being a permanent club employee, Billy was given the same complimentary treatment regarding tickets, food on the day and, in the case of Champions League finals, flights.

*

When United reached the 2008 Champions League final after defeating Barcelona 1-0 on aggregate in the semi-final, I received an email stating that all staff could travel to the final against Chelsea at the Luzhniki Stadium in Moscow free of charge. I never dreamt that I would receive such an opportunity.

To illustrate the point that I never expected this invitation, at the time, I didn't even have a passport. I really tried to get one in the four weeks before the final. I went to the passport office in Liverpool but it was to no avail. In fact, I found going to the passport office quite a stressful experience and I felt a little bit like a criminal going through the door… the staff were unfriendly, bordering on rude, uncooperative and needlessly stern. It was horrible.

Four months after this, I went for a passport interview in the now closed office in Wrexham. I was very nervous due to my past experience. Fortunately, they were courteous, understanding and considerate of my autism, and I found it a painless and stress-free process. I got my passport in case United ever reached another Champions League Final.

Fortuitously, I didn't have long to wait as United reached the final the following year in defence of the trophy after a 4-1 aggregate win over Arsenal in the semi-final. I remember running upstairs when Cristiano Ronaldo made it 2-0 on the night and 3-0 on aggregate at the Emirates, and bringing my passport down while kissing it. I felt joyous and slightly emotional while watching the television with my nephew, Louis.

In the run-up to going to the Stadio Olimpico in Rome for the day, as I had never been on a plane before, I was a little scared and nervous of the unknown. In addition to me going on a plane for the first time, Bill has a fear of flying. This scared me slightly more! Ma decided to phone Manchester Airport up and we arranged for me to visit the Airport Chaplain in the days before my flight. As I have mentioned earlier, I am an atheist; nonetheless, I have now realised that chaplains are well versed in counselling people's fears and worries, as in this case. I found going to see the chaplain worthwhile as he showed me around the airport and helped me to have a good time in Rome.

The actual day of the final began for me at 4am after Ma had arranged a wake-up call from the General Phone Operator. I have never gone a single day without at some point seeing my mother even when I went to the Champions League final in the Italian capital. Some people may believe this to be sad, but I am sure many of my mates, and many people generally, would love to see their mothers every day if they are fortunate enough, like me, to still have them living.

After getting to the airport and checking in, I remember seeing future Northern Ireland International Corry Evans in the queue ahead of me. I then went for a coffee before meeting up with my M.U.T.V. mates and co-workers. On the plane itself, I felt unsettled by the steward's instructions in preparing for a potential accident – I felt as if I was getting ready for my impending doom. I found take-off and landing a long, drawn out process, but whilst in the air, being on a plane didn't bother me. However, I didn't particularly like losing my hearing for 15 minutes after landing as it made me feel disorientated, and I didn't like the lack of leg room.

On the way from the Leonardo Da Vinci Airport, I remember the bus's tour guide was a bespectacled, blonde-haired girl, who appeared to be in her twenties and was quite attractive. I don't think she always knew where we were going, but nonetheless, she was very polite. The day itself was a great day as in the early summer afternoon warmth, I enjoyed going to a pizza restaurant. It wasn't in the nicest area of Rome, but it was sufficient enough despite the boarded-up windows and graffiti covering many of the adjacent buildings.

After the coach had parked at our designated meeting point on the way to the Stadio Olimpico, I was very conscious of Lambretta scooters as mobile weapons and made sure they never got near me. I was slightly terrified on the numerous occasions that a scooter went past me on the walk to the Stadio Olimpico.

In addition to Lambretta scooters, on Ma's advice, I didn't let my bag out of my sight all day; quite a lot of the time I kept hold of it while sitting down, especially in the airport. I was aware, on Ma's instruction, that there were thieves everywhere. This instruction, I felt, was reminiscent of when Homer Simpson owned a sugar pile in his back garden in Evergreen Terrace in the season six episode "Lisa's Rival", when he goes on a diatribe about how "the strong must protect the sweet".

During the ninety minutes of the final, United were thoroughly outplayed by Barcelona, losing 2-0 to the Catalan giants. The result was an aside to the experience of going overseas for the first, and currently, only time. I will never forget it as long as I live. When I got home the next morning, I was tired and knackered for three weeks afterwards as I then came down with sinusitis. It was a very small price to pay for such enjoyment.

The Rome trip was the best example of how Manchester United looked after their regular staff when the team reached finals, but another good example was that meals at the staff canteen at Old Trafford were complimentary, even for Billy. I know for a fact that this wasn't the case in a lot of workplaces, where employees have to pay a subsidy to eat in the canteen. This is how good M.U.T.V. and United were to me. In addition, I always enjoyed the food.

Unfortunately, the Rome trip turned out to be the absolute pinnacle of my time in my "dream job". Just a couple of months prior to Rome, my boss and mentor had left M.U.T.V. for another position in another company. His departure was announced before he even had the chance to tell me, or anyone else, face to face. Although he worked his notice period, it was the very beginning of the end for me at M.U.T.V. and the first sign of any real unhappiness I had working there.

Whilst my mentor and I had sometimes bickered, it was just between close mates who cared about each other and we always made up within moments. I cried when I found out he was leaving and was allowed to go home for the rest of the day. Any potential issue at M.U.T.V. always seemed to be sorted out by my mentor.

At times, I struggled with certain situations at work. For example, if I had to change desk if a new employee joined the company. I hated doing this as it unsettled me and, to start with, I could be awkward with the new worker, as they were now in my old seat. I also struggled for quite a while when my set three days were changed as it was my autistic routine to work the previously set days.

My workload lessened significantly after my mentor's departure as the commentators now undertook their own research. Accordingly, I was asked to log clips of archive matches of United rather than my beloved job of researching stats and facts.

In addition to this, there had been a few redundancies around the time and with the lessening workload, and the fact I had become extremely lazy due to this, I really feared for my job and started to feel trapped for the first time ever. I remember that when I went to Shaughssa's house for his birthday, he privately took me outside in the gathering autumnal gloom and said, "If they call you into the office and they tell you that you are to be made redundant – ask them why. Whatever the reason, accept it and shake their hand and walk out of the room with your head held high."

Although at this stage, I wasn't ready for such an event and I didn't want it to ever happen, if it did, I was determined to do Shaughssa proud and heed his wise words. In the end, however, I was not to be made redundant and continued at M.U.T.V. for a number of further years.

Work had become very stressful and a chore rather than enjoyable. I felt everything had been taken away from me and I didn't know how to cope. During my working day, I would ring Mel repeatedly – moaning, whinging and being generally miserable or just acting in an obnoxious or antagonistic manner. This pattern repeated itself with alarming regularity during my last four years at M.U.T.V. Without the stats, I felt worthless and useless in my job and could see no end in sight as M.U.T.V. was all I knew. My family felt helpless.

I was sent to an occupational health doctor by M.U.T.V. The doctor recommended that the National Autistic Society come into M.U.T.V. to see me and give a talk to the rest of the staff at Old Trafford. Although a representative from the NAS helped with the theoretical side of autism, it was all very textbook and lacking in any sort of emotion.

In fact, they were so textbook that they cut me short in the middle of a sentence, in our meeting, as it was the exact minute they had planned to finish the meeting. I would never do that as it is far too literal. In my opinion, the representative seemed more autistic than I am! Nevertheless, after the NAS came into the office, some good did occur from it as people started to understand why I would say certain things or act in a certain way, whereas they hadn't previously.

A typical trait of autism is an inability to accept any change easily. The alternative to what I knew appeared non-existent or too scary to contemplate. I freely admitted to everyone that the only reason I stayed at M.U.T.V. was the familiar, understanding faces being more preferable to strangers and the 'unknown' alternative option. In all honesty, although I stayed for another four years at M.U.T.V. after the change of job description, I never really felt fully happy again. I was quite broken up. This sent me into a state of depression, which lasted for several years. Depression frequently goes hand in hand with autistic spectrum disorder.

Although I never contemplated suicide, I did suffer from some of the symptoms described – like increased stress. I was struggling with work and I had difficulty controlling my emotions during this juncture. Due to this, I started to have occasional days off from work struggling with the depression. My autism had also got worse and I started to suffer from bad obsessional behaviour. I became angry with the family, and unhappy. At times, on my days off, I would struggle to leave my room to drag myself to the gym or away from BBC 6Music.

We decided that I should go visit my GP and I was prescribed anti-depressants, which I still take to this day. I eventually went to see a counsellor, who understood me well and had had experience with disabilities. I seemed to be making progress, but due to cutbacks from the recession, unfortunately, I had to stop seeing them.

However, the night of Thursday 22nd November 2012, when I was at a work social quiz at a bar in Manchester city centre, was a shock to others and even me. I had previously attended quizzes and found them enjoyable. At quizzes, I always wanted to win and took them seriously. I was on the winning team on a couple of occasions, including a fortnight earlier in a quiz at Old Trafford, and I prided myself upon my general knowledge. On this occasion, they were strict on the non-use of mobile phones, which I wholeheartedly agreed with. Quiz players had to put their phones into a cooler normally used for champagne and wine; the organisers would know if someone took them out.

I hated people looking up answers on their phones at quizzes. That was a no-no in my book. I thought, "What is the point in that?" You go to quizzes to learn, be educated, have a chat with mates and, hopefully, win. What was the point in cheating? I would rather know nothing, get every answer wrong, and finish last than that. In my mind, it is the same as deliberately and knowingly using banned substances in sport. Bend the rules as everyone does, but to out and out cheat is wrong, very wrong in my eyes. Although, admittedly, my way might be an autistic way of looking at matters.

On the evening of Thursday 22nd November 2012, a former United player was on one of the teams. At the halfway stage of the quiz, I heard people comment that he was "looking up answers on Google". His team couldn't win, could they? Surely someone would say something and deduct points, especially when his actions were so blatant?

When the results were read out, the ex-player's team were declared the winners. At this point, I was confused and upset. I felt I had wasted a night as I had come from Wrexham on my day off for this. I wanted a word with him to tell him that cheating was wrong. At this point, a couple of people were holding me back, but I broke free and a table went flying and a glass or two smashed on the floor. I grabbed the ex-player's jumper to remonstrate with him as he turned and shouted "Championi!" in my face. This annoyed me more, but by then I was ushered away.

The following day, I was informed that I was suspended from work on full pay with immediate effect, pending an investigation.

Even though it was understandable that I couldn't go into the office or speak to any of my mates from M.U.T.V., it hurt greatly not being able to talk to them. This really affected me as Christmas was coming and it was tradition to ring all my close friends on Christmas Day and Boxing Day, including the ones I had met at M.U.T.V., and also exchange presents and cards. As soon as it happened, I was so ashamed. I felt a shame that I had seldom, if ever, felt in my life. I dreaded having to tell Ma when I got home as her stress levels would go through the roof. Why had I reacted in such a way? Why had I probably thrown away my job in such an act of temper and fit of pique?

I went to an investigation hearing four days later on Monday 26th November 2012. En route to Old Trafford, the perspiration poured out of my hands and forehead like a fountain and I used four hankies during the journey to dry the sweat. My heart bumped with fear, my knees trembled and I drank an entire two-litre bottle of lemon flavoured water. Ma attempted in vain to support me through this, but she was on a hiding to nothing.

I arrived early to the hearing with Ma, who had come to Manchester with Bill and me. Ma wasn't allowed into the meeting; however, Bill was – as my support worker. I had written a letter of apology to the ex-player and took it into the investigation hearing with me. As it turned out, the ex-player was placed on record as saying he didn't want me to lose my job. I voiced nothing but total remorse for what I had done and begged to keep my job. I knew my reactions were deeply wrong and that I certainly should have dealt with the situation differently.

*

I was home day in, day out, for several weeks in the run-up to Christmas. Every second felt like a minute... every minute an hour... every hour a day... every day a month. I barely got out of bed some days during this time. I had tickets to see Robin Ince at Sale Waterside Arts Centre, near Manchester on November 29th 2012, but I stayed at home as I was so ashamed of what I had done. I didn't want to navigate far in case I saw someone I knew as I was so embarrassed by what I had done. The one thing that kept me sane during this time was waking up to see England's first Test series win in India in 28 years.

I only existed, but wasn't living or capable of being particularly merry in what was the festive period, which was unusual as I adore Christmas. Why had I been so stupid? Why had I brought such shame upon my family? They only existed, like me. When we put up the Christmas tree, Ma was so ill with stress that she stayed in bed and wasn't able to come down. I would ask the same question a million times over... "Am I keeping my job?" My family were in the same boat as me. A final disciplinary hearing was arranged for the week before Christmas, when my fate was to be decided, but I was too ill and stressed to attend.

The decision hung over the family and me over Christmas and New Year. It was all I talked about. It was a very emotional time and, understandably, won't go down as my favourite festive period. I remember we went to Cheshire Oaks one night, just before Christmas, and seeing the lights on the big tree there made us all very emotional, especially me. This was very hard and made us contemplate what life would be like in the New Year if the worst-case scenario happened. Another workplace would be reluctant to take me on due to the nature of what I had done; probably, even volunteering would be hard to organise.

Somehow, we managed to scrape through the long holiday period. Eventually, in the first week of 2013, I was informed that the disciplinary meeting had taken place and I was to receive a final written warning. Along with my family, I was delighted. I was to be kept on. I was to have a chance to make amends. I would be returning to work in the New Year. I was to be released from HMP Gwersyllt, which was what I had dubbed the house during this period. I would be released from my personal torment, albeit that I myself had created. I would be given a final chance.

Although I was delighted to be kept on, in all honesty – like I have explained – I hadn't been happy at M.U.T.V. at that point for a couple of years. At least I now had the opportunity to make amends and, if the day when I left were to ever arrive, I would have the chance to leave on amicable terms. By no means was I thinking about leaving at this juncture. I was just happy to be still in employment, have something to fill my weeks, and was happy that my mates at M.U.T.V. would get the opportunity to forgive me.

The night of Thursday 22nd November 2012 has undoubtedly changed me. Quite often, when I have gone to a gig, a sporting event or somewhere socially, I have been petrified that something stressful would happen. I have had to talk through my emotions with my family regarding this. I get very nervous and anxious at times at the thought of some social events, and it can take away some of my enjoyment. That night will now stay with me for a long time.

Although I didn't mention it at the time, I have been told subsequently by quite a few people from different parts of my life that my actions on Thursday 22nd November 2012 were textbook autism. With my autism, I take things very literally and it is all black and white. I have attempted to improve over the years, but these traits will always be there.

*

For the rest of my time at M.U.T.V., I felt like I was hanging on a wire over the precipice like a trapeze artist. On most occasions during this time I went to work with a nervous, worried feeling in my stomach. I would make frequent trips to the toilet. I would be snappy and antagonise Ma and Mel. This routine must have repeated itself three days a week, every week after the unhappiness started.

During my suspension from M.U.T.V., I went to see a psychiatrist to try to tackle my depression. This lasted half an appointment as he seemed deeply uninterested in my case. In fact, he was so uninterested he left me halfway through the appointment to go to another clinic and left me with his understudy. Ma and I did likewise. They phoned Ma to apologise, but I was never going back anyway.

According to *mentalhealth.org.uk*, one in four people in Great Britain are said to suffer from depression in any given year. Anyone can have depression at any given time. The condition doesn't discriminate. It doesn't say you are so and so and have a certain type of personality. It can happen to absolutely anyone.

Like a lot of people in life, I didn't realise how lucky I was until it was almost too late – when I may have lost everyone and not had the opportunity to have a second chance. Even though I now, on the whole, realise my strengths, I still waste a lot of energy on the negativity of my weaknesses… although a lot less than before. I feel more accepting of myself now.

Although things have got better over time, I can well imagine many sufferers with depression being in a similar place as me. What helped me was talking through my feelings and emotions with my family and close mates. This also controlled the anger, although I still rant at the television, at the news on my phone applications, and the radio. However, this is part of my autism and my personality. I still get down, but not depressed. This, and persistence over time, has helped me. I can't guarantee it won't come back in the future, but I know that I wouldn't wish it on my worst enemy.

*

In April 2014, after four and a half years, the logging at M.U.T.V. was coming to an end and I was called into a meeting room to see the bosses. They discussed the possibility that I would be made redundant. They were going to attempt to find another position for me by looking at the vacancies available, but redundancy was a distinct possibility.

A few days later, I was emailed a list of vacancies. None seemed suitable as they were full-time positions, rather than my three days a week, or I wasn't qualified or suited to the different roles.

At this stage, I was getting more and more stressed at home – taking my emotions out on my family, who didn't know what the future held for me. Partly due to my personality, but mainly due to my autism, I needed to know the final outcome. I couldn't see any light at the end of the tunnel. I just wanted it all to end. At this point, I no longer wanted to work at M.U.T.V., but I didn't know anything else. What was I going to do? Mel then came up with a plan as we believed (rightly as it turned out) that my support hours were probably going to be taken away if I was going to be made redundant. Her plan was for her to work with me voluntarily and take me out between certain hours. In the long run, I would begin volunteer work, I would start writing this book, and, whenever possible, take trips to see my friends in Manchester.

After Mel told me this – and I could tell she had put in plenty of thought – she ran out the room in tears. The plan was great and that is when, for the first time in four years, at the drop of a hat, I felt at peace with myself and felt that I could feel the way I previously did.

Rather than beating around the bush for a month of "consultation", Mel helped me to "grab the bull by both horns" and accept the inevitable redundancy.

With Mel's plan in my head, I went into the room with my bosses for the second meeting in a much more relaxed and comfortable place than I had been for the vast majority of the previous four years. I had accepted my fate and was looking forward, as my mind was made up. I told the bosses that rather than go through the procedures for a month – and probably not find a job at the end – I wanted to cut to the chase and be made redundant.

I don't feel bitter at all about losing my job – in fact, quite the opposite. If I had been sacked after the night at the staff quiz, it would have been very difficult to keep friendships on such a low note. Fortunately, I had an extra 16 months in this respect. I could lift my head high upon redundancy, rather than feeling ashamed for the rest of my life at being sacked.

Over the course of my final four years at M.U.T.V., my interest in football had eroded almost completely. I couldn't watch 90 minutes and enjoy the action unfolding on the field without mentally logging what I was seeing on my television or at a game. In my head, while watching the game, everything became the metadata labels that were part of the logging… name of the player, headers, on target (saved), and more.

One day, I really hope to return to loving watching football, either in person or on television. I hope it is just a temporary break I am taking from it.

Although I now have little interest in contemporary footballing matters, an example being that I only watched three and a half minutes in total of the 2014 World Cup in Brazil on television, I will always remain a scholar on the history of the sport. In recent times, I have visited the National Football Museum at the Urbis in Manchester with our Louis and, to quote the late legendary broadcaster, producer and writer Sid Waddell, "it was akin to giving Dracula the keys to the blood bank". I absorbed the information with an enormous smile on my face, even gleefully noticing mistakes on the displays like the pedant I am.

For instance, United's record victory was erroneously credited as 9-0 against Ipswich Town on Saturday 4th March 1995, rather than the 10-0 victory over RSC Anderlecht in the European Cup first round, second leg at Maine Road on 26th September 1956. In fact, the 9-0 win over Ipswich Town isn't even United's biggest League win. That is the 10-1 win over Wolverhampton Wanderers on 15th October 1892. Although named Newton Heath at the time, it was the club's first ever Football League win after being accepted into the League after finishing the previous season as runners-up to Nottingham Forest in the Football Alliance.

In addition to this, I recognised the incorrect year of formation for my hometown club Wrexham being acknowledged as 1873. Research from February 2012 revealed that they were formed in 1864. Hitherto, my old club Cefn Druids were recognised as Wales' oldest club after being formed in 1868.

Nevertheless, looking back on my decade or so at M.U.T.V., I have thousands of fond memories. Far too many to remember, even for me! I met some of my closest mates in the world at M.U.T.V., and I would never have swapped my friendships, life experiences or memories for anything. As well as all this, it was never in my wildest dreams that I would go to Rome for free to watch my club in a

Champions League final and attend three Wembley finals in 2009, 2010 and 2011 or do the job I did for the club I had supported since the age of five. I never thought any of this would have happened when I required two support workers at St. Christopher's before going on to enjoy so many happy, wonderful experiences.

M.U.T.V. gave me a purpose in my life, as well as something, for the most part, to look forward to on the three days a week I was there. It also offered a little bit of financial independence and social mobility, which is rarely there for adults with autism. I entered the office as a child, but left as a man who had learned so many social and emotional skills whilst wisening up significantly and learning more about what life is about.

Even though I no longer work there, M.U.T.V. were always very accommodating towards me, especially my Line Manager Janette Horrigan. Even when I needed to swap my days at short notice, to either a Wednesday or Thursday, it was never a problem. I will be forever thankful that M.U.T.V. were like this as it is unusual for an employer to be so understanding, flexible and caring of your needs. Compared to other companies, I believe few – if any – would have been so considerate of anyone, never mind someone with a disability.

Being made redundant gave me my emotional freedom back and I felt it gave me another, new lease of life. Towards the end of my time at M.U.T.V. the often-used anonymous quote, "If you're not living on the edge, you take up too much space" swirled around my head. By pushing myself into new things and situations I felt a renewed vigour, zest and hope in life that had left me. I believe you can't put a price on happiness – but if you could, I now started to feel like a million pounds!

Chapter 10
Pastime Paradise

As I explained earlier, my first real interest was with toy cars. Then, by age seven, besides Manchester United – and football in general – I developed a love of cricket. Even now, summer begins for me with the commencement of the County Cricket season in early- to mid-April. When I was growing up, the summer would then progress to the end of the football season, first Test of the summer, along with Wimbledon, the Open Golf Championship and, finally, the school holidays.

Although, in Britain – with our maritime climate – we can have chilly summer days, as well as hot days, I would wear shorts every day of summer. This was despite Ma's usually prudent advice on the weather. Shorts wearing lasted until I went to watch Lancashire in the opening County Championship Division Two match of 2005 against Somerset at Old Trafford. It was really cold that Friday and I must have looked completely out of place dressed as I was. I was quite lucky that there was only an hour's play that day due to rain, otherwise I might have had hypothermia!

The first Test series I can vividly remember is England's exciting and controversial home Test series against Javed Miandad's Pakistan in the summer of 1992. Pakistan were the defending World Champions after beating England in the World Cup final earlier that year at the Melbourne Cricket Ground. Legendary captain Imran Khan had retired after this success and passed the reins over to the rather feisty Mr Miandad.

The memories of Waqar Younis and Wasim Akram bamboozling England with pace and bringing reverse-swing to the cricketing mainstream are still in my memory. So is David Gower breaking England's all-time record for Test match career runs in the third Test at Old Trafford, which was also his first Test since the Tiger Moth incident in a meandering tour match against Queensland at the Carrara Oval during the 1990-91 Ashes Tour.

Unfortunately, the series was forever tarnished after the fourth One Day International at Lord's, which saw accusations of ball tampering – which, in turn, ended up with the high profile lawsuit by Allan Lamb and Ian Botham against Imran Khan at the High Court in July 1996. Nevertheless, I prefer to remember the exciting aspects of this summer, which saw a seven-year-old autistic boy hooked on the sport for life.

Around this time, when I started to play cricket in the garden with Ma, there was only one man I wanted to be and that was Alec James Stewart. I would try to play hook and pull shots like him while pretending I was him doing jacks, which was a superstition of his between deliveries at the crease to keep his feet moving effectively. In the same instance, Stewart would also twirl the blue handle of his Kookaburra Bubble bat like a cheerleader would twirl their baton at an American sporting event. Needless to say, I attempted to replicate this motion with my bat in the garden. He was my first cricketing hero.

On Wednesday 30th May 2001, at Old Trafford, prior to the second Test against Pakistan, he signed a copy of his 1998-99 Ashes Tour Diary – a series when he was England's captain. I treasure the book as I told Mr Stewart I was taking my G.C.S.E. History at the time and he signed the book wishing me good luck. In the match itself, Stewart was stand-in captain after Nasser Hussain had his notoriously brittle thumb broken by Shoaib Akhtar in the previous Test at Lord's. I actually have an amusing picture with Mr Hussain putting his broken digit, which was in a cast, up at the camera. He had noticed I had a habit of lifting my thumb in every picture I had taken that morning.

The Old Trafford Test of 2001 ended rather controversially in the final session of day five, with Pakistan winning with several wickets being taken through no-balls that were unseen by standing umpires Eddie Nicholls and David Shepherd. This would be extremely unlikely to happen now with the perpetual referring of wickets to the Television Umpire to be checked for the possibility of a no-ball when a wicket has been taken.

Growing up, I was also hooked on the television commentaries of Richie Benaud on the BBC and Channel Four. I was fortunate enough to meet "The Doyen of Cricket Commentators" on two occasions. The first time was after a punctuated third day's play at the third Ashes Test of the iconic 2005 series at Old Trafford. I waited for an hour after the close of play at 6.30pm, and during the hour that I waited for "The Great Man" (not to be confused with the other "Great Man" Sir Alex Ferguson), Louis and I had our pictures taken with a host of cricketing personalities. But Richie was the one we really wanted to see and meet, especially as he had announced his intention to retire from commentating.

As he approached down the green creaky, decaying steps of the old Media Centre at Old Trafford, my moment had arrived. There was no one around as the sell-out crowd had long since departed for either home or the pub, except for a few old-school autograph hunters, who seemed to be at every day's play at Old Trafford. At this point, I asked him for a picture. I will always remember, as it's what I always did for pictures, I put my arm around his shoulder. Mr Benaud, with his trademark sharp, succinct delivery, told me to "keep your hands to yourself". However, he still posed for the picture that is treasured at our home. I then rang Ma to tell her in my excited, happy, but quite emotional state that Louis and I had just met him and had our picture with "The Great Man".

Almost a year to the day later, on Monday 31st July 2006, on what was scheduled to be the fifth and final day of the second Pakistan Test at Old Trafford – a match which had concluded, and I had been present, on the third day with England winning comfortably by an innings and 120 runs as Pakistan capitulated – I again met Mr Benaud. This time it was on my lunch break from M.U.T.V. The venue was Waterstone's on Deansgate in Manchester. Mr Benaud arrived around 20 minutes early for a 12.30pm start to the signing.

Clearly remembering what he had said a year earlier, I said to him, "I shouldn't put my arm around you". This raised a pleasant, polite smile from Mr Benaud as he signed my copy of his then latest book "My Spin on Cricket" and a cricket ball that I have mounted in my room. Despite Benaud's passing away on 10th April 2015, aged 84, his distinctive voice and delivery will forever be implanted on my brain, whilst transporting me to the summers of my youth where the sun always shone and rain never stopped play. Impressive passages of play will forever be described as "marvellous" – as they will always remain.

Latterly, I love David "Bumble" Lloyd, Nasser Hussain and Michael Atherton commentating on Sky. I like their commentaries for contrasting reasons. I like Atherton for his deep intelligence, articulation, knowledge, humour and dry wit. Hussain for his tactical and technical insight, his research, his no-nonsense approach and the way he gets his point across when he is putting together an analytical piece, such as the "Third Man", when displaying a potential game situation in the nets or on the pitch. And finally, "Bumble" for his humour and our shared love of Half Man Half Biscuit.

I have counted that up until the end of the 2014 season, I have been to 25 England Internationals, spent 119 days watching Lancashire, and attended one Australia v Bangladesh ODI at Old Trafford in 2005. My first match was the first day of Lancashire v Glamorgan in the County Championship on Wednesday 18th June 1997 at Aigburth, Liverpool. This was the day before the start of the second Ashes Test at Lord's when England were bowled out for 77, with Glenn McGrath taking eight wickets for just 38 runs, but they drew the match as most of the match was rain interrupted.

As a memento of my years of watching cricket at Old Trafford, I even own a piece of the turf that all my cricketing heroes have played on. Be it Jim Laker's match figures of 19 for 90, Warne's aforementioned "Ball of the Century", the 1960 Ashes Test where Richie Benaud cleverly changed the course of the match, Cork's "Champagne" moments in 1995, The West Indian barrage against forty-somethings John Edrich and Brian Close in 1976 or Botham's Ashes hundred in 1981, which is still the quickest Test century in balls by an England player; these memories are some of the sport's finest.

I was so chuffed putting my piece on the lawn and, needless to say, it is still there to this day. Although it is bedded in now, I still know the part of the lawn that holds my Lancashire grass.

*

The biggest interest of my youth, apart from sport, was *The Simpsons*. At one point of my adolescence, I literally couldn't go out of the house when it was on television. I never used to miss an episode, even if I had seen it 50 times previously. Eventually, I was convinced to tape it sometimes. However, if it didn't tape, I would have a "turn" and hit out. I was that obsessed with the show. I just couldn't help it. I just had to watch every episode over and over again, even though I had literally seen it on hundreds of occasions.

Even every Christmas, Mel and I would look through the T.V. Guide with a fine-toothed comb writing down on paper, that I would laminate, the times and dates of every episode on the BBC and Sky One over the festive period. Never mind *The Queen's Speech*, we – as a family – wouldn't even sit down for Christmas dinner until I had watched *The Simpsons* at approximately 3pm on BBC2 or Channel Four.

After just over a decade of being obsessed with *The Simpsons*, I suddenly stopped watching in autumn 2007. In all honesty, I hadn't enjoyed it in some time. It had become a chore but I had to keep up a record of watching every new episode as it was the convention.

Despite not watching *The Simpsons* regularly in years, I can recite the dialogue for the episodes of the first nine seasons, possibly a couple more. This is mainly down to my memory, but also possibly due to watching some episodes repeatedly over the course of a decade. Funnily enough, on the occasions that I catch a few minutes of an old episode, I can now understand the cultural references more, some of which could be niche to non-American viewers, and find them even funnier, but I only watch a few minutes in passing. Looking back, these cultural references were possibly one of the reasons I watched the show. Some of the references were probably well beyond my years, but have helped my general knowledge immensely over the years whenever the opportunity has come to answer a question on a reference. My favourite episode was the season six episode "Homer Badman" as I believe it to be an excellent satire on the round-the-clock news coverage that is now everywhere we turn. I love this episode as – I believe, in the UK at least – it was several years before the saturated news and comments we now experience. It was a prescient view into the future we now live in.

Looking back with hindsight, I believe if *The Simpsons* had been cancelled or finished production in the late 1990s or early 2000s, it would have gone down – in my eyes at least – unequivocally, as the best television comedy of all-time, but others have surpassed it since.

While *The Simpsons* is very much from my formative and early adult years, latterly, music is one my main interests. Initially, I was introduced to music by my mate Pazman in the summer of 2001 when Ian Brown released his opening single entitled "F.E.A.R." from his third solo LP *Music of the Spheres*. For a few years, "King Monkey" (Ian Brown's nickname) was, narrow-mindedly, my only musical interest. I even have the nickname "Monkey Boy" off Cunnah due to this obsession.

Prior to meeting Pazman, I was rather dreadfully into Robbie Williams. If it wasn't for Pazman I wouldn't be going to gigs, listening to BBC 6 Music or even have such a large physical music collection of CDs and vinyl. I dread to think what my musical taste would have been! Fortunately, over the years, my musical horizons have expanded far beyond just one man. I was still pretty much a "white indie kid", specifically "lad rock", before I started listening to BBC 6 Music in late 2009. BBC 6 Music has broadened my tastes more than I thought, at one point, possible.

My musical palate now encompasses such performers and genres as Half Man Half Biscuit, William Onyeabor, Homeboy Sandman, Public Service Broadcasting, El Perro Del Mar, Lykke Li, Animal Collective, Bibio, Connan Mockasin, Ghostpoet, Motown, funk, northern soul, samples, African, Latin and world music, electro, jazz, especially fusion, acid jazz and hip hop jazz, folk, dubstep, new and old school rap & hip hop, experimental, and a little helping of the self-indulgent progressive rock.

All this whilst also loving technically highly accomplished female vocalists like Warpaint, Anna Calvi, Agnes Obel, Natasha Khan A.K.A. Bat for Lashes, Alice Russell, Vashti Bunyan, Nadine Shah and many others. The funny thing is that most of my mates haven't heard of the musicians, rappers and performers I like these days. I have the vast majority of my mates furrowing their brows.

I have listened to up to 12 hours of 6 Music some days. My favourite shows are Shaun Keaveny for his comedy and self-deprecating wit, Lauren Laverne, Radcliffe and Maconie, Steve Lamacq, Mary Anne Hobbs and, most of all, *The Huey Show*. Latterly, I have got into listening to Gilles Peterson as well, with his eclectic, esoteric mix of styles, grooves and genres, and Stuart Maconie's *Freak Zone*.

Needless to say, I was delighted that the BBC decided against the closure of BBC 6 Music in summer 2010 after a public furore. I feel they treat their listeners with the respect, intelligence and the knowledge that they deserve. I feel that BBC 6 Music is worth the license fee alone.

Proudly, I was the mystery guest on BBC 6 Music on Steve Lamacq's show on Tuesday 29th April 2014 as I was musically profiled by comedian Robin Ince. To explain the feature in more depth, Robin Ince guesses everything about your life – from your favourite book, age, what newspaper you read, where you are from, where you grew up, favourite subject at school, and what job you have or have previously worked at. He does this from just six musical selections that you submit.

Mr Ince actually did pretty damn well as some of his guesses were spookily true, including guessing that my favourite subject was in some way related to media. I couldn't tell him at the time that I was in the media myself, so was doubly impressed by that.

I had really wanted to be on this segment for over a year. Nonetheless, it couldn't have happened at a better time as I was now clear in my head of what to say and not to witter on.

Before the show, I explained to the producer that I was autistic and my spot was pre-recorded the day before it went out on air, which was a great assistance.

Due to listening to 6 Music, I now collect vinyl as well as CDs after Mel and Billy bought me a record player, for my 28th birthday in November 2012, that converts records onto my iPod. I can't stand downloads as I feel the sound is far too decompressed and you lose the purer sounds of vinyl and, to a lesser degree, CDs. I love owning the physical product and I wholeheartedly agree with the Sheffield troubadour Richard Hawley who, in 2012 on 6 Music, analogised downloading music to "downloading steam".

A collection of downloads is non-existent in the physical sense, whereas I can show off all my CDs and vinyl, which are lovingly – obsessively, some might say – alphabetised and, if I have more than one by the same performer, they are placed in order chronologically. Granted, it is splendid to be able to conveniently carry your iPod or other MP3 player around, with all your collection, when you are on the move – but nothing beats the sound of vinyl, or to a much lesser extent, a CD. Nothing, in my eyes, beats the sound of the needle hitting the groove – with the palpable tension this brings, waiting for the track to start, and the end which crackles in a soothing, comforting fashion. It is almost as if the performer is in the room with you.

I love listening as it transports me to another place, with each piece of music I own reflecting a certain feeling, emotion, thought or time in my life. I can be transported to a happy time and place or taken away from negative thoughts with the appropriate music in my collection.

The music can suit almost any emotion – whether it's humorous, satirical, a mundane occurrence (in the case of Half Man Half Biscuit) or quiet contemplation – as classical or ambient music can offer. Also, the beat and sound of intelligent dance music makes me happy, especially the likes of Daniel Avery or Aphex Twin. Samples of hip-hop can really excite and enthral me, or the sometimes witty lyricism of rap can make me laugh out loud. It is all dependent on my mood.

I also love nothing more than to go to an independent record shop. In fact, events like Record Store Day on the third Saturday every April have got significantly bigger by the passing year, with just as many teenagers and twenty-somethings, like myself, queuing up for specially released limited edition vinyl. It can get rather hectic around the country on Record Store Day. Going to Manchester to Piccadilly Records isn't an option as customers queue up to 24 hours before in the quest for the best limited releases.

On Record Store Day 2013, I went to Vinyl on Decks Music in Mold, Flintshire, which is one of the smallest independent shops in the country. Due to my autism, I struggled with the lack of personal space, which, as I have mentioned before, is always an issue with me. It was extremely hectic and, by the time I nipped into the adjacent Record Fair, my head was blagged and I was really stressed buying a couple of CDs without really thinking.

However, what I like most about independent record stores is that the owner or manager is easily identifiable. They are behind the till or loading stock – unlike a chain store, which tends to be a faceless corporate monster lacking even the infinitesimal personal touch. The employees are also usually genuine music enthusiasts who are greatly knowledgeable, like in Piccadilly Records in Vinyl Valley, Manchester, which is my favourite record shop. The staff at Piccadilly are extremely friendly and I just can't compete with their knowledge of music despite being autistic.

As well as collecting my music, I put colours to the respective sounds of each track that I listen to. I don't know if many people do this, or if it is weird or strange. Although I haven't had any tests, I believe I may have chromesthesia, or sound to colour synaesthesia, like the South-East London-based experimental electronic producer Kwes. To give an example of this, I put a dark maroon colour to his single "36" off his debut 2013 album *ilp*.

As well as buying and listening to the music, I love to watch live intimate gigs at smaller venues like The Soup Kitchen, Academy 2, Gullivers, Gorilla, or The Deaf Institute in Manchester rather than stadiums or arenas. I adore the sound reverberating through your entire soul and body at tiny venues, with each word, piece of musicianship or nuance profoundly affecting you viscerally rather than the performers being like tiny crushed ants in the distance.

My first gig was on Monday 19th October 2004 at the Manchester Apollo to watch Ian Brown. For the vast majority of gigs I attend, I can afford three, or perhaps even more, in a small venue to any one in an arena or stadium. Plus, it is cheaper than attending nearly all football matches past the Northern Premier League, which is the seventh tier of the English footballing pyramid, Welsh Premier or Cymru Alliance level.

Billy, "The Beast", and Louis are my regular gig companions at most locales these days. I have consciously passed on my love of music and comedy to Louis as I always wanted him to grow up culturally open-minded rather than watching reality television and mainstream media of that ilk. I also wanted to give him the opportunities my autism didn't always afford me when I was younger. My niece Chloe has also recently started collecting vinyl and loves several Half Man Half Biscuit tracks.

I love collecting music as a hobby because it is something that will never be complete, although this used to annoy me some time ago.

The fact that there are so many genres, cultures, nationalities – an infinite smorgasbord of creativity and ideas – excites me. I hope musical creativity never runs out, although it has been going in some semblance since the dawn of time and the fact that there are fantastic genres still to be created or derived from what we already have. I hope I am around to hear some of these.

I love the fact that with sporting success and making music, or even in our thinking patterns, there is no one-size-fits-all approach. This, in my opinion, represents a microcosm of all our actions as human beings. We are all individuals. Just because something works for one person doesn't mean it can work for you. It is certainly the same with autism as the condition is so varied, but there are obviously some core traits.

As an adjunct to my love of my music, I have a playlist for my funeral, which I have updated regularly since I was 21. I read that Mani [of The Stone Roses and Primal Scream] had one for his big day too. So, I thought, if it is good enough for him, then it is must be for me too!

The current track listing reads

- "There's A Ghost in My House" – R. Dean Taylor
- "God! Show Me Magic" – Super Furry Animals
- "Going Underground" – The Jam
- "Atomic Bomb" – William Onyeabor
- "Sexy Boy" – Air
- "Sadness Is A Blessing" – Lykke Li
- "Race for the Prize" – The Flaming Lips
- "Hypocrisy Is the Great Luxury" – Disposable Heroes of Hiphoprisy
- "I Follow You" – Melody's Echo Chamber
- "My Brothers" – Homeboy Sandman
- "Dead Men Don't Need Season Tickets" – Half Man Half Biscuit

- "When an Old Cricketer Leaves the Crease" – Roy Harper

For the big day, I have decided it will be a Humanist Service as I don't believe in religion and I have read that a service of this nature has no hymns, no sermons and no religious figurehead talking about someone they never actually knew in life. The service does have the music that you loved and have chosen for the occasion. It also includes people that cared for you when you were alive talking about your life with anecdotes and stories that arose in their relationship with you. I want to be celebrated in death, but also for people to comically remember my many human deficiencies as it gives a realistic picture of me.

From week to week, I generally love working out as it clears my mind. Over the years, I have tried circuit training, boxercise, bodypump and spinning at Plas Madoc Leisure Centre in Wrexham. In addition to this, I also undertook weekly Referee Interval Running sessions. The Referee Interval Running saw me lose almost three stone and I looked a lot skinnier. But I wanted to bulk up and become more muscular while also being athletic and decided to enlist the help of a personal trainer named Gary "Guru" Jones in my quest to get pectorals in August 2013. Before I recruited "Guru" as my personal trainer, I had hit a wall with my training. I couldn't see the results I desired. My chest wasn't altering much and my arms weren't getting any bigger.

Gary is a great motivator and I know there is always room to improve. He helps me focus on one exercise at a time. He explains things to me in a calm and positive manner.

Another hobby of mine is going to watch stand-up comedy. My favourite comedians are Stewart Lee, Richard Herring, Kevin Eldon, Mark Steel and Robin Ince. I feel these acts are certainly part of the intelligentsia. Although I use that word rather ostentatiously, and in a pretentious manner, their routines make you reflect and reward you for being a thinking human being. This is one of the reasons I enjoy going to watch comedy along with a brand new tour and act every year. I admire their work ethic and, in some cases, improvisation. Also, the sheer energy, thought and articulation they express when on stage is, in my opinion, to be admired.

Nevertheless, just because I can undertake these hobbies, pastimes and interests, like going to gigs and sporting events, it doesn't mean every autistic person has been blessed in the same way. It is different for each person, and various things like social skills, family, mates, or even the opportunity to do what you want to do, are relevant.

Chapter 11
Mr Personality Man

From a young age, I have always had easily identifiable traits in my personality, whether it is my memory, extremely strong opinions, insecurities, obsessions or general knowledge. Whether this is me or my autism, or even a combination of both, I am not totally sure.

Whilst I was at SEC, I was referred for a neuropsychological assessment to a Principal Clinical Psychologist to assist in understanding the nature of my abilities and behaviour. I always recall he had a thick ginger beard that I thought, as a six-year-old, was scary and threatening, but his friendly eyes belied his formidable facial hair.

Several tests were administered, including the British Ability Scales, Kaufman Assessment Battery for Children, Test of Motor Impairment and the British Picture Vocabulary Scale.

My behaviour was also monitored during these sessions. Looking at the report now, there are several facets of six-year-old me that are still prevalent, including trouble with concentration, only being interested in subjects that engross me with my "almost obsessional level of interest" (Orbis Football Collection stickers being noted at the time), and extreme highs and lows in my emotions. On this last point, I have improved slightly.

Six-year-old me was also aggressive, although to a much higher degree than I can be now, and struggled with balance and motor skills. Coincidentally, I still can't tie shoelaces to this day. I also used to spout words and phrases that I didn't understand. This final one certainly isn't the case now, thanks to looking up definitions on Google!

The Clinical Psychologist's final conclusions from the tests were as follows:

From the British Ability Scales results [we see] *that Andrew is functioning generally within the below average range of ability. This conclusion is based on an interpretation of his test scores in relation to factors such as Andrew's difficulties with attention, the inflating effect of his previous intensive exposure to object labelling and verbal stimuli in general, and his difficulty with using a pencil.*

When I was younger I would only perform tasks in a structured environment due to a short attention span. Due to this, I was required to be taught in a small group with specialised individual attention.

Unusually, when I was younger, I would ask how old someone was, and (from that) work out what year they were born. I even did this to some of my peers, who didn't understand and were rather taken aback. Nowadays though, rather than people's age, I try to place regionalised accents and, even though I have just met that person, I ask them where they are from. I then attempt to come up with a fact about the place that they hail from.

When I was younger, my conversation always tended to go off on a tangent. This would not always make sense to whomever I talked with; subjects could drift seamlessly from one to another without me taking much of a breath or for an observer to even distinguish the difference in topics involved. I still do this today.

Nonetheless, it all makes perfect sense to me most of the time, even if I baffle my family and closest mates with it. I can be three or four steps ahead of people. It is very much a chain about something that is completely unrelated to what people think is the next link in the chain, when it is actually several links well down the line of the chain, or going from "Step one to Step 66", as my family call it.

However, my main autistic "power" is my memory. I believe my memory, due to my autism, enabled me to have a job at M.U.T.V. I also feel that when it came to my job it gave me an unfair advantage over the rest of the staff in remembering vital dates in the club's history. Who can compete with someone with autism when remembering dates? Not many people on the street, I'd hazard a guess. To quote T.V. detective Adrian Monk, who has OCD, my memory "is a gift...and a curse". I remember a lot of things I'd rather forget. For instance, I still remember phone numbers from years ago, even of people I don't particularly like.

Sometimes, due to remembering certain events, my memory sends me into a state of panic and worry. I have to look away in queues in shops, or near a cashpoint, as I will memorise people's chip and pin numbers. I just cannot help doing this. I have to look away to cope with the situation. I don't want to be able to remember these things, but the memory just does it. See what I mean with it being a curse as well?

As with many people with autism, there are few grey areas with me. I hate situations in my life when there may well be more than one possible outcome. I like to know where I stand rather obsessively. I like each step of a process to be explained to me clearly and not in a convoluted manner. I don't like surprises either, even for birthdays or Christmases. I like to know what is in front of me, even in a black cab. Some people may think this is being a control freak, but this is a typical autistic character trait. I really hate the not knowing, whether it be waiting to find out if one of my mates can meet up or any situation that requires a wait for it to unravel itself. I find it to be one of the most frustrating aspects in my life. Like I have explained earlier, I like to plan days, weeks or even months ahead. Quite often, though, I do it when it may not be required. I have to do this with gigs or some big sporting events; I need to get in first with the buying of tickets.

Nevertheless, for some events like the 2012 London Olympics this forward planning is unavoidable. I bought my tickets for the boxing at the ExCel Arena 13 months prior to the event, due to the demand that comes hand in hand with an Olympics on home soil. Another example of this forward planning is a Lord's Test, where you have to send away for a place in the public ballot five months before the May Test and seven months ahead of the July Test at "The Home of Cricket". I do worry, though, about the availability of tickets for just about every event or gig I attend as I hate them to be sold out before I purchase them. This is why I organise so far ahead even when, in most cases, it isn't always required.

A lot of the time, though, I blow my head apart with all the planning, worrying and panicking about it all. I worry, stress and panic about all the different scenarios that can happen. I even used to plan my exercise a week ahead, sometimes a bit further in advance if it was a holiday period. The vast majority of the time I have found that things fall into place if I am more laidback. However, I still fall into the same trap time and time again as I plan when it is not always needed.

I also get very excitable when I am happy, but get very miserable and whinge relentlessly when what would be considered minor events for most people go wrong. On these occasions, discussions I have can often turn into rants and I have to be careful not to get too excited or too down as it can be hard to get my mood back onto a normal level. I wear my heart on my sleeve and don't really have any hidden feelings. If I don't discuss my feelings, then I usually start to rant and rave, sometimes from quite an innocuous conversation.

Patrick Howells, who was my Community Nurse when I was growing up, came up with a really brilliant piece of advice for the family, telling Ma and Mel that I should "stay on an even keel" and never get too excited as it can lead to aggression. I also shouldn't get too low as it can lead to more bad behaviour. Patrick's observation has helped the family enormously over the years.

Although I can come across as confrontational, cocky or extremely confident at times, people that don't understand me don't know that I am really very insecure, don't like confrontation, and that confidence is sometimes a façade. All I want is for people to understand me – which, admittedly, is far from easy.

One instance that sticks in my mind – when I was easily hurt – was when a girl that I used to know criticised the clothes that Ma and Mel had bought me for Chrimbo. I was dressed very smartly, as I am greatly conscientious in what I wear, so this was hurtful and I felt was also deeply lacking tact. Also, the same girl always thought I was cocky when, of course, I am closer to being the exact polar opposite.

My emotions can sometimes come over in different ways; for example, if angry, or if I am worried about an issue or someone, I can get abrupt and verbally aggressive when most people would show empathy or get upset. I can also be very insecure and I require constant reassurance when I am worried or panicky. This usually comes from Mel, Ma and Louis. Sometimes, in the not so distant past, I was still insecure about events from when I was a teenager, when some people let me down – which required reassurance. Mel and Ma have tried to get me to talk about feelings of anxiety so they don't turn into an argument and to express these emotions to keep my stress levels down. This is something I find very difficult. One day I can talk about things, but the next day it may start again and everything has to be explained all over.

116

Typically, for someone with autism, I hate to have routines broken. Especially in the mornings. For example, I hate sleeping past 7.30am in the morning as it sets me back for the day. I am always up and about in my room well before then. It makes me more dozy if I sleep past then. I have never overslept when I have *needed* to get up and I hope I never will. I love to be up before 7am to listen to BBC 6 Music as Shaun Keaveny is on every weekday and he makes me laugh with his self-deprecating wit, satire and faux miserable style of humour.

I can be indecisive and overthink constantly, yet, at times, I can be impulsive. I usually like to get advice from all-comers before making a decision, but sometimes – like when I started to get swimming lessons in early October 2012 – I just crack on. I booked them, on the spur of the moment, thinking that within a year I would be in a triathlon even though, at the time, I was petrified of water and couldn't ride a bike. Nonetheless, it was a wise decision as I made great progress, gaining confidence in the water after starting lessons, and could swim 20 metres non-stop on my first attempt of the session. I might not be very streamlined but I have come an awfully long way from being totally petrified of having even a squirt of water on my face.

Towards the summer and end of 2014, I would get stressed and frightened before every session and get quite snappy. I still worried, ever so slightly, that I would drown as my fears took over, even though I knew that my instructor, who was very considerate of my autism, would not let this happen. Nonetheless, after my first swim of the evening, these fears would fade almost entirely and I could carry on with the session to the best of my limited abilities. This repeated week after week like clockwork.

Unfortunately, the anxiety and stress got too much as I decided to stop having lessons after Christmas 2014. Besides, I could swim to a small degree. As I was a very late starter, I think I may have achieved as much as I was ever going to do. If I ever go swimming again in the future, I am sure I will enjoy it and swim to the degree I could when I finished lessons.

As well as swimming, I have also struggled slightly emotionally during my workouts. This was clearly evident when the Bootcamp – Guru's Tuesday evening class – went from being outside to inside in the late autumn of 2014 as the weather turned for winter. Even though I knew all the people that attended the session and they are nice and friendly, I couldn't cope in the barn that the session moved to. I can't fully explain the reason, whether it was just the change from outdoors to indoors, but it was very cold and I felt claustrophobic. It could have been all three. I got nervous and grumpy prior to Bootcamp each Tuesday, and my personal training session, which was also in the barn, on a Friday morning.

To attempt to solve the problem, Ma phoned Guru and explained the situation. Fortunately, Guru fitted me into a session on a Tuesday in the daytime and Mel could see a big difference in my mood almost instantly as I really enjoyed the session outside. I was chilled afterwards, rather than stressed.

Also, at one point not so long ago, if I was unable to train due to extreme weather like snow, or illness, I would be pacing around the house bemoaning the unforeseen situation that had arisen. Hitherto, I used to moan that I was going to gain weight and lose vast levels of conditioning. I had been told that I didn't give illness the respect it deserves. I wouldn't rest at the best of times even when I was ill. I don't sleep during the day or relax when I should.

*

Along with my other personality traits, I hate to have my personal space invaded. An example of this occurred when I attended a Christmas lunch in 2011. I had started to queue up in the cold weather as soon as I arrived. Moments later, while excitedly looking forward to my meal, I received a shock to the system when a security guard touched me, on the shoulder, to get past me to get to the door. This completely freaked me out as I don't like people coming from behind me at the best of times. I hated it and I felt slightly violated.

When I entered the room where the meal took place, I was taken aback and felt more uncomfortable by the cacophonous sound of the festive music. When I was younger, I disliked loud noises, but over time – in controlled environments like music gigs – I have coped better. Nonetheless, I found the festive music overpowering. It was ridiculously loud and I had expected it to be in the background, adding to the general ambience.

However, it was significantly louder than nearly every one of the guitar-based gigs I have been to over the years. I can still hear the loudness of the music in my ears as I am typing this. It was horrible. I couldn't cope. I had all my festive cheer knocked out of me for a short time. Although other people present at the meal found the relentless cacophony annoying, they just coped with it. About twenty minutes after my arrival, I simply had to leave. It had become totally unbearable. I never returned to attend a festive meal at this venue. When I got home, Ma decided to make me a Christmas lunch to make up for this unpleasant experience. This made up for it somewhat, but the horrible memory remains.

As well as situations like that Christmas dinner, I struggle with my personal space and the smells in certain shops in Wrexham Town Centre. I used to go into one card shop before they, fortunately, significantly widened the aisles, and the same routine would repeat. I would struggle to go in there, have a slight panic attack at the lack of space and would have to be taken out of the shop by either Mel or Bill as I was stressed and panicky at the situation. I only kept going into the shop as I wanted, desperately, to overcome my fear, but this was making it worse. I didn't want to let it beat me.

*

Most people find the experience of going on holiday relaxing and enjoyable. Like me, however, many autistic people find going on holiday stressful with the unfamiliar environments and different routines. Indeed, for me, holidays could be mind-blowing.

In 1991, my family went to a camp called Glan-Y-Mor in Clarach Bay, near Aberystwyth, in our touring caravan. In the camp shop, I would get excited trying to buy a toy car as this was my obsession at the time. The owners of the shop would help me to wait in the queue until it was my turn to be served. At the time, I found waiting very difficult and would shout (as mentioned in Chapter 1) "I'm autistic and hyper-bloody-active" whilst not understanding the meaning of what I was saying. The shop owners, who were named Brenda and Gwyn, even got more toy cars in stock for me when they knew we were next to visit.

The manager of the camp was also very understanding and friendly. It became more of a routine going to the campsite and, over time, I found it less stressful. Brenda and Gwyn, the shop owners, even got in touch when I won *Redheads* a decade after I last went to the camp as they read about it in the *Daily Post*.

On another holiday, in July 1997 in Prestatyn, an amusing tale unfolded when Ma phoned the owners of the caravan we were staying in to inform them that their television wasn't working and could they take the television away since we had taken our own (I liked my own television). They said they would call by, that evening. Later on that evening, after we had been out for the day, I got stripped off to get my pyjamas on. This was my routine if we weren't going anywhere for the rest of the day. However, before I had the chance to get my pyjamas on I realised that my television wasn't there. The owners had taken the wrong one!

At this point, I ran out of the caravan undressed and hysterical. Ma charged after me, but as she was cutting an unsliced loaf with a bread knife it must have been quite a scene to onlookers. I was running through a caravan park naked – with my Ma chasing after me, brandishing a breadknife. This prompted astonished looks from other people on the camp. When I had calmed down, we phoned the owners of the caravan, who came from Manchester. Luckily, they understood fully how we felt as they had an autistic relative. As we mulled it over later in the evening, my Ma couldn't help but laugh at the situation as she half expected the police to arrive.

Another trait that is brought on by my autism is that, on occasion, and without even realising it, I talk to myself in the house. Unfortunately, it is not quite as eloquent as a Shakespearian character taking on a soliloquy. This behaviour is usually prevalent when I am enthused or my thoughts are running away with me. I speak to myself when I am stressed and also when I am excited and happy. On the latter occasion, I have a propensity to smile to myself. It is something that could appear strange outside of the home, but I'd like to think I limit this to the point of no-one noticing, except Ma and Mel.

*

As previously stated, I really adore Christmas. That Christmas dinner in 2011 aside, generally, with the change in routine that comes with the festive period, I can get stressed. Along with the change in routine, I struggle once I have passed gifts over to my close mates, their children, and my family as I have kept them safely for months prior to the 'big day' after I have bought them. I see the box I have lovingly protected for months being emptied and it upsets me a little. With the presents I receive, I get an enormous thrill wondering what wonders may lie within the carefully wrapped packaging. I get a little stressed and empty after all the gifts have been opened. Nonetheless, I get a big thrill when my mates and family inform me that they have enjoyed my gifts as it makes it all worthwhile.

I also keep a collection of all the Christmas and birthday cards I receive as I believe just by sending the card my mate or family member has shown great thought, and I think they deserve to have them kept, hopefully, forever. I put up all the Christmas cards from past years that I have received. To illustrate my point, there are some cards I have which date back to 1992 off my Nanna Nell, which was the last Christmas before her passing. Nevertheless, when I am putting the Christmas cards out I get stressed, as I hate my belongings to be moved in the lounge, and also over-excited – which can boil over into antagonistic behaviour while putting the tree up as it signals a change in routine and the house suddenly feels strange. It always feels weird when it goes down, but not in the same vein.

Generally, apart from at Christmas time, I hate to have my things moved – be they books, CDs, DVDs, VHSs or vinyl. We have to have discussions that suit everyone as it has to be explained thoroughly to me, so that I understand why we need to accommodate the extra space and why some of my belongings have to be moved. I notice quite quickly if something has been moved or altered as it really upsets me. This has been a trait throughout my life. When Mel moved around the corner in August 1995 and took the television that she owned, which we used in the lounge, Ma and Mel had to get a television/video combo that was exactly the same type of Amstrad so I wouldn't notice when I woke up the next day. I did, though, as the picture quality was not as good.

When all is said and done regarding Christmas – or Chrimbo, as I term it after "Sinbad" off *Brookside* – I love it so much, although, as I have explained, I find certain facets of it worrying. I much prefer giving presents to receiving them, as the latter is just a way for me to save money on products I was going to buy myself during the course of the year anyway. Nonetheless, I love the fact that family and close mates have taken the time, trouble and effort to pass gifts and cards on to me.

After Boxing Day, however, and our traditional feast of a buffet, I really want my routine back to normal as I really dislike New Year. It is, in my opinion, just glorified clock watching. In addition to this, I feel disorientated and struggle with the evening's lack of routine so I just go to bed. The only good things about New Year are *The World's Strongest Man* (after which I retire to bed) and the darts from Alexandra Palace. However, there are arrows on all year long and, ironically, none on New Year's Eve itself. *The World's Strongest Man* is filmed during the Northern Hemisphere summer, which leaves little redeeming features regarding New Year.

As well as Christmas and birthday cards, I like to keep my text messages. Over the Christmas period of 2014, I accidentally deleted two years' worth, dating back to 2013 and 2014. I attempted to get them back, even paying £47.55 to get them back and being ripped off in the process, but it was no use. It upset me. Fortunately, I got the money back, but it taught me a lesson. When I told a close mate that I had kept two years of texts, his succinct reply was "Why?" In future, I will delete my texts more regularly.

All in all, my personality is a contrasting mix of traits. I can be confident and outgoing (even cocky), yet deeply insecure. I can be thoughtful, yet come across, at times, as selfish. I can clumsily attempt to help, but come across as domineering. I can be caring, yet harsh. When I come to think of it, I suppose I am a bit of a contradiction, perhaps even slightly paradoxical in some respects. Will the "real" Andrew please stand up? Which parts are me? Which are due to autism? Am I an enigma, even? To quote the late sports broadcaster Tony Gubba, who was glorified in song by my favourites Half Man Half Biscuit on their eighth album *Trouble over Bridgwater* from 2000, whilst reading out the Romania team, who had all dyed their hair blonde, in a 1998 World Cup finals group match against Tunisia, he exclaimed, "I'm buggered if I know!"

Chapter 12
Freedom of Speech

Due to the open way I have been brought up with my autism, and the fact that I thought it would be good for me to share my experiences with others, I began to give talks on my condition. My first talk was at a Wrexham Autistic Society meeting at Wrexham Rugby Union Club whilst I was still at school in June 2002.

This appeared to be well received as someone who was at the meeting then asked me to go to the Autistic Unit at Darland High School in Rossett, Wrexham. I still have the letters and notes that the pupils sent me, to this day, in a safe place at home. I remember one pupil liked wrestling and, as someone who had previously had an obsession with it, I had empathy with him and the other students.

I also found the pupils seemed to relate to me as I was only 18 and my then encyclopaedic knowledge of football, especially United, appeared to be something of an ice breaker. I felt quite important and that I was making a difference to people who, like me, suffered from autism. I felt that if they could take a little hope and encouragement from my talk, then perhaps it could help them with the condition.

I then had a bit of a hiatus from giving talks and speeches as, to be honest, I wasn't asked to make any. I returned to give talks to the Wrexham Autistic Society, which was now run by Ray Clarke, who the family has known for years via his work in the 1990s and early 2000s. I gave two talks in the space of 15 months – on Monday 6th November 2006 and Monday 11th February 2008. For both of these talks, I invited my mates from home, and the attendees at the meetings joked that I had brought a fan club with me. The audience, my mates aside, seemed really attentive, interested and, I think, were taken aback by my energy. Nonetheless, inside, I was always nervous, as I am of a nervous disposition generally, especially when I am going somewhere.

To coincide with the 2008 talk, I gave a talk to my mates and co-workers at M.U.T.V. regarding my autism to help create a better understanding of myself and the condition. It was intended to help my co-workers understand why I acted the way I did or sometimes made certain inappropriate comments. They realised it wasn't due to me being awkward, it was due to my autism. I feel this would have helped them significantly more coming from the horse's mouth, than when the National Autistic Society representative recited lines from his "manual" over four years later. As stated in the prologue, only 15% of people diagnosed with an Autistic Spectrum Disorder work. It is a shame.

The later talk I gave to the Wrexham Autistic Society started a chain of events that would see me giving talks on a more regular basis and start me on the path to winning two awards and a trip to Buckingham Palace. At the end of the talk on Monday 11th February 2008, the day after United lost to City at home for the first time since Denis Law's backheel on 27th April 1974, a lady named Lowri introduced herself to me and asked me to give a talk to the teenagers at the Youth Club she ran in Llay, Wrexham.

On Tuesday 26th February 2008, the day that I got my first mobile phone contract, I gave the talk to the youngsters at the Youth Club. I was impressed by how Lowri had got the kids to come to the Youth Club in an age when you hear constant stories about kids hanging round the streets with nothing to do. I enjoyed giving the talk and found the kids very receptive. I had been slightly concerned that I was dealing with a different demographic so I consciously altered the material and pictures on my projector for a more teenage-friendly audience, making it less dry and more laidback. I used pictures that I felt would connect more with a secondary school audience rather than adults or parents who had a child with autism.

It must have worked to some degree as one lad who was present at the talk remembered me when I walked through the Town Centre and when I went to a boxing match in Llay on Friday 8th May 2009. At the end of the talk, Lowri approached me and asked me to sign something so she could enter me into a competition for Welsh Young Volunteer of the Year. I signed it, not thinking anything else about it.

Almost three months later, on Friday 16th May 2008, I received a letter before going to M.U.T.V. – informing me that I had won, and asking me to attend a presentation at the Norwegian Church in

Cardiff Bay on Thursday 5th June 2008. I bought a shirt and tie for the event as I, unbelievably, didn't own one at the time. I must now have about 25 ties and several shirts! Lowri was also invited to the presentation as she had nominated me for the award.

Sensibly, she took the train. Personally, rather stupidly, I didn't go by train and got Billy to drive. I will never put Billy through that again as I much prefer going on the train now. I didn't want to go on the train at the time as I was slightly scared as to what the train would be like. Would it be punctual? What would I do if it didn't turn up on the way back? Would I get home? All these concerns worried me greatly. However, I now much prefer going by train than by car, for the extra room. Although, in the few instances a train is delayed I can get stressed, even though it may not come out until a few hours later.

For winning the Young Volunteer of the Year Award, Ma rang the *Daily Post* and a very positive article about me was written by Carl Butler and printed on Wednesday 19th June 2008. This was put across in an extremely supportive manner, even making light of me not having a passport in time for the trip to Moscow to see United in the 2008 Champions League final against Chelsea.

Unfortunately, everything snowballed into a negative direction after this. BBC Radio Wales wanted me to go on their *Drivetime* show to talk about Cristiano Ronaldo's potential move to Real Madrid. Although he didn't move until the following summer, there was plenty of speculation regarding this in the aftermath of Euro 2008. This was just because I worked at M.U.T.V. I had been warned at this stage about the situation, but it had come just too late.

While I was at the BBC's Wrexham Bureau, they conducted an interview and took a picture for their website and we weren't happy as we hadn't been told about any picture and I was not very smartly dressed by my standards. On Louis's 12th birthday, on Friday 21st June 2008, we were going to the Roses T20 match at Old Trafford. BBC Wales rang up and said they would like to make a feature on me at the game with cameras following me. This was after we had rejected previous offers of them coming to the house or to M.U.T.V.

After this, I thought it was all over. We celebrated Louis's 12th birthday on the Saturday with a buffet, after inclement weather put paid to an arranged barbecue with my mates. This was really enjoyable and I slept in the next day, which is really unusual for me. When I got up, I noticed Pazman had texted me. He informed me I was on page 13 of the *News of the World* in a one-paragraph article. They had, rather crassly and unimaginatively, dubbed me "Rain Man". Ma and M.U.T.V. both rang the editor. I just wish I had listened to M.U.T.V. at the time, as they had rarely, if ever, steered me wrong. They were again right and showed great prescience.

It was very stressful. When I went back to work after my holiday, I was told that Richard and Judy wanted me on their Channel Four teatime show. Fortunately, M.U.T.V. flatly turned them down. I was very glad at that. My family and I were very naïve in all this and it taught us a big lesson. Even a nice article about winning an award can turn into something very derogatory and upsetting, if you are not careful, on page 13 of the *News of the World*, even though it is just one paragraph.

That article changed me in some ways and I have only just returned to my old self, as I am very dubious of similar issues arising again. When I am now interviewed by the media it has to feel comfortable, be by an organisation which is not interested in stitching people up, be considerate to people with autism, and be generally respectful, like when I was interviewed by John Humphrys on *The Today Programme* on BBC Radio Four about my autism and this book on Easter Saturday 2015. They must also not be sensationalist in the slightest.

When I publicise this book, or anything again, I will think very carefully about which media organisations I will speak to and only choose ones I feel have a caring attitude towards me and my condition. I won't divulge which ones I am distressed at the thought of talking to, though.

Although I worked in the media, I now realise that not all facets of the media are as above-board as my mates at M.U.T.V. For several years after the *News of the World* episode, I went through a phase of hating being autistic. I felt upset, bitter, and angry that I suffered from this condition. I started looking at other people's lives and became unhappy with my own. I didn't realise, however, how much I had and how much I had achieved.

Around the same time as the article in May 2008, the first metaphorical darkness descended on my speeches after a talk at the

Association of Voluntary Organisations in Wrexham. It was poorly attended and knocked my confidence somewhat. For the first (but not last) time, I began to question whether the speeches were worth persisting with. I used to get obnoxious and nervous, and generally moan on the day of the speeches after this. This was the time I started to question what I was getting out of it. Was it worth the stress? Was I making a difference or was it a vicious circle repeating itself?

My next talk was in Bangor, Gwynedd, which was further than I had travelled previously to give a speech, on Tuesday 21st October 2008. I vividly remember there was a gentleman from Gainsborough in Lincolnshire in the audience. I rattled off the stat that Gainsborough Trinity were the first club to face Manchester United after changing their name from Newton Heath on Saturday 6th September 1902 at The Northolme, which is Trinity's home to this day, with the attendance just 4,000. United won 1-0, thanks to a debut goal from Charlie Richards.

Subsequently, I have also found out that Gainsborough was also the capital of England, briefly, a thousand years ago. That would have been a good stat!

I noticed – when giving these talks – that some autistic people have university degrees or are very academically capable, but, unfortunately, lack the requisite social skills to interact in everyday life. I feel I am fortunate to have social skills and to have coped in a working environment for so long. It is my belief that good social skills can be more important, at times, than a high intellect, especially if a person has the latter but not the former, although I believe it is helpful to have both.

One lady who attended one of my talks worked at the local police station and asked me to visit the station as a guest. I had mentioned at the speech that, over the course of time, I had developed a fear of the police as I had been stopped on a few occasions while travelling in Bill's car and in Wrexham Town Centre. I now carry an autism alert card to inform the police of my difficulties after these incidents.

Whilst at the station, I remember that I asked one police officer how hard it was to attain the phone records of suspected criminals compared to the television programmes, when it seems they have access to them almost instantaneously. The officer said that it took weeks rather than the hours or a day or so in the T.V. programmes and movies. I also had a new respect for the physical prowess of the police when I tried on one of their heavy vests. The vest I tried on must have weighed around three to five kilograms. Bearing in mind the men and women in blue have to chase after criminals, who may just be wearing trainers and light clothing, the pursuit of criminals cannot always be easy.

The tour around the police station to see the officers at work made me see them in a more friendly light. Fortunately, I don't fear them as much now, but I can still feel slightly scared if I see a police officer in the street as I immediately, rather ludicrously, think to myself that I have done something to catch the officer's ire. But I recognise they only stop people they suspect of crimes rather than just anyone.

What turned out to be my final speech was also by far the best attended, on Tuesday 27th January 2009, at the Talardy Hotel in St. Asaph. The speech went really well despite my projector playing up briefly. After this talk, however, I decided the stress in the build-up to the event had been far too much and I wanted to move on to concentrate more on my own difficulties.

My favourite part of my speeches was always answering questions from the audience. I tried to make my ripostes light-hearted and jokey. Unfortunately, that night my favourite part of the speeches would also turn out to be my undoing.

An audience member wrote an article on the evening and quoted me saying something that I thought should rather have stayed in the room. I was fuming at this; for the second time in six months or so, I was found to be naïve and trusting. At this point, I decided to stop giving speeches as it just wasn't worth the stress.

In the end, with the speeches, I also found that – quite literally – no two autistic persons' condition is the same. I lead a completely different life, I have been told by some experts – a unique existence for someone with an Autistic Spectrum Disorder. What works for me probably doesn't work for another person with Autistic Spectrum Disorder. It is far from a one-size-fits-all uniform approach and was a peripheral reason I gave up the speeches.

Nonetheless, one final piece of good news did come from the speeches as on Thursday 12th March 2009, after a gym session, my phone rang and it was the Welsh Council for Volunteer Action, who had awarded me the Volunteer of the Year accolade the previous 5th June. They had been trying to get in touch via email the previous day.

The email read as follows:

Good afternoon Andrew.

I hope you are well.

I am pleased to inform you that the Welsh Assembly Government would like to nominate you to attend one of the Royal Garden Parties this summer, as one of last year's Wales Volunteer of the Year Award Winners. The dates of the events are as follows

TUESDAY 7 JULY, TUESDAY 14 JULY, TUESDAY 21 JULY 2009

I hope you will be able to attend on one of these dates. If so, could you please email as soon as possible with the date and I can send you the relevant forms you will need to complete. If you have any questions please get in touch.

With kind regards

Welsh Council for Voluntary Action

I initially turned the invitation down as I am an anti-Monarchist. Indeed, at first, I was rather taken aback by my invitation on the phone as I don't like surprises due to the autism. I had ignored the email from the Welsh Council for Voluntary Action, that I had received the day before, thinking it to be a spam message. I then rang my mates and one of them bluntly said, "Now then, you're not Albert Finney. You're not famous enough to turn down the Queen. [Salford-born Finney rejected a knighthood at the turn of the millennium after previously declining the CBE in 1980]. You're going to Buckingham Palace." After this brief conversation, I quickly relented and decided to go to the Garden Party! After all, it would be a once-in-a-lifetime opportunity and I would only regret it later in life.

On the train to London, I rang and texted everyone, asking if they knew where I was that day. I was deeply nervous, excited, emotional and honoured. I was suffering from a multitude of emotions. When we got out of the black cab outside Buckingham Palace, I cried tears of joy at the enormity of the experience. Rather hypocritical for someone who claims to be an anti-Monarchist!

Amusingly, some tourists outside the Palace must have thought we were important – we were wearing our smart attires – as they asked for our picture! I thought Old Trafford was packed full on a non-match day with tourists from both home and abroad, but it paled into insignificance when compared to Buckingham Palace. I can understand now why the Monarchy has not been abolished, with the number of people visiting the outside of the palace on a daily basis. *Brand Finance* says the net value of the Monarch to the U.K. is £44bn, although the method behind this is disputed somewhat, but after researching the figures, it is safe to say they bring more money into the country than they take away.

When the time came for the Royal Family to meet and greet at the Garden Party, I shook hands with Camilla, Duchess of Cornwell. I also saw Prince Charles and Queen Elizabeth II. The Queen looked very petite and not in the slightest bit frail. Prince Phillip was also there.

I'll always remember other guests at the Garden Party included long serving ex-Hereford United manager Graham Turner, who also guided Wolves to successive promotions in the late 1980s, and "Fiz" off *Coronation Street*. It seemed surreal that I was at a Garden Party at Buckingham Palace just for talking about my autism.

The third and final award I received was presented to me on Thursday 8th October 2009 by outgoing Welsh First Minister Rhodri Morgan at Plas Brereton in Caernarfon, Gwynedd – a big, stately home in need of renovation. We shared a table with several people, of whom the only two who were friendly were the then Mayor and Mayoress of Wrexham, who came from Rhos. One of their chosen charities for the year was for autism. Sadly, the then Mayor of Wrexham has passed away since, but he and his wife at least made our day pleasant.

Although Buckingham Palace was a momentous day, I stuck by my decision not to do any more speeches. Don't get me wrong. I enjoyed some of them as I felt honoured to give speeches about my autism and how I have lived with it. I hope they helped some parents and carers. I know it would have helped Ma greatly if she could have listened to speeches like mine when I was first diagnosed, or when I was young, to help guide her and give her the confidence to carry on. She would have known she was going in the right direction and that there was light at the end of the tunnel for parents with autistic children.

Latterly, progress has been made in the mainstream regarding autism. Some businesses in Britain now have provisions for youngsters with the condition. There are now autism-friendly screenings of films at the local cinema and football matches where arrangements are made for autistic children. This would have been beneficial for both my family and me when I was a child but they were never forthcoming. In addition to these events, there was an autism-friendly solo, acoustic gig performed by ex-Supergrass frontman Gaz Coombes, who has an autistic daughter, at KOKO in Camden Town, North West London on 15th December 2014. As well as his gig, Coombes has also written a song about his autistic daughter, entitled "The Girl Who Called to Earth", which is on his 2015 LP *Matador*.

There was also a test flight for autistic youngsters who were booked in (or planning to go) on an overseas holiday with their families at Belfast International Airport in January 2015. This was reported on the BBC News website in the section specifically for autism-related stories. This, in my opinion, signals further progress in the understanding of the condition, and how much more recognised it seems to be.

On television, there was recently the four-part series on Channel Four entitled *The Autistic Gardener*, which focused on the green-fingered skills of people with autism rather than what they couldn't do. It clearly showed the traits of their condition to the several million viewers watching each week. In turn, the best-known personality in getting publicity for autism is Keith Duffy of Boyzone and *Coronation Street* fame. Duffy has an autistic daughter. He has raised money for the National Autistic Society through several physical challenges like long distance runs and bike rides as well as opening a specialised autistic school in his native Republic of Ireland and publicising the condition whenever he appears on charity television quiz shows and interviews.

All in all, understanding is a damn sight better than when I was first diagnosed. Most people seem aware of what autism is to a small degree. You also don't receive blank stares when you tell someone "I am autistic".

In July 2015, *The Guardian* went as far as to dub autism "the new baking". Perhaps if this book goes well then Paul Hollywood and Mary Berry might be out of a job and *The Great British Bake Off* gets replaced by "I've Got a Stat For You" as the television show on primetime BBC One! Who knows? Stranger occurrences have happened.

Although facilities and understanding have improved greatly for children due to an increased presence in mainstream life, it appears that when you reach adulthood, things are very much down to you and your family. This is something that needs to alter greatly as when you reach adulthood, autism is not recognised by certain organisations and there can be great difficulty with self-sufficiency or coping in the outside world without your family's help. I have been fortunate with Ma and Mel prodding me every day to self-improve, and move on. They fight my corner incessantly and prod me "for the autism not to win"!

Chapter 13
Everyday Life Has
Become a Health Risk

During my formative years, I was under the combined care of the Health and Social Services Departments. After my Chapter 4 incident, I would hit out at people before they had a chance to hit me and therefore I was on 2:1 support.

In March 1997, as I was struggling to socialise when away from the family, I began to attend a Special Needs Youth Club that was based at Wrexham Maelor Hospital, which then moved to Oteley House in Wrexham shortly afterwards. The hospital building was a pre-fabricated hut that had seen better days and which you may have expected a Scouts weekly meeting to take place in, apart from the fact that it was based adjacent to the maternity ward at the hospital.

Whilst at the Youth Club, I would play pool and listen to CDs on the hi-fi as well as being cooked a tea – something like sausage and chips covered in oil. When the Youth Club moved to Oteley House in September 1997, I recall the meals being far better: delicious and evidently memorable in a positive sense, if I can remember them all this time later!

Oteley House, since renamed Bradbury House, was built in 1867. It is a Grade II listed building with a strong Gothic design, which – if I have learnt anything from watching Michael Portillo's *Great British Railway Journeys* – the Victorians couldn't get enough of. Before being used as a Youth Club for people with disabilities, it was occupied by the architect that designed it, a brewer, and it then became a convent.

The house, to this day, is one of the biggest I have ever been in. From memory, it contained two downstairs lounges, and an enormous reception area that separated the two lounges. The reception area had a stone floor and was open plan with large stairs leading to the second floor of the house, which seemed to contain at least five bedrooms.

I remember what could have been a wine cellar, which was like an underground cave that our prehistorical brothers would have dwelled in. I used to get lost in the maze of the twisty staircase. The garden, I recall, was like a small park with benches and steep concrete steps that divided the land into gradients.

Whilst I attended the Youth Club at Oteley House, I gave a brief talk to the rest of the staff and youngsters on autism. I seem to recall that I mainly talked about obsessions and, at the time, not always knowing when I was full after a large meal. I hope the people present were a little more aware of my condition and difficulties. I also made a bottle of "my dreams" that we still have in our home. It was made up of different coloured sand very similar to a rainbow. I was immensely proud when I gave it to Ma to use as an ornament. Unfortunately, my autistic powers can't recall what "my dreams" were in late 1997, early 1998, but I hope that some of them have come to fruition over the subsequent period.

Although I really enjoyed Youth Club, there were only a couple of people I socialised with. Due to my autism and the black and white way I dealt with matters back then, I didn't integrate with people who didn't like sport, especially football and cricket. Needless to say, the people I socialised with from Youth Club were either fans of football and/or cricket. Although it may come across as narrow-minded to some, it was typical autism. If you didn't like football or cricket I wouldn't bother with you. It was that clear cut.

In February 1998, due to a change in my routine, I stopped attending Youth Club on a Thursday as I was worried that I wouldn't get there for a 3.30pm start. My thinking was that if I couldn't get there for the start, what was the point in going at all? Looking back, I should have persisted longer with it, but then again, Youth Club wouldn't have suited me as much as I went deeper into my adolescence.

*

On Saturdays, as well as attending Youth Club, I had two well-trained, experienced support workers from the Intensive Support Team, who handled me with no great difficulty if I started to misbehave. As well as being adept at their jobs, they were also caring, knowledgeable and understanding of my difficulties. Unfortunately, this was only to be a short-term measure.

Around the same time, I met my community nurse Mai Rees-Moulton and we greeted each other with a memorable exchange of, what could be deemed, offensive insults. In my juvenile attempts to shock, mimicking the late and much lamented Rik Mayall character Richard Richard off *Bottom*, I said to Mai, "Hello, big tits." To which Mai's quick witted riposte, as she was in no way shocked by my behaviour, was, "Hello, fat arse."

Mai is extremely caring, understanding of my condition, and not easily offended – as my comment above proved. As I was at the age of puberty, it was her job to teach me Sex Education and how to act appropriately in many situations, including knocking on someone's room door, rather than just barging in as I once had done. Mai was a great confidant for me in my teenage years if I had any worries, issues or problems that had occurred during the previous week. I saw her every Monday morning, initially at her office before, eventually, in school.

Mai was also very supportive of the family. Ma felt that there was someone out there who understood and cared for us. It felt good to talk to someone outside of the family and, as a family, we missed this greatly when I had to be transferred over to Adult Services – I had built up an excellent relationship with Mai and I trusted her enough to tell her any issues. Due to her compassion and understanding of my condition and the family's worries, Mai is still a family friend and we meet up whenever we can.

Apart from Mai, another caring community nurse was Patrick Howells. I used to see him at Marchwiel Centre in Wrexham during 1997. As part of the sessions, I vividly recall that Patrick created a Football League Table to help monitor my behaviour over the previous week. This was ushered in due to my love of football. At the beginning of this, I was at the bottom of the division which was then entitled The GM Vauxhall Conference. If I behaved well in the last week, I went up places in the division and down if I had misbehaved. I used to take the league table home and we hung it on the kitchen door in the intervening time. Nonetheless, when I got to Division Three, or what is now League Two in my League Table, I ripped it up in anger.

In addition to this, Patrick put forward theoretical scenarios I would encounter in my life; like how I would behave if United lost and how

I should deal with it. He would issue red and yellow cards if I misbehaved or didn't concentrate during a session. This helped me deal better with situations in the future.

One day in my session, I was being generally antagonistic towards Patrick as I was in a mood, so to get me out of this he decided to shock me by stating, "You're really pissing me off now". I backed off in surprise and stopped what I was saying and doing. Such tactics can sometimes have the required effect.

Around this time, I had a bit of an epilepsy scare. Autism can be associated with epilepsy, as well as other conditions, so it was not a massive surprise if I had been diagnosed as epileptic. The suspicions first arose in July 1996 when Ma filmed me in the garden and I was just staring rather blankly. In addition to this, a vehicle went past and I didn't get up to look at it, which is the norm for me. It made the episode all the more unusual. Due to this, we arranged an EEG scan at Glan Clwyd Hospital near Rhyl on Thursday 29th August 1996. On that day, England beat Pakistan in a One Day International at Old Trafford.

I was wired up and made to look like Uncle Fester from *The Addams Family*, which I watched religiously during the summer holidays of 1996 on BBC Two. I remember that my hair was very spiky and sticky after the scan, thanks to the hard gel that connected the electrodes to my head.

While I was at the Youth Club on Thursday 21st August 1997, which was the opening day of the sixth and final Ashes Test at The Oval, where Phil Tufnell took match figures of 11 for 93 to give England a consolation win, epilepsy concerns came further to the fore when I fainted after cutting my finger playing pool. So, the day after fainting, I had another EEG scan, this time at the Wrexham Maelor Hospital, before being referred to a specialist at Alder Hey in Liverpool. At the time, my specialist was appearing on the primetime BBC One "fly on the wall" series about Alder Hey – called *Children's Hospital*. Fortunately, the tests concluded that I didn't have epilepsy. It was something of a relief.

*

Apart from Mai and Patrick as community nurses, I went to see my psychiatric consultant, initially on a weekly basis. He was originally from Malta and was a rather Falstaffian figure. His personality and nature certainly had an air of the Mediterranean about it, and I could well imagine that when he went back home it would be similar to the scene in the Olivio television commercial where the whole family sits down to a big feast after a day's work.

He was very easy-going, but deeply intelligent and extremely opinionated, which he was never shy of showing when he felt the need. He also used to be tickled pink by some of Ma's colloquialisms, like the time Ma said during a meeting that "there's more go in a bottle of pop than in you lot". When he got home that night, he keeled over with laughter and couldn't speak whilst explaining to his wife why he was laughing. He really got Ma's sense of humour!

I always recall that the consultant psychiatrist had a penchant for old battered Honda Accord cars despite the fact that he must have been earning enough for a significantly better vehicle. He changed to a 4x4 at one point, but soon switched back to his trusty Honda. He was always smartly turned out, but his appearance was characterised by a big beige mac he used to wear. On one occasion, when he visited our house, he fumbled for what seemed an age to answer his phone. He couldn't get to the phone in time, but he was so laidback that he said they would call back. That summed him up in a nutshell.

For my appointments with the consultant psychiatrist, I visited the part of the Maelor Hospital reserved for mental disabilities and mental illness. It seemed to be a varied waiting room with outpatients having a full range of conditions. Nonetheless, the waiting room was a far more welcoming place than some other rooms I was to encounter in later years. I remember that the receptionist was very nice and made me feel comfortable. I have subsequently seen her outside the hospital as she goes to the same hairdressers as me.

When my consultant psychiatrist left, his replacement was of Nigerian origin. If I remember correctly, he had moved positions from London. It took me a while to get to know him as he was new, but after this initial period, I really liked him as he was dry and witty. I vividly remember his big wide smile. In build, he was the polar opposite to his predecessor: he was quite tall and slim.

On one occasion, I asked him if he was any good at sport as, at the time, I stereotypically believed that he must be very athletic due to his West African origins. He gave his trademark wide grin and told me that he was terrible at sport and only occasionally played five-a-side football. Looking back, I should have asked him about the legendary musician and political activist, Fela Kuti, who was from Nigeria, but when I was a teenager I wasn't aware of Kuti. An amazing fact about Fela Anikulapo Kuti that I picked up from the documentary movie about him shown in U.K. cinemas in 2014 is that he was once married to 28 women at the same time.

However, just as I was getting used to the Nigerian doctor, he left – and this signalled the beginning of the end of having a helpful, caring, considerate and understanding service for my needs as I had now reached the stage when I was to be transferred to the department that dealt with adults. This is where the care completely alters and money appears to be more of a driving force behind decision-making.

In line with this, many professionals in the system seemed to think that once you have reached adulthood you no longer should demonstrate traits of your condition or the difficulties that these entail. It would seem, in their eyes, that I had to suddenly make certain decisions in life that are difficult, if not impossible, for me to make without the help and input of my family. They seemed to think that you have to learn the hard way from your mistakes, but with autism this is seldom the case. I need guidance, help and support – not to be condemned for being born with a condition.

They should have listened to my family as they are the people who live with autism 365 days a year, 24 hours a day, seven days a week. They are the ones who best know my capabilities. Certain professionals didn't seem to understand that autistic people have more nerve cells in the brain than a "normal" brain. This is why autistic people react in certain ways, which can appear as over-reactions to some people. People with autism can't help this, and this is why I need a lot of guidance that needs repeating, sometimes on a daily basis, rather than learning the "hard way".

Another example of their lack of understanding was that they couldn't fathom how I could attend gigs, cricket matches and other sporting events but, at times, struggle going into certain shops in Wrexham. As explained previously, I feel, on occasions, quite uncomfortable in Wrexham Town Centre because of the people who hang around on the streets. However, I am very comfortable in Manchester City Centre, Chester City Centre or when I visit Chiswick in West London. I even much prefer going on the tube rather than going to some places in my hometown, and I have memorised most of the District Line between Ealing Broadway and Upminster. I even helped a Liverpudlian family find Earl's Court in May 2015.

Some professionals found this bizarre and didn't understand how I could feel more at home in some areas of a big city rather than certain areas of my home town. Some professionals thought this was unacceptable behaviour in an adult.

For years, the professionals appeared happy for us to plod along with my support worker, whose training we believed was not up to date, including at the time of the incident that led to my suspension from M.U.T.V. He was also (we believe) not up to date in restraint techniques or how to deal with me should such a situation arise. In my opinion, the professionals put a lot of people at risk, including myself. I deserved to have someone with me that was trained to do the job. In addition to not being trained, my support worker wasn't asked for years if he even had a valid driver's license or insurance. In my opinion, they were responsible when he was taking me in the car as he was employed by them.

After almost a decade of everything being left alone, things seemed to change overnight. Suddenly, and conveniently after the incident at work, my support worker had to undergo training. Just a couple of months prior to this, he was told not to use his own car for work and to use a pool car. We were given only a day's notice for the change to occur, and the stress of the changes became immense.

When I was assigned a new community nurse, after going a substantial amount of time without even being aware that the previous one had left, we did not get on. I found the nurse to be rude, nasty and liable to "forget" basic information. Reviews into my condition and needs took place sporadically. At one point, there was no review for many years and the support package was ongoing without any alterations. But around the time that the cutbacks in the system were starting to take hold, various reviews were brought in and changes began to take place. The stress, panic and worry of the reviews and changes come back to me as I am writing this now.

During one of them, the nurse had lost information on my medication and my doctor's letters stating which medication I was on. This was terrible for Ma and Mel, who both had to attend these reviews.

The social worker was no better as, in our opinion, he was arrogant and lacking in any empathy for Ma – a septuagenarian lady, who, as well as suffering from angina, arthritis and two strokes, had had a difficult job caring for her autistic son and, due to her age, got tired quite easily. Ma and Mel even attended meetings when there were no rooms available and the relevant people didn't turn up. It was like they did not care.

On one of these occasions, it was winter and had been snowing – making the journey treacherous. Nonetheless, they didn't care that Ma and Mel had turned up and that they hadn't booked a room for the meeting. They only appeared interested in getting me off the books and saving money.

We made numerous verbal complaints to one of the managers, but nothing was ever done. I know we should have put all this in writing to cover ourselves, but we were deeply stressed and at our wits' end with these people. Towards the end of the review, we were told that my support worker would look to leave me on my own in coffee shops after our meetings in the future, so that I could get used to being on my own. There was no one independent to help us as the community nurses and social workers appeared to have the same superiors.

When I was made redundant from M.U.T.V., we had to inform the professionals that my circumstances had changed. It was a task we were obviously not relishing. Even before my future at M.U.T.V. was officially decided, all support work was removed. We went from having a support worker during my three days at work (and three other days for attending exercise and social events) to nothing. No support for the family at all.

Dr. Carole Buckley, a clinical champion for autism within the Royal College of GPs, told the BBC in January 2015 that:

If we [healthcare professionals] *treated people in wheelchairs the way we treat people with autism, we'd be in court – because we're not making the reasonable adjustments and we're not managing things as well as we should.*

To help with autism, the Royal College of GPs has launched a three-year training programme to make doctors more aware of the condition and the problems. In all honesty, in all my life, I have never had a single problem with the GPs at my local surgery at Pen-Y-Maes in Wrexham. My care at the surgery has been exemplary, especially from Dr. Glen Willis, Dr. Garry Bates and the Tattersalls, who left the surgery in 2005. The problems that we, as a family, have had have not come from our surgery.

Nonetheless, speaking to other people, it seems that the type of "care" I received from many professional people in the system is endemic of the way they seem to work. We are in the process of taking it further and campaigning to try and prevent the removal of care happening to other autistic adults. These are the ones who may not have families to support them. We are determined, perhaps naively or idealistically, to try and change the behaviour of so called "professionals". We fight on but I am not holding my breath.

Is it any wonder that people with autism, or other disabilities, fall through "the cracks" of society? These people are going to find it harder to cope than they do already if they are treated, in my opinion, with such disdain. We have to at least try to stand up and not be scared to voice our opinions to these "professionals", who think they know better, but in my opinion, seemingly know little.

Looking ahead, there are a number of things that could be done to improve matters for people with autism.

Firstly, take on board the advice of family members who know the person best, and look to implement the family's views fully into the care of the person.

Secondly, if changes have to be made, then a lot of notice needs to be given. Changes should be introduced over a long period of time. For over a decade, I had the same support package and same support worker. Then suddenly it was suggested that a new support worker would be introduced.

Thirdly, have a Plan B for when problems arise. If my support worker ever had to be off sick (fortunately, he very seldom was) it appeared the system had little to no alterative in place.

Chapter 14
Finished I Ain't

As she said she would, Mel now takes me everywhere on weekdays. After my redundancy from M.U.T.V., I now feel happier than I have done in years. I now express my feelings even more, as well as in a more constructive manner.

Nonetheless, the initial transition from being at M.U.T.V. for over a decade and having my brother-in-law, Billy, as my support worker for 17 years was not without hiccups. The change of routine, with Mel taking me to everyday events such as my personal training sessions with Gary was a big adjustment. Everything felt unusual.

Although I knew nearly all of the changes were undoubtedly for the best, and were what I personally wanted (I couldn't take much more meandering through life), it was still a big alteration for Mel to be my carer during the day. This was not the routine. In addition to this, Mel finishes working with me at 2pm in the afternoon, in time to pick up Chloe from school. I found this adjustment extremely difficult as the autism was trying to stand in the way and tell me differently.

What helped me was that, since Mel knew me so well, she would pick up on signs that I was stressed with the new routine or I was a little grumpy. She would ask me what was wrong and bring the feelings out as I would eventually tell her what was the matter and inform her about what had been worrying me. This is something that I struggle with. Many people with autism do. Talking through my feelings has helped my stress levels enormously. However, Mel had to notice the signs and start asking me as I struggle to express what is wrong without this support.

Initially, Mel and I spent a lot of time together on our own before starting voluntary work, although we had always planned for me to undertake volunteering. We got used to being together in our new setting. Although we have always spent plenty of time together, it wasn't the norm for Mel to "work" with me in these environments.

Initially, this is something I struggled with – typical autism – and it is difficult for people to understand without the experience of living with a family member with autism.

To help me with our new routine, Mel would write down a plan of action for the week ahead so I would know in advance what I was doing daily – with dates and times clearly set out. If anything needed changing we would sit down together and discuss it beforehand and make an alteration. We would discuss why it was changing whilst confirming a new date, and plan what was happening instead.

A key example of Mel helping me occurred when we were stuck in a two-hour traffic jam on the A483 Wrexham to Chester road on Thursday 22nd January 2015 as we made our way to the train station. Previously, I would have panicked beyond belief. However, after a brief (heated) discussion which quickly became far more constructive, we caught a later train to Manchester and adapted our plans accordingly.

This is something that I struggle with, at times, as some days are better than others – depending on the change. For example, if any of my mates have to postpone meeting up, I struggle with the change as I can take the change very personally. This is an issue Mel and I are still working on. Planning and structure are the two things that help my autism, but I try not to plan too far in advance as this "blags" my head.

I did get used to the new routine, but sometimes, I would feel like a layabout as the new routine wasn't as time consuming as before. When I was at M.U.T.V. I would set out on my three work days at roughly 9.10am and not return, sometimes, until 5pm, perhaps later – depending on circumstances. Today I don't feel like this.

*

Even though I still lead as full a life as possible, autism will always be a part of my life. I have learnt to accept this over the years and have attempted to work around it. I will always need support, guidance and understanding to deal with situations in my life.

Unfortunately, on Saturday 19th July 2014, Ma broke the neck of her femur after slipping on chicken grease in the kitchen. It was very stressful and scary seeing my Ma on the floor, on her side, being seen to by a paramedic. She underwent an operation the next day. It was really hard in the aftermath of Ma's accident as she had never been away from home and I had seen my Ma every single day of my life, but Mel kept the new routine in place in spite of our sad emotions around this time. It was even harder seeing tubes attached to Ma during her stay in hospital. After Ma returned home from hospital, after eleven days, she had her bed in the lounge as it was going to be a long recovery for her. I cried dozens of times in the time she was away. I really missed her.

Nonetheless, this time actually enabled me to appreciate my Ma more than at any time in my life. I was determined to enjoy all the time I would spend with her. Although her accident only had a small chance of being life-threatening, it gave me the opportunity, when she returned home, to be mates with Ma – probably for the first time in my life. We now enjoy each other's company as we have tea in the kitchen and also have an afternoon cup of coffee together, which previously seldom happened.

Hitherto I was bossy and demanding, and expected far too much of my Ma. I now cherish every moment I spend with her as we generally enjoy our time together. I feel more fulfilled due to this as a new sense of letting certain events "go over my head" now prevails. Previously, due to my high stress levels and bottling up some of my feelings – this did not occur.

With Ma's accident I have had to become more self-sufficient, something I had never really been. Prior to this, I could come across as self-centred. If someone was ill in the family, say Mel, as long as I could go where I had planned to go, that was fine. "Bugger everyone else." In turn, Mel and Ma have been known to say, "We may have two heads – but as long as you are OK, then that is all you care about." I have been told that this is typical autism.

Fortunately, Ma is now recovered and lives a full life. She walks with the aid of a crutch but her mobility is almost as good as previously, although she struggles with aching limbs and gets tired after walking through the Town Centre or supermarket. If she has a lot of walking to undertake, then Ma will intermittently use a wheelchair, as well as walking with her crutch. The fact she lives such a full life after such a serious accident is testament to the determination and strong will that has always pervaded through her personality. A pivotal example is the way she has raised me to this point.

Just after I finished at M.U.T.V., we received a pamphlet through the post from Brymbo Heritage Centre asking for volunteers to undertake certain roles. Several of these were tailor-made for me, like historical research and several other skills I learnt in my time at M.U.T.V. I arranged to visit Brymbo Heritage on Monday 12th May 2014, which is on the site of the former Steelworks, with a view to volunteering for work.

Although the visit went well, it was definitely too soon to have that sort of structure at the time and I was noticeably stressed during the visit. I also had a meeting with a voluntary organisation in Wrexham on Tuesday 15th July 2014, but I was even more apprehensive during this and clearly not ready to return to any routine involving a working environment.

After agreeing to go to Brymbo Heritage Centre during the visit on 12th May 2014, I eventually started volunteering on Tuesday 7th October 2014 under Heritage Officer Gary Brown. This gave me time to get used to my new routine with Mel and to deal with the severe stress of Ma's accident. When I first volunteered at Brymbo Heritage, I was extremely tense and talked too much, which tends to be how I behave when I'm in an unfamiliar environment or feeling apprehensive. Gary Brown noticed very quickly that I preferred being in the top area of the Heritage Centre, which is part of a post office and local enterprise centre, rather than where the actual steel and ironworks are based. He realised that I found it cold as well as uncomfortable because of the mud and dirt that inevitably carries into an old steel and ironworks (my old working environment was a relatively clean office, where I wore a shirt and tie).

After going to Brymbo every Tuesday morning for around a month, my interest in cricket was noticed by staff at the Heritage Centre. Initially, it was decided that I should undertake a project for a wall display on the history of Brymbo Cricket Club. As 2014 gave way to 2015, and a month long Christmas break that I took away from writing this book and volunteering, I came up with an idea to compile a book on the twin subjects of Brymbo Football Club and Brymbo Cricket Club, entitled "Steel, Bat & Ball". My initial thinking was to undertake this after I had finished this book.

Nonetheless, after an informal discussion regarding ideas on Thursday 15th January 2015, Gary Brown came up with the great idea that I could work on it alongside this book and hopefully have it published locally in time for the 25th anniversary of the closing of the Steelworks in September 2015. During the time I researched the book, I felt a self-worth and usefulness regarding my work that I hadn't felt since my research days at M.U.T.V.

I really have been enthusiastic about the Brymbo book, some days slightly obsessively. It hasn't taken anything away from this book as Mel and Ma have helped me to separate my thinking from this book to the Brymbo book. I feel, all in all, I have separated my differing work heads quite well. The Brymbo book is on a small scale locally, compared to what I hope for this book, but it is still a rewarding experience as researching stats is my forte in life. It sums me up and makes me very happy when I am compiling stats and finding out pieces of trivia that a lot of people may find useless. This makes me happy, though, and probably always will.

Fortunately, the characters that have been involved for the two sporting clubs of the village have been extraordinarily helpful. I am delighted to say that it was quite refreshing that they weren't resistant to someone who had never previously been a follower of either club writing a book on their respective clubs. These people loaned me their cherished scrapbooks and newspaper cuttings, some of which were half a century old, with one picture in a photo album taken in 1924. The pride felt in their village's sporting achievements since 1882, which has included a combined total of six National Cups for the two clubs, has empowered me to write the book. I will always cherish the help these people gave me on their subject, most of which isn't readily available online.

Three hundred copies have been printed and I sold the book for the first time on Saturday 15th August 2015. The official launch was on Saturday 5th September at the site of the football and cricket clubs, which went fantastically well. People were showing me photographs from close to 85 years ago of their family members in the cricket and football teams of the day. I felt that I had made an impact with these people, who were proud of their village's sporting heritage. The factual and statistical part of the book is what comes naturally with the autism, but what has made a lasting impact on me during the project is the pride felt by these people. I was quite touched when one lady, who went to school with Ma, told me she was buying a book to send to her brother in Melbourne, Australia.

Hopefully, I can cover my costs, but if I don't – in the long run – make my money back, the project was never for that reason. Seeing how chuffed the people of Brymbo have been more than makes up for it. At times, the project has helped me come out of my comfort zone in a very positive manner and I have gained tremendously from the experience.

Despite the big changes in the family's life, and mine, I get to see my mates as often as I possibly can with Mel – or Louis, when he is on Uni holidays. I still attend my plentiful gigs in Manchester, too, which Mel does not attend. This would not have been possible if I had still been at M.U.T.V. and didn't have my new-found routine, which has given me more flexibility. My mates have commented on how they see a big difference in my happiness levels as I have talked through my feelings more, which has paid dividends.

In recent times, I have undergone a lot of changes, and due to Mel's help I have become more self-aware. In this time, it has felt like a journey of positive self-discovery, which may sound slightly pretentious. I wouldn't say I lacked awareness of my personality traits before, although everyone must believe that, but Mel has aided me enormously in a short period. She has also attempted and helped me to be more flexible.

After Ma's accident, my redundancy from M.U.T.V., and the challenges with the services, Mel has helped me regain my self-worth and confidence, and she has lowered my stress levels despite our various recent worries. All this I have achieved whilst getting into a new and fantastic routine. I have learnt to talk my feelings through, no matter how small. We have written this memoir and compiled another book through my volunteer work, plus maintained my personal training sessions and trips to Manchester to meet up with my mates, just like she promised.

However, despite the improvements, the autism will always be there and I still struggle on a daily basis. I still get down days, just a lot less frequently, and I deal with them infinitely better with the support of my family. Weekends can be problematic with less structure compared to weekdays. I control the autism most of the time now, rather than the autism controlling me.

All in all, I think the little autistic boy who went around at 1,000mph would be proud of the man, who, admittedly, now only moves at the slightly more controlled pace of 100mph. I am sure, if the little autistic boy could have expressed the feelings that the autistic man can – with the life experiences that I have had in working for Manchester United Television for over a decade – he would have exploded with delight.

Nonetheless, I now look forward to the future with a sense of renewed vigour and sense of excitement that, as I have previously stated, were not there in the recent past. I hope the future has a great time in store for me. I now feel in control of my destiny.

In all honesty, though, who knows what the future has in store? My life has been far from predictable so far. Who would have predicted when I was diagnosed autistic at age four that I would have lived as fulfilling a life as I have done? I think I have proved wrong the doctor who told Ma, "In all probability your son will be institutionalised", don't you?

I hope every day I continue to achieve in life whilst overcoming my difficulties. In fact, the future is so unpredictable, who can say with any certainty that there won't be a sequel to this book? As British hip-hop artist Ghostpoet put it in 2011, on his Mercury Prize nominated album *Peanut Butter Blues and Melancholy Jam*, "Finished I Ain't".

A nurse at Wrexham Maelor Hospital holding me before
I was discharged, following my saliva gland infection.
Ma is seated next to us.

Me sitting next to a line of toy cars.

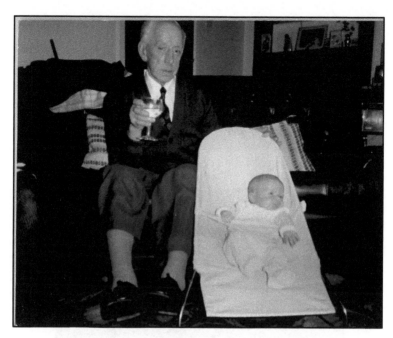

My Taid, Samuel Davies, sitting next to me.

Me and Ma at Mel and Bill's Wedding on
Saturday 3rd February 1996.

Billy, Louis, Mel, Chloe and Me near the banks of the River Thames
in Chiswick, West London on Wednesday 14th August 2013.

Me throwing a sponge at my Headmaster, George Darby,
from Special Education Centre at a Fete
on Saturday 21st September 1991.

St. Christopher's Headmistress Maxine Pittaway (née Grant) MBE
and Mark Powell, who were two extremely understanding
and positive influences on me during my time at the
school between February 1998 and July 2003.

Rene Bruce-Pinard and Me at a St. Christopher's Sports Day.

Kevin "Beast" Apsley, Myself, and Stephen "Pazman" Parry at
Heaton Park, Manchester, on Friday 29th June 2012.

(Clockwise) Steve O'Shaughnessy, Kevin Apsley, Gary Jones, my
nephew Louis and Me, at a meal at Anise, Wrexham, celebrating my
30th birthday on Saturday 22nd November 2014. My friendships
mean the world to me and have helped my social skills tremendously.

Receiving my G.C.S.E. from Sir Alex Ferguson.

Me sitting in the old M.U.T.V. studio on Wednesday 2nd October 2002. This was the evening after a 4-0 win at Old Trafford against Olympiakos in the Champions League Group Stage.

Louis and Me with "The Doyen of Commentators", Richie Benaud
outside the old Media Centre at Old Trafford Cricket Ground
on Saturday 13th August 2005 after truncated
Third Day's Play of the Third Ashes Test.

Me flipping a Tractor Tyre with Personal Trainer Gary "Guru" Jones looking on. Guru has helped my mentality and conditioning levels no end over the last two years.

Mel and Me outside Buckingham Palace, Tuesday 21st July 2009.

My niece Chloe and Me outside the main house at Erddig
National Trust in Wrexham, Sunday 11th October 2015

My Godparents Jim and Shirin Nelson at the book launch of my
local history book "Steel, Bat & Ball" on Saturday 5th September
2015. One of my two middle names is after my Uncle Jimbo.